FOLLOWING SUNSHINE

A Voyage Around the Mind,
Around the World,
Around the Heart

Niamh McAnally

Black Rose Writing | Texas

Some names and identifying details may have been changed to protect the privacy of
individuals.

ISBN: 978-1-68513-477-8
LIBRARY OF CONGRESS CONTROL NUMBER: 2024936739
PUBLISHED BY BLACK ROSE WRITING
www.blackrosewriting.com

Printed in the United States of America
Suggested Retail Price (SRP) $22.95

Following Sunshine is printed in Garamond Premier Pro

*As a planet-friendly publisher, Black Rose Writing does its best to eliminate unnecessary waste to
reduce paper usage and energy costs, while never compromising the reading experience. As a result,
the final word count vs. page count may not meet common expectations.

FOLLOWING SUNSHINE

"Gripping and heartfelt, Niamh's beautifully written memoir unfolds with warmth, courage, and a touch of cinematic magic. A truly brave, enriching read that will take you on a global adventure in pursuit of purpose, and leave you uplifted by the impact one person can have. A MUST-READ for anyone seeking inspiration and a deeper connection to the world."
–**Liam Neeson**

"A story of an ordinary woman doing an extraordinary thing. As Goethe said, 'Whatever you can do or dream you can, begin it; boldness has genius, power and magic in it.'"
–**Jeremy Irons**

"A brave, honest memoir, at times introspective, poignant, and often funny. McAnally tells her story with humor, empathy and intelligence."
–**Book Reviewer,** *Caribbean Compass Magazine,* **Caitlin Richard**

"Few people see all the things Niamh's seen and even fewer have the ability to put pen to paper and record their experiences with such beautiful vividity. Niamh's writing is stunning."
–**Author of** *The Midnight House,* **A Richard and Judy Book Club choice, Amanda Geard**

"Niamh McAnally is a brave, fearless adventurer, who grabs life and lives it to the full, picking herself up when she falls and moving forward, always with hope in her heart. An uplifting read that will warm your heart."
–**Best Selling Author of** *The Seven Letters,* **Sinead Moriarty**

"An astonishing story of human courage, achievement, and endless surprise. Niamh travels the world and wraps herself around your heart."
–**Songwriter, Singer, TV presenter, Max McCoubrey (Maxi)**

Note to my North American readers.

Just a heads-up — this book will not only take you on a journey around the world but also on an expedition through British English. For those not familiar with the UK/Irish spellings and idioms, get ready for a language vacation packed with extra letters like 'u' in harbour and 're' in theatre, and of course, the extra 'l' in words like travelled.

A metre is 3.3 feet. A kilometer is .62 of a mile. 10 kilos is not something you want to add to your waistline because it equals 22 pounds! And since we don't want you to fall asleep while reading, many of the 'z's have been replaced with 's's.

Enjoy!
Niamh

For my parents,
actors Ray McAnally and Ronnie Masterson,
for giving me the mindset that
Anything is Possible

FOLLOWING SUNSHINE

I am a child of the ocean,
The water draws my soul.
It drags me deep beneath the waves
Where mermaids might exist.
And every time I come undone,
There's a rolling surf to turn me,
An ocean spray to cleanse me,
And another rock on which to grow.

–Niamh McAnally

Prologue

We were twelve minutes into the dive that morning when I knew something was wrong. It was 1993. Thirty of us were living in a disused wooden convent on a tiny islet in Central America, fifteen miles off the coast of Belize. We had come to volunteer for a company dedicated to marine conservation on a project designed to help Belize protect its system of barrier reefs. As a certified scuba instructor, and the appointed diving officer in charge, I was exempt from the daily chores of cooking and cleaning. Instead, my task was to consult with the on-site scientist and organise dive teams to conduct underwater surveys twice a day.

Volunteer divers, some of us from Ireland, most from Britain, came for one, two or three months at a time. My boyfriend and I had come for four. After ten days of intensive study — learning the names of fish, corals, sponges and invertebrates — divers were ready to play a vital role in identifying life on the reef. After each dive, we uploaded the data to the home office where GPS coordinates of the surveyed zones were superimposed on satellite imagery of the area, which helped identify the underwater terrain further down the reef.

That morning I was leading one team of four, navigating the tract. My buddy diver, documenting fish, swam to my right. When I turned to check on the pair in the rear, I realised Maureen was upside down. Her mask was pointed towards the seabed, her feet towards the surface. It was not an unusual position for a diver documenting algae and miniscule invertebrates. She had to get as close as possible without making contact. But something was off. Her slate, attached to her wrist by a cord, was not in her hand, but floating above her head. Her pencil lay in one ridge of the brain coral beneath her nose. I swam back, grabbed her arm and leg, and turned her right-side-up. Her vacant eyes held no fear, but I'm sure the alarm must have been obvious in mine. We were thirty metres below the surface and she was non-responsive. I had been trained to assist an unconscious diver at such depths, but, at that time diving was still my hobby, not my profession, and I'd never done it for real. If we didn't act quickly, she would die. If we acted too quickly, she would also die. And so would we. I signalled the others to abort the dive, and we started kicking our way to the surface.

On our way up, two questions focused my mind. One: how fast could we push the swim to the surface without getting the bends? Two: how to manage the air expanding in our bodies? If everyone didn't keep exhaling, as the ambient pressure decreased, we risked bursting a lung. Easy for us — we just kept breathing. For the unconscious Maureen, however...

Her regulator was still in her mouth like a baby's pacifier. With the heel of my hand, I held it in place so she wouldn't drown. My fingers covered her mask and pushed her forehead back to extend her neck and open her airway. My other hand gripped her weight belt in a fist and punched against her belly, forcing the expanding air up and out of her lungs.

Next problem was our jackets. If we didn't purge the air from our buoyancy control devices (BCDs), they would fill like balloons and whisk us to the surface. Bubbles would form in our blood and decompression sickness would follow. I had no free hands, so I nodded at Maureen's buddy and he alternated between venting her jacket and his own. Mine did the same for me. Had Neptune been out on a daily survey of his vast underwater world, he might have believed we'd invented a game of subaquatic Twister. The four of us became a tangle of arms and air bubbles as we kicked for the surface, ascending towards the light.

Since that time, there have been studies and different recommendations made on how to rescue a submerged, unconscious diver. Whether it was the best procedure, or the safest thing to do, it was all I knew back then, and therefore what I did. With that training also came the decision to abandon the safety decompression stop. We needed to be topside, and we needed to be there *now*.

We were so close. Shafts of sunlight reached us. A couple more kicks and we'd be there. I could see the underside of waves rolling above our heads. Whether it was the motion of the surge or the reduced pressure against her eardrums that shook Maureen awake, we will never know. Between my spread fingers, I saw her eyes come to life. She was alert and breathing by herself. I removed my hand from her confused face, but kept a hold of her belt while we broke through the surface together.

She wasn't sure what had happened. Neither were we. We hauled her into the dive boat and sped back to base, where the doctor examined her. By the time I had stowed my kit and come to check on her, she was sitting on the back porch, drinking a beer and laughing and joking with the rest of the team. I wasn't ready to join them. My legs were weary from the adrenalin rush and I needed some space to get over the fright.

Just like I had in a Dublin pub in 1987. Rory Golden, the explorer who later founded Flagship Scuba and dove the *Titanic*, three times, had introduced me to the subaquatic world the previous year. From the moment I'd completed my first exercises at the bottom of the swimming pool that winter, I'd fallen in love with the freedom of neutral buoyancy and breathing underwater. I also loved the camaraderie of the Nautilus Dive Club and being one of twelve students (nicknamed The Dirty Dozen) preparing to plunge beneath the surface of the Irish Sea that spring. After months of training, we made our first two dives from the beach at Sandycove, swam in a loop for about twenty-five minutes, and gradually came to the surface close to our departure point.

By the Easter weekend, we had progressed to boat diving. On the Saturday morning, twenty of us boarded our club's three Zodiac inflatables and motored about a half a mile off the coast of County Wexford. My instructor for this dive — let's call him "Patrick" — had two students assigned to him, myself and a girl I'll call "Mary". All three of us rolled backwards off the inflatable. The waves were choppy this far out from land.

As soon as we regrouped on the surface, Patrick gave the signal to descend. I started heading down, pinching my nose and gently blowing against it to equalise the pressure building in my ears. When I reached the bottom, my depth gauge told me we were twelve metres below the surface, the deepest I'd ever been. I was aware of Patrick off my left shoulder, but of Mary there was no sign. We looked up and saw she was still on the surface. Patrick motioned for me to stay put; he would go up and get her. Unlike in Dublin Bay, the visibility was such that I could watch him swim to the surface. I sat down on a bare boulder. I waited. I looked around. Brown kelp grew from the seabed and I counted several crabs scurrying about. When I looked up again, all I could see was the underside of waves. No Patrick, no Mary.

I thought about the systematic searches I'd heard about for people who are lost, how they'd often be found sooner if they stayed where they were. Patrick had told me to stay put. He knew where he left me, so I reasoned that I'd better not wander off. As I sat there, I wondered from which direction they would come. Maybe I should keep looking over my shoulder so they wouldn't startle me. I breathed in; I breathed out. Nothing else to do. Breathe, and keep wondering when they would come for me. I had no sensation of time. The only instruments I had were a depth recorder and pressure gauge that showed the amount of air I had left.

By the time I got cold, I had breathed through more than half my tank. Now what? Do I still stay? Then, when I realised the obvious, the chill came from my insides. No one was coming for me. That moment of disbelief spread from my belly to my chest, to my fingers, to my toes. Although I had been alone for probably twenty minutes, now I felt truly on my own. There was just me and this watery environment, an environment in which I didn't belong. Not permanently. Not today, anyway. I had no choice but to surface, but I'd never done it by myself. Later in life, I recognised this was the precise moment when I learned what it means to be self-sufficient, that we are all born with that power, that courage, that instinct to survive.

I kicked off from the bottom and started to rise, careful not to hold my breath. Eighteen metres per minute was supposed to be the safe rate of ascent. I didn't have a watch and dive computers were luxuries of the future. Was I going too fast? Was I going too slow? I had no reference point in the middle of the blue, no other diver to monitor my speed. Then I remembered "smallest bubbles". As I exhaled, large bubbles burped to the surface, but the smaller ones seemed to hang around. So long as I kept pace with the ascent of the smallest bubbles, I'd be OK. Right?

Ironically, when I broke the surface, I felt more scared than I'd been underwater. I couldn't see land. I bobbed up and down in the half-metre waves and kept searching the horizon. But all I saw was ... the horizon. Until I figured out to turn around. Good news: the shore had been behind me. Bad news: it looked very far away. Too far to swim, especially with all my gear. I considered dropping my weight belt.

But then, in the distance, I saw our three zodiacs zipping across the waves in a random pattern. There must be an emergency, that's why they hadn't come back for me.

I inflated my life jacket. It helped buoy me up in the rolling waves and gave me a chance to think. What should I do now? One boat broke off from the others and started heading out to sea. I waved, but they kept disappearing from view each time I dipped into a trough. I yelled, blew my whistle, and wished I'd had a neon orange inflatable sausage among my safety equipment. One boat changed direction, it looked like it was getting bigger. When I reached the crest of the wave, I whistled long and hard. I waved. Yes, it was definitely getting bigger. Someone waved back. They were coming.

But when the boat arrived, and Patrick leaned over the side, I saw dried blood on his face, and I really got scared.

"Oh my God! What happened?" Had he come up too fast? Had I? How long before I'd know? Why was there blood?

"Get in."

I got a hold of the grab lines along the side of the boat and kicked with whatever energy I had left. Two of the guys in the boat had to haul me onboard by my arms.

"Where were you?" Patrick yelled at me above the roar of the wind.

"What happened to your face?" I yelled back.

"It's nothing. I got kicked in the nose when I rolled off the boat. Where were you? We've all been worried sick."

"I was right where you told me to wait."

"*What?*" He was incredulous. "Everybody's been looking everywhere for you."

"You told me to stay put."

"Mary couldn't get down, so I had to bring her back to the boat. I assumed you would have surfaced."

"You told me to wait."

"Jesus! We thought we'd lost you. For once, I wish you hadn't listened!"

We humans have a funny way of handling fear and then relief. How many stressed parents bargain with God when their child goes missing, only to yell at the poor kid when they return?

I still thought I'd done the right thing. I'd been congratulating myself on staying calm and making a solo ascent, but now I was being yelled at for doing what I'd been told to do? Patrick's reaction told me how fearful he had been. It was only then I realised *I* was the emergency. I'd followed the rules and look where that got me. Had I not surfaced when I did, things could have ended in tragedy. I started to shake. (Of course, nowadays, if divers get separated from their buddies, they're trained to look for each other for just one minute and then surface.)

That night in the pub the pints and comments were flying.

"What kind of eejit sits on the bottom, thinking someone will find them?"

"Sure wasn't she two rocks past the third lobster on the left."

"If you didn't want to dive with any of us, you could have just said so."

Somehow, *I* was the butt of the slagging. I laughed politely, but I'd had enough.

Patrick was sitting quietly in one booth, still nursing his first beer. I went over and sat beside him.

"Hey," I said.

"You scared the crap out of me," he said.

"Sorry, I was only—"

"I know ... doing what you were told."

"Why didn't you come back for me?"

"I did! By the time I got Mary on the boat, we had drifted so far, I couldn't find you."

"I'm sorry."

"We looked everywhere. I'm glad you're safe. All I kept thinking was, how was I ever going to tell your father, of all people, I'd lost his youngest daughter?"

Looking at Maureen now, sitting on the porch on South Water Cay in Belize, I could imagine the type of banter she was probably enduring:

"Hell of a time to take a nap." or

"You do realise you gave that brain coral lead poisoning?"

Yes, relief shows up in many forms. I understood now how Patrick had felt. What if I had not brought Maureen safely to the surface? How could I have told her parents?

The rest of that month went by without incident. Surveys were completed and lifelong friendships were forged. When the morning came for Maureen and the rest of the February volunteers to depart, everyone descended on the dock. Those who were staying helped those who were leaving, and, before long, the boat was stuffed with backpacks and tearful goodbyes. Scraps of paper with addresses and phone numbers were exchanged, along with promises to keep in touch. Seems archaic now, but we still had to wait four more years before social media was invented, and another eleven before we could find our friends on Facebook.

As I drove the boat towards the Dangriga shore on the mainland, from where they would be transported to the airport for their transatlantic flight, I listened to Maureen lament the end of her trip. She was going home to the cold, wet, English winter. Two days later, she would be back at her desk, looking out a window at a blank wall, sitting next to people who could neither relate to her experience, nor comprehend what she had achieved. Her month of living on a tropical island, contributing to the conservation of the second largest coral reef system in the world, not to mention surviving what could have been a long swim with the fishes, would all fade into the corners of illusion. Reality would return.

"It doesn't have to be like that," I said, above the hum of the outboard.

"How do you mean?" she asked.

"You could live this vibrantly your whole life, if you wanted."

"No," she said, "maybe you could, but not me. It's easy for someone like you. No baggage."

In what Oprah likes to call an *aha!* moment, I realised two things. Maureen was right. She would go back to England and follow the rules. She would work at her desk, whether or not she enjoyed it. Her life would be exactly how she had described it, because that's what she believed. She was right, but so was I. Somehow, I had an innate knowledge that the power of my intentions could manifest everything from a mundane existence to a life of dreams. I had stumbled on *The Secret* before it became one. I understood the *Law of Attraction* without ever being told. That didn't make it any easier for me than it could have been for Maureen or anyone else. I still had to monitor my internal chatter because, whatever I focused on, the good and the bad, I would draw more of the same to me. I also knew that desire was not enough, I had to take action when appropriate. My unintended solo dive had taught me that sometimes breaking the rules might be the only way to soar. And so, I knew my life would become the sum of my thoughts; my experience would become the result of my choices.

PART ONE
Around the Mind

Chapter 1
The Tightrope

Despite being raised Catholic, I am not religious. I don't think I've ever read the back blurb on the Bible, but, somewhere among its pages, I believe it says something about it being easier for a camel to pass through the eye of a needle, than for a rich man to get into Heaven. I never understood where the camel got the sewing kit, or why the rich man didn't offer him a pot of gold for it, to even out their odds. However, taking all that into account, I reckoned, if I could carry everything I owned on my back, I would have as good a chance of squeezing through the Pearly Gates when the time came as anyone else rich in scriptures. My addiction to minimalism began on 15 June 1989, the day my perspective on life changed. I was lying on a white shaggy rug that had allegedly once adorned the back of a rather fat sheep, performing side leg-raises, when the phone rang. I scrambled across the room to lift the receiver on the cream contraption, wondering if the curly cord would stretch to the middle of the room so I could continue my exercises.

"Hi."

"Hi Conor," I said, surprised to hear from my oldest brother, who was working in England. Like myself and my other brother Aonghus, the three of us had careers in TV. My sister, Máire, was the only one who hadn't followed our parents into the entertainment industry. "How are you? How's London?"

"I've something to tell you."

Pause.

"Dad's dead," he said.

"What? No. I had lunch with him yesterday."

"I know."

"No," I said again. "He's home on a break from filming." I tried to explain to my brother that he was wrong. Something about those two words — "Dad's dead" — would not compute in my brain. Ray McAnally, actor, director, husband, father — my dad — is dead? No. He is very much alive and I am meeting him tomorrow to give him his Jacobs award, the one I'd collected on his behalf at the RTÉ Television awards the previous year. He'd been away in the Orkney islands filming *Venus Peter* and had asked me to deliver an acceptance speech on his behalf. It was my second time in front of the TV cameras, but the first time as myself. No. My dad was not dead.

"I'm on my way to Heathrow now," Conor said. "Aonghus will collect me at Dublin airport and we'll go over to tell mam together."

Oh God, my mother!

After we hung up, I walked through the apartment I shared with a roommate as though I had never seen it before. I wondered where I kept my car keys. On the kitchen counter? In the hall? Or maybe my handbag? Bingo. I don't know if I took the lift or the three flights of stairs down to the car park. It was so noisy inside my head. Dad's not dead, Dad's not dead. My granny's dead. Been dead seven years. I was even in her hospital room. We all were, praying decades of the rosary. Mam was holding her hand. Granny was almost ninety-four. Her breaths were shallow, growing further apart. One more breath in, one last breath out. Then the strangest thing happened; her face changed. Wrinkles faded. Colour disappeared. It was like she was home one minute and then she went out. She wasn't there anymore. I had just watched my mother watch *her* mother die. So, no, my dad was not dead.

I'm sure someone could tell you how many traffic lights there are along the twenty-five-kilometre stretch of coast road between Dublin's Blackrock and Sutton — I don't remember any of them. What I do remember is seeing one royal blue Jaguar after another. I checked the driver of each one, but none of them was my dad. I sped on. I had to get to my mother's house first. If she opened the door and saw Conor and Aonghus, standing there *together* … barring Christmas, the sight would be such a rare occurrence I felt it would have been as subtle as sending two policemen — followed by an ambulance!

I rang the doorbell, and heard her singing, as she often did when she walked up the long corridor. Through the diffused patterned glass of the front door, her approach looked like an animated film by Picasso. Green jumper, plaid skirt. Fractured.

"Hi darling, come in," she said. "I'm on the phone with Olive. Do you want to stick on the kettle?"

She turned and headed back down the corridor to the lounge. I made the tea. Weak. Cup and saucer. Two saccharin and a squirt of lemon. She was still on the phone chatting with her sister when I brought the tray, complete with tray cloth, and placed it on the coffee table by her armchair. I sat on the couch opposite and waited.

What will I say? How will I say it? I have to be strong. I have to be gentle. Can I keep a neutral face until she gets off the phone? Help me. Is there a tutorial on breaking bad news? Oh. Ask them if they are sitting down, right? She already was. Make them a cup of tea. Done. As I listened to her for the next few interminable minutes — planning a trip to the theatre with her sister for the following day, plans I knew she would have to break — it hit me. Dad wasn't dead, but he had died. He'd passed away. He'd crossed over. Dead came after died — something you say years later, something you can say when the tears have dried up, when it's a status on an official form you have to complete, when you've lived in acceptance of the reality. That was why my brain couldn't grasp it before. There'd been no period of transition between alive and dead.

"Mam," I said, when she'd put down the phone. "Today … today, Dad's heart stopped beating. He died."

Her eyes widened, her hand flew to cover the O her mouth was trying to form. Actress, Ronnie Masterson, wife, Mrs McAnally, my mother, despite having been separated from my dad for several years, was devastated.

She had never stopped loving him and never would. Seeing her heart break shattered my own. My lungs tried to push against my ribcage, tried to suck in some air. My dad had died. Suddenly. In his prime. He was only sixty-three; I was twenty-seven. I felt robbed. Cheated. Abandoned. My dad had left his baby girl. I held my mother as we sobbed.

Hours later, my brothers arrived. We all hugged. Deathly silent hugs. Those hugs that cause a volcanic eruption in your heart. Our shoulders shook violently as we spewed those ugly tears.

By eight p.m. the phone started ringing. Reporters wanted to confirm the death of Ray McAnally.

"Please," my mother begged them, "please hold off. We haven't been able to reach my daughter yet."

My sister, Máire, was on a hill-walking holiday somewhere in the Austrian Alps. But, by 11 p.m. the news had broken. I don't know which would have been worse for her: hearing it on the radio or the way she did — from an Interpol policeman who tracked her down. After twenty-four hours and crazy connections, she finally arrived home. Those wordless, all-speaking hugs started the avalanche of tears all over again. But we were all together. We would get through.

And then came the food, lots of it; in hushed tones, neighbours and friends tried to help in the only way they knew how. For the first time in my life I lost my appetite, but during those endless days that followed, days spent waiting for the services to begin, my thirst found its way into the wee hours of those mornings and to the bottom of several bottles of wine. It didn't numb any of my pain, just offered an escape to float above it for a while.

We glued ourselves around the Formica-topped kitchen table – talking, laughing, crying, riding the emotional roller-coaster of memories unleashed by death. We laughed at events that hadn't been funny at the time, anecdotes that had become family lore. With a ten-year spread in age between us kids we each had our own experiences and stories to tell. One we shared in common had occurred eight years earlier when our dad had been about to undergo an open-heart triple bypass. Back then there was a two per cent possibility that he might die on the operating table. The evening before surgery, he had called us all, individually, into his hospital room, for a potentially permanent goodbye. Afterwards we learned that, as each one of us had given him a hug, wished him well, and had a hand on the door to leave, he'd cracked a joke, making sure we were laughing as we walked out.

During my one-on-one, he had handed me two envelopes. Inside each one was a note addressed to his fellow actors and crew, because I also worked with him at the Abbey, The National Theatre of Ireland, at the time. Depending on the outcome, I was to put one of them on the notice board. The first said something like:

Good news, I made it through the op.

If he had died, I was to put up the second:

Ah well, that's show business!

Around that kitchen table we remembered his sense of fun, laughed at his craziness till our bellies were sore. And when the convulsions eased, and the chuckles petered out we passed around the tissues and cried some more.

So many friends, fans and celebrities wished to attend Ray McAnally's funeral that it could not be held in our local parish, but was moved to the Pro-Cathedral in the centre of Dublin. Every pew was filled, and those who couldn't squeeze in lined the street outside.

"Gabriel's Oboe", Ennio Morricone's theme music from the film *The Mission,* filled the cathedral. My dad and I had spent months together in South America working on that movie. When the cast list was announced, I had just finished training under the director, Sir Peter Hall, at the UK National Theatre in London and had nothing else lined up. Dad invited me to accompany him to the film set. What a privilege and special opportunity. I cherished every moment we spent getting to know each other as adults, no longer just parent and child. I loved helping him learn his lines and watching him craft his portrayal of Altimirano, a major supporting role to Robert De Niro and Jeremy Irons, for which he won a BAFTA. My experience as an outdoor adventurer, kayaker and canoeist, earned me a spot as the stunt assistant in the jungles of Colombia and by the Argentinian Falls of Iguazú. Our admiration for each other grew, our respect deepened. Dad was so proud of me. He loved to tell everyone that I had taught the Guarani tribes how to paddle. A *slight exaggeration*! But, I did have the honour of spending an afternoon up-river in a small dug-out canoe, showing another Irish actor the basic strokes he'd need for his canoeing scenes above the falls, an actor whose film career was about to take off – Liam Neeson.

As I listened to those haunting notes of "Gabriel's Oboe" on that funeral day in June, I felt a sorrow I had never known. A hole, a loss, a crushing disbelief. When I cried, TV cameras captured my tears in time for the 6 p.m. news. My dad had been a private man, but Ray McAnally was a public figure, so my family and I had to share our grief with the people.

What most of them didn't know, what they couldn't have known, was the sacrifices both he and my mother had made to raise four kids while following their creative calling into a financially precarious profession. The tightrope they walked together had no net. My dad might get cast in a show that would run for only three or four weeks at a time. He was both talented and dedicated so he had confidence the next role would come his way, but he never knew for sure, and he never knew when. During gaps in his employment, no matter how lucrative it might have been, he refused to do voiceovers or appear in commercials. His reasoning? If he became known as the guy who spread butter instead of margarine, or recommended one hotel over another, how could an audience find him credible as Willy Loman in Arthur Miller's *Death of a Salesman*, or the Bull McCabe in John B. Keane's *The Field*. To him, typecasting was the kiss of death for a freelance artist. Playing a Shakespearean role would be impossible if he became known as *yer man from that carpet ad*. His integrity on this issue never wavered.

In the days following his death, praise poured in from the entertainment world. Many newspaper tributes commented on his fastidious attention to detail and how you could rely on his theatrical performances to be equally brilliant, night after night. The consummate professional. He instilled this work ethic in all us kids, too. We often heard him say:

Good work, done consistently, over a long period of time, never goes unnoticed.

Towards the end he was getting noticed with film and television awards. He joked about becoming an *overnight success* after forty years. He was only one or two movies shy of international stardom before he died. The *big money* had been right around the corner. Someone once asked how he achieved his consistency on the stage, if he pretended it was always the first night.

"No," he'd replied, "because my brain would recognise the lie. Instead, I tell myself it could be my last, so it had better be my best."

And one night it was both.

My mother had to make hard choices too. She was already a leading actress at the Abbey Theatre by the time Ray figured out the priesthood wasn't for him. They met on stage and were married four years later. When Dad was cast in the film *Billy Budd,* and in TV shows like *Spindoe* and *The Avengers* in the UK, he would be gone for months at a time. Mam put photos of him above our beds so we could kiss him goodnight and remember we had a father. I missed him, but to me, his absence separated him from the ordinary. He was not like my friends' dads – home for tea each night and going for a Sunday drive on the weekends.

One day, when he'd been gone a long time, I found an old newspaper article in a green leather box my mother kept in her dressing table.

Ronnie Masterson turns down a role on Broadway to raise her two young daughters

A mixture of pride and guilt swept through me. I found her in the kitchen, stirring a pot on the cooker and hugged her as fiercely as any young child could.

"What was that for?" she'd asked, half laughing.

"To say thank you."

"For what?"

"I'll tell you when I'm twenty."

I was hardly going to risk the punishment for snooping.

Chapter 2
Afternoon Sparkles

Never a dull moment was a common phrase in our home. And there wasn't. Variety was the norm. We weren't monetarily rich, but my parents always provided a solid roof over our heads and nutritious meals for our bellies. The privileges I enjoyed as a child were those that made me feel special. If the Christmas panto was sold out, I knew we would still get a seat. At the curtain calls, the star of the show would mention us by name. My sister and I would beam as people turned towards us to see who we were. Renowned, innovative performers like Marcel Marceau had dinner in our kitchen, simply because Ray McAnally thought to invite them.

As work became more plentiful, my parents stretched themselves, moving us to a three-storey house on the northern coast of Dublin bay. The mortgage must have been weighty. But I was still a child, cocooned from any of their worries. From the bright bedroom I shared with Máire, I could see the sea. On summer days, when the sun glinted on the crests of waves, I loved to watch the pretty sailboats dance against the afternoon sparkles, although joining the yacht club was financially out of the question.

One night I was awakened by a scary storm directly overhead. My dad came to our room and brought my sister and me to the window. He said if we watched the lightning and listened to the thunder we'd never be afraid again. Snuggled under my daddy's arm, with my nose pressed against his brown woolly jumper and one eye out the window, I felt protected from every flash and every clap. Minded. The next morning, the tide had gone out so far I felt as if I could skip across the puddles in the rippled sand, all the way from Sutton to Bull Island.

But my dad couldn't protect me from the enemy he didn't know. He knew its face alright, had hired it to work on our house, but didn't know its deeds. No one in the family had any inkling that down in our dark, dingy basement, a certain tradesman had snatched my innocence, giving me lifetime membership to the undesirable club of molested children. I was eight years old.

As a family, we had all pitched in with the renovations. I remember many a day we hacked old plaster off the thick walls of our Georgian house. It was slow and dusty work; only inches of mortar came away at a time. Except for that one time when a huge piece, at least two foot wide, fell off in one lump. To celebrate, work stopped. Everyone went upstairs to make those thirst quenching cola-floats. Except him. And, for some unknown reason, me too.

He perched himself on the side of the newly installed bath and scooted me to stand in front of him. He unzipped his jeans, reached for my hand and shoved it down his underpants. I couldn't see it, but I felt this long warm thing, smooth like the skin of an unripe banana. He wanted me to pet it. My small hand barely reached the whole way around it. When he pushed his face to mine and parted my lips with his tongue, a whooshing noise started in my head. I couldn't hear. But I could smell. Damp. Coffee breath. Stinky-sweat. Then he pushed me away, stood up and zipped up. Quickly. The drinks had arrived. I drank my float through a long, pink hard plastic straw with a wee spoon on the end. I scooped the ice-cream from the bottom of the glass. I couldn't look anyone in the eye, not even my Crolly doll when I hugged her later that night.

Over the next several weeks work progressed and so did he. To this day, I can't walk past a building site without the smell of fresh sawdust or wet cement plunging me right back into that basement. Every time it happened

I knew it was wrong. I knew I was naughty. I knew it was a secret – a shameful secret I kept hidden in the folds of fat for years and lovers to come.

When I was in my early teens, Dad saw the play *Kennedy's Children* performed in London. He loved it so much he produced it in Dublin, offering our house as collateral. But the large audiences he'd expected stayed away and the house was no longer our home. Resilience was his middle name, however, and he found a way, drawing up designs for a smaller house which he had built nearby. The tradesman came back. I was almost fourteen. But apparently not too old for him. By the time he was done with me I had a built-in wardrobe and a bedroom to myself but it was dark and my view of the sea was gone. I missed the solace it brought me, that tidal feeling of ebb and flow, every six hours a new chance at life, permission to begin again. But I felt I had no right to complain. There were children starving in Biafra.

My parents were breaking up, but they weren't very good at it. My dad moved out, he moved back in. They split up a second time, but got back together again. The rows were loud. Two actors in a small house who both knew how to project their voices. I'd go to bed at 4 p.m. so I could take cover during the worst of it and rise in the quiet of 3 a.m. to study. Then, when the house was still asleep, I would escape to school, to normalcy. But each afternoon as I pedalled home a feeling of dread would rise up my throat like bile. I'd hold my breath as I put the key in the door, anxious about what the day would bring. If I heard voices in the kitchen, I would try to gauge the mood. If it sounded volatile, I would sneak down to my bedroom as fast as I could, shut the door and hide.

Other times, if I felt brave, I would march right into the kitchen and try to fix them. Or when I'd hear my dad slam the kitchen door, pound his way down the corridor to the lounge and slam that door, I'd quietly open it and slither onto the couch beside him, put my hand on his beating chest and try to calm him down. I'm not sure if he ever noticed I was even there. When his breathing slowed and his colour returned to normal, I'd go up to the kitchen and try to wipe away my mam's tears and sorrow.

I wasn't sure if they were keeping it together "for the sake of the kids" but secretly I wished they wouldn't. Each time they vacillated, I found the anti-climactic climax emotionally exhausting. By the time they legally split I was sixteen and the last one left at home. Friends and teachers consoled me. "How awful for you!" they'd say. But I felt only relief. Yes, I was sad to come from a "broken home", especially such a public one, but for me it meant the noise had stopped and the feeling of daily dread began to fade. According to the nuns at school, the tension on my face, which I didn't know I'd been wearing, vanished.

I tried to live with my dad for a while, but he was working long hours and I was studying for exams. I needed clean clothes, home-cooked meals and the stability my mother could offer. She and I moved into a small rented house three miles away. My bike ride to school was replaced by a bus.

Dad was always generous of spirit and of wallet. One winter's day, when I was about twelve, he came home from work and announced we were going on our first overseas packaged holiday. To Spain! Excitement reigned. I had no idea he'd been fired on the first day of what was supposed to be a five-week film shoot. Allegedly, the main star didn't think they would work well together. But the producers paid out his contract and this was how he chose to spend it.

Swimming in outdoor pools in November, plucking oranges off heavily laden trees, and riding burros through slanted vineyards were alien activities for a kid raised north of the fiftieth parallel. It took time for my brain to process the possibilities, but process them I did. I learned sunshine brought me joy, I wanted an atlas for my birthday and, as soon as I was old enough to leave home, I knew I was going to follow the sun and live in places others visited on vacation. I was going to be like my dad. Away most of the time. Different.

Paris was first.

Chapter 3
No Baggage

In the late 70s and early 80s in Ireland it was not automatically assumed that every second-level student would progress to college. Some got jobs, some apprenticed in trades. It seemed to me those who signed up for a four-year degree were intent on becoming teachers and professors themselves. In my experience, our career guidance counsellor took the counselling element to heart, lending more of an ear to a troubled teen than any genuine attempt to guide us towards careers.

Included on our English Language curriculum, however, was a series of essays by Cardinal John Henry Newman entitled *The Idea of a University*. While many a scholar and student has since discussed the purpose and their own interpretation of his work, what resonated with me was how he described it as a "school of knowledge of every kind, consisting of teachers and learners from every quarter". To my mind, that meant a bringing together of peoples from varying ethnic, spiritual and economic backgrounds. Back then, the institutes of higher education in Ireland seemed to be filled with a fairly homogenous group of young Irish adults. The only diversity I imagined I would encounter was students from the countryside coming up to Dublin on a Monday and bringing their laundry home to *the mammy* at the weekends.

So, "At Seventeen", right around the time Janis Ian was singing that "love was meant for beauty queens", I left home for the first time, moved to Paris for a year and joined thirty international students enrolled at the Sorbonne University. My new schoolmates were not from County Wexford or Galway city, they were from countries all across Europe and the Middle East. The only thing we had in common was that French was not our mother tongue and yet it was the only means by which we could communicate. After class, we would sit on the terrace of *Les Deux Magots* sipping cafés-au-lait outside this historic haunt of writers and artists from days gone by, discussing Sartre in our broken and borrowed language. As staccato as our parleys were, I felt incredibly animated. Everything was new, schoolmates were cultured, and the city seemed to vibrate with creativity. I felt grown up, independent, and I loved the fact that no one knew who I was. Gone was the identity, Niamh McAnally, daughter of... I got to be just me.

On Sundays, I would visit the Louvre for free, and marvel at how Mona Lisa's eyes seemed to follow me as I moved across the room. Other days, I'd climb the seven hundred and four steps to the second floor of the Eiffel Tower, bypassing the tourists waiting for the elevators, or when I craved the sea, I would saunter the banks of the Seine and watch the river flow. In Versailles, I visited the home of the Sun King, Louis XIV, and teased my reflection in the Hall of Mirrors. It was invigorating, enlightening, and I felt educated in the ways of the world because I had talked to the people who lived there. By the time I'd returned to Ireland, aged eighteen, I had a thirst for travel and a longing to quench it.

It was hardly surprising I followed my parents' freelance footsteps into show-business, because it gave me the opportunity to work for a while, take off and travel to places like Belize, then return and work some more. But I didn't want to trade on the fame of their name, a name that, to my mind, was synonymous with talent, in case I had none. Initially I changed mine to McShane, and started out where many thespians begin – on the bottom rung of the theatrical ladder, as an assistant stage manager. Several acting roles came my way, on stage and on camera, but ultimately it was to the director's chair that my creativity was drawn.

"Five seconds to wrap. Standby camera three," I said. "Take three. Cue Derek."

Tina, the vision mixer to my right, punched the output of camera three into the live transmission feed and downstairs in the TV studio its red light blinked on. Johnny, the floor manager, cued Derek and Thelma's closing piece to camera.

"...and we'll see you tomorrow for another edition of *Live at 3.*"

"Cue music. Roll credits." I said, watching the names of everyone I'd worked with roll up on both the centre and top screens of the bank of monitors in front of me. Mine, as director, was second to last.

"Standby presentation," said the production assistant to my left.

The top screen, which showed what was going out live in people's homes across Ireland, switched to a commercial for washing powder.

"And we're clear! Thanks everybody." I muted my microphone and took off my headset.

"I can't believe this is your last show," said the PA.

It was four years since my father's death and I'd just directed my last television programme. My bags were packed, sentimental valuables put in storage, and I'd sold the rest of my stuff. Why?

Apart from my dad's drive for professional perfection, his curiosity for knowledge and his thirst for truth, he'd been a great man for collecting things – not of the stamp, coin, or ship-in-bottles variety, but of vinyl records he played over and over, or hardback books he read again and again, or the paper clips and rubber bands he kept in jam-jars because he never knew when he might need one. Treasures. But after he died, I realised they were *his* treasures. Any meaning they'd had when he was alive died with him. Now they were all just *stuff*. Stuff to be cleared out, passed on, or stored in boxes till the rawness of grief wore off and someone in the family had the emotional detachment to dispose of them.

It had been less than a year since I'd returned from Belize but the months I'd volunteered there, and lived without *stuff*, had made a deep impression on my soul. Things didn't make me happy, new places did. I was thirty-one and itchy. My boyfriend wanted to travel and I didn't want to lose him. He'd sold his apartment and his business. We could make a living teaching scuba across the globe, he'd said. Had I been rational and career minded, I might have stayed in Ireland, continued to hone my craft, built an independent name for myself, and become a director of movies, theatre, and TV. But my dad's life had taught me to take risks; his sudden and untimely death to embrace them. My security came from the traits I'd absorbed growing up – an ability to see the big picture, a belief that anything is possible, and a craving for variety.

Our human experience is finite and within that undisclosed timeframe all we have is *now*. We can reminisce about the past or plan for the future but we can only live in the present. So I condensed my possessions down to two bags – one with five tee-shirts, two pairs of shorts and a swimsuit, the other filled with diving gear. Passports in hand, visas applied for, we were off to see the world.

Chapter 4
Settling on Shifting Sands

We flew first to America, got off in New York, and turned left. I couldn't have asked for a more uncluttered life than teaching scuba in the Florida Keys, but even the wages were minimalist and my income took a plunge down several tax brackets. However, gone were the low-clinging clouds of Irish winters, the early evening darkness and the damp cold that would seep in through your pores. Here, the water was warm and the sun shone every day, even in February. I hadn't yet heard of seasonal affective disorder (SAD) but I knew the colours of Florida – aqua pools, green trees and deep blue skies – made me happy.

The Keys were laid-back living and life fell into a groove. We worked on the ocean by day and socialised on shore at night. I loved being on the water so much I barely noticed two years slip away, along with the dream of world travel. What woke me up, startled me to the core, was when the boyfriend called it quits. As with many breakups, one person knows it's coming, the other not so much. I was shocked. Didn't understand. To me, the only reason we were not yet married was because we were waiting on an annulment from his first wife. Divorce was still not legal in Ireland then. Because of that, I had shied from the early white gown and veil. I'd had other boyfriends, dated some, lived with another, but having seen my parents separate after twenty-five years of marriage, I'd been waiting, waiting to find that mate for life. I'd thought I had, so the breakup was devastating. I'd been so sure he was the one that I'd not just travelled, but actually emigrated to be with him, leaving everything – Ireland, my family, my career – behind.

Now, after I'd invested five of my prime childbearing years in our relationship, he was leaving me. We weren't getting married. We weren't having kids. Bewilderment overshadowed hurt and paralysed my pain. I wasn't sure what to do. Should I go home? Should I stay? Would I ever find *the one*?

On sleepless nights I watched TV. Hosts of the late-night infomercials became my new companions. On one despondent night, I saw videos of children in underdeveloped countries, flies darting across their innocent faces, children who needed to be sponsored so they could wear shoes and go to school. It only cost $21 a month. I called the charity the next day and within two weeks I was looking at a photo of Ivan, "my" ten-year-old boy from Bolivia, the boy I could write letters to in English, which the charity would translate into Spanish, the boy I'd promised to sponsor until he was eighteen. I had never undertaken such a long-term commitment before. I made two promises to myself. One, no matter what bills came my way over the next eight years I would always find that $21 each month. Two, I would tell no-one.

Another night, another man spoke to me and I made my first ever home shopping purchase – a thirty-day audio course by Tony Robbins. Listening to his *Personal Power* tapes over the next few weeks helped me reset my thinking and regain my senses. What was the lesson I was supposed to learn? Since I'd been in America, men, women and children had been traversing the turbulent waters of the Florida Straits, in questionable boats and makeshift rafts, risking their lives trying to flee Cuba and reach *the land of the free and the home of the brave*. I was already here. Perhaps this land of opportunities had one waiting just for me. Maybe the boyfriend had been the vessel to get me here. With little more than a Green Card in my pocket and sunshine on my back, I quietly packed away my dream of world travel and decided to stay.

I needed a grown-up job with benefits. Even though my mam would've loved to see me back working in TV, I didn't want to live in big cities like New York, Chicago or Los Angeles, so I turned to what we Irish are supposed to be inherently good at – hospitality. The local Sheraton Hotel took a chance on me and within two months of learning the trade I repaid them with my abilities to take on a supervisory role. An increase in salary afforded me a kayak and I spent many an evening soothing my soul with the dip of a paddle and a sighting of dolphin.

For my birthday that year, a co-worker gave me a miniature compass she'd purchased at the Monterey Bay Aquarium, California, and a book edited by Susan Fox Rogers called *Solo: On Her Own Adventure*, a collection of true stories told by women who travelled alone in the great outdoors. I was in awe of them. I wanted to be one of them – a self-sufficient outdoor adventurer who could paint her story in words. Between the book and the compass I saw a sign. The greatest thing about working for hotels is that they can be found in every town. I was ready to leave the Keys and I challenged myself to drive solo across the United States, pitching a tent at every stop. For my safety, colleagues wanted me to carry a gun, but I refused point blank. Of greater concern to me was that, by now, my possessions filled more than two bags. I put a map of America on the wall, stuck raffle tickets on cities along my potential route, and held my own going away party. When my workmates drew a ticket, they received the prize marked on the corresponding one on the map. At the end of a hilarious evening, staff exited the hotel's car park with an array of household items that couldn't fit in my car, or inside the kayak on the roof, including an ironing board, Christmas tree lights, and a set of tools missing a hammer. Of course, if I wasn't going to shoot a nefarious attacker, I was hardly likely to club them to death.

It's difficult to imagine making a cross-country trip without a cell phone or GPS today. Nervousness fuelled my wits. I never stopped in the big cities and got off the road by 4 p.m. every day. With the crumpled map I'd taken down from the wall I got as far as Alaska without getting lost. Given the spectacular scenery and a wonder of wildlife to cherish, it's surprising I didn't stay, especially when I heard there were eight men to every one woman up there. While the statisticians may have been correct in their figures, it seemed to me the eight men were either all away fishing or drinking their profits from their last bountiful catch. I headed south.

Driving the Pacific Coast Highway, through Washington and Oregon, and crossing bridges like San Francisco's Golden Gate heightened my sense of adventure. These were places I'd seen on TV as a child. If only there'd been someone to share the excitement. The miniature compass that lay on the empty passenger seat beside me seemed to steer me back to its origins in Monterey. Someone had told me I would love it there, and at a training course I'd attended in Atlanta, I'd met the general manager of the Hilton. I called from a payphone along the way and accepted the job he offered. By the time I came through Santa Cruz and drove around the bay to Monterey, I was ready to turn off the engine.

The only thing still running was my biological clock. Eighteen months later, it tick-tocked my thirty-five-year-old body into a marriage, in search of a family, but found an unsuitable union plagued with incompatible values instead. Friends and family knew it was doomed to fail long before the wedding ring had indented my finger. I knew it too. Yet, I couldn't give myself permission to leave. Old tapes and cultural conditioning played loops in my head:

Until death do us part.

I thought if we could afford to buy a house and settle down, the fairy-tale would begin. Two days after 9/11, we flew on a less-than-full plane to Tampa, Florida and moved into our new home.

You've made your bed, now lie in it.

I stayed, desperate to prove I hadn't made a mistake. But I had. I'd sold myself out. I'd been flattered by a good-looking man in a sports car (how could someone that cool want me?) and driven by maternal instincts and a desire for the white picket fence. I'd confused touch with love. If someone hugged me, cuddled me or wanted to have sex with me, I thought that meant they loved me. For eight and a half years, I compromised who I was to try to make it work. And it did work – so long as I suppressed my feelings and existed as a superficial version of myself. The marriage was wrapped in material success; we had a nice house, a pool, two cars and two businesses, but the union was fundamentally flawed. The absolute irony? The babies never came. I was still fertile, but doctors with turkey basters couldn't make the sperm and egg hold hands. My heart bled for the mother I would never be.

Two years earlier, even Ivan, "my" Bolivian boy, had been ripped away. His enrolment in the sponsorship programme ceased when he turned eighteen. The charity refused to give me the details to contact him directly, but instead offered a photo of another young child, inviting me to start all over again. I just couldn't. My financial commitment was over. I'd done it. I was proud of myself, but this wasn't a mortgage I'd just paid off, this was a little human I'd watch grow into a healthy young man, ready for the world. I still had all his handwritten letters, along with the typed translations, all his school reports showing his wonderful progress, all the photos they took of him proudly wearing gifts I'd sent him, including an Ireland soccer shirt because he loved the sport and played it at school. It was still the era of pen-pals and I always assumed we would continue to write, that I would be in his life and he would be in mine. I felt sad. I thought about him throughout the years and always wondered what might have happened to him.

So, there were no children or surrogate children in my life, but still I stayed in the marriage. My brothers and sister were all married with kids. I loved my nephews and nieces dearly, but I was acutely aware of the difference between my siblings' lives and mine. I felt empty. Directionless. Lonesome. I felt more lonely inside the wrong marriage for me than if I'd actually been alone. But still I stayed, locked in a misconception that I could fix it, change him, change me, change the relationship – find a way.

It was a wise young woman, Dana Vince of Healing Hearts Counselling, who finally gave me the sentence to free myself:

Why wait one more day to be happy?

That one question unlocked my self-imposed bars, and heritage was no longer my jailor. Blame was banished, guilt gutted. I was free, free to be me.

Where would I go, where would I heal? Texas. Family. Support. As we go through the various periods of change in our lives, there is nothing more comforting than the love of family. Through hormones and acne, boyfriends and breakups, marriage and divorce, my family has always been there for me no matter what. My brother, Conor, was now living near Austin and he and his wife, Kay, opened their arms and unconditionally welcomed me in.

Long walks by the river, chats by the fireside, and hours of sleep in down-filled comfort helped stretch the distance between disillusion and hope. Within months I was re-nourished. But I couldn't stay. I still yearned for a relationship and the type of close marriage Conor and Kay shared, but Texas was not in my blood. I was fearful of falling in love with a ten-gallon hat (with or without the cattle) and having to make living on the land my way of life. I feel claustrophobic in the wide open fields. It's the water that draws my soul.

Time for a paradigm shift. Instead of bemoaning being childless, it was time to ask a better question: what could I do that others with child-rearing responsibilities could not? Maybe it was time to unpack that dream of world travel.

The islands of Fiji seemed like a good place to start.

Chapter 5
The Next Rung

I didn't hear the usual flight attendant announcement to stow my table and return my seat to the upright position. Not surprising, since there was neither aisle nor crew. I could see the back of the pilot's head two rows in front of me as he began his descent. The short flight from Nadi on the main island to Savusavu on Vanua Levu took no longer than sixty minutes; time enough to clear my ears and relish the alluring waters below. As we screeched to a halt on the one-strip runway, paralleling the aptly named Hibiscus Highway, men in bright-coloured shirts scuttled about the doors and deplaned us with such cheer I felt like I'd won the Lotto.

"*Bula!* Welcome to Fiji!"

It was 2009.

Tony Robbins had come to my town last year; now I had come to his. It had been thirteen years since I'd first listened to his message. When the opportunity to attend his seminar *Unleash the Power Within* arose, I couldn't resist the chance to see if I, too, could walk barefoot on burning coals. Along with thousands of other participants chanting *cool moss*, I'd got myself *in state* and traversed the three-and-a-half-metre stretch of embers without incurring so much as a blister. Afterwards, when the euphoria was effervescent, I met a girl who had her sights set on another of his seminars, this one called *Life Mastery*, staged near his Namale Resort in Fiji.

"You'll love it, Niamh," she'd said. "You'll be put through your paces, physically, mentally and emotionally, all while juicing."

"Seriously?" I asked. "You get nothing to eat but juice?"

"The greatest thing is," she continued, ignoring my question, "you can get a visitor's visa for four months. We can probably rent a house after the course is over, and maybe volunteer on future courses. I bet it won't be expensive to live there either."

Four months? Could I give it all up for four months in the South Pacific? I was childless, divorced, unemployed and dabbling in a less-than-successful online businesses trying to be mobile and global – sadly, there was nothing to give up, save the connection with friends and family. Couple that with the deeply engrained freelance mentality I'd inherited from my parents, the idea of knowing where and how I'd be living for a whole four months had felt like the security of taking on a career with a pension.

So here I was, south of the equator, feeling alive! A friendly busman drove us twenty minutes out of town and up a hill to the Wasawasa Conference Centre. Scattered along the ridgeline, overlooking the coral reef, were simple wooden buildings that had accommodated many a *Life Mastery* graduate. Jovial women with flowers in their hair gave us a tour of the grounds, culminating in the grand hall.

A lunch of fresh raw vegetables, hummus and salads was laid out on a wooden table. Alexandra, a lean woman in her thirties introduced herself as our facilitator, and invited us to eat our last meal with pleasure. She knew more about the week-long juice menu than we did. No sooner had the last cucumber been swallowed, and although many of us had flown across continents and oceans to get there, we were loaded onto buses and brought back down the hill.

"There they are," said a guy named Tom sitting behind me.

We'd pulled up at a grass field. In the centre stood three eighteen-metre-high wooden poles. Each had metal rungs evenly spaced from the ground to the top. Tom seemed nervous. He had been here before. Alexandra gathered us in a circle around the base of the central pole.

"Welcome to *Life Mastery*," she said. "You'll each be given a helmet and harness which will be hooked onto the safety line. When you're ready, you'll call out, "Belay on" so that the crew will take up the slack as you climb. When you get to the top, stand on the top of the pole, enjoy the beautiful bird's eye view, and jump to the trapeze suspended in front of you. Any questions?"

I wanted to ask if you could get altitude sickness at eighteen metres, but didn't. Once the challenge began, we morphed from a diverse gang of individuals into a united team of supporters, rallying around the person making the climb, calling their name, encouraging their progress. Some made it look easy. Some got halfway up and froze. Others fell off and swung around the pole, saved by the guide rope and safety crew on the ground.

When my turn came to be clipped in, I looked at the tableau of unfamiliar faces and wondered how they could possibly support me when most wouldn't even know how to pronounce my name. But, undeterred, I took the first step, thinking, *This is easy.* One arm after one leg, and up I went with a gusto of such momentum that the three-quarter mark was right in front of me before I looked down. Mistake. My zestful clamber came to an abrupt halt. Fear snuck up the back of my neck. Why was I here? Why would I put myself in harm's way like this? Could I climb down again, could I climb up? I was about ten rungs from the top. When I looked down all I could see was a collection of colours: green grass, blue helmets, a rainbow of upturned faces. The pole grew disproportionally wider as it stretched all the way up to my feet. Instead of enjoying a regal view from the top of the world, my brain perceived the vision as a threat. Adrenalin swarmed my body as it fell into fight-or-flight mode. The slight vibration in my left leg became a shaking and then a wobble. I had a chat with my knee, but it shook without care. I heard Alexandra call out:

"Niamh, what would this mean to you, to get to the top?"

And there it was, that competitive streak that had to be satisfied. Why did I feel I had to be the one to show everyone how to climb the pole perfectly? Why did I have to be the leader? Why did I *think* I had to be the leader? Did I really want to, or was this feeling a reflection of how it used to warm my heart when my dad would boast about my accomplishments? Was that because I cherished his pride in me, or because I knew it pleased him? It always seemed so important to him. He was completely supportive of my choosing to do, or be, whatever I wanted, but once the choice was made, he encouraged me to be the absolute best.

From six years of age I was taught piano by a nun. It was laborious, tedious, and it hurt. If I played a wrong note, she would rap my knuckles with a wooden ruler and make me start again. I wanted to learn music but I hated the process. I couldn't understand how to read what was on the page on the little ledge that hung above the keys in front of me. Instead, I cheated. The nun pencilled numbers above the notes. Each one corresponded to a finger. So, I used to sit there on the piano stool, gazing at the sheet music, allegedly playing by sight. What I was actually doing was hitting the key in front of my index finger if it said the number two or with my ring finger when it said the number four. It worked well, and everyone was happy, until I'd get to the exam and the grumpy old man who conducted the tests would put brand new, unnumbered sheet music in front of me. It was about as mystifying as trying to comprehend the instructions on how to knit an Aran sweater. I tried to convince my parents I didn't want to learn to play the piano but they felt I would regret it later in life. So the crotchets and quavers remained part of my after-school lessons for another few years.

Eventually, after one particularly painful knuckle-rapping session and ensuing tears, I was let off the hook. Perhaps my parents had finally heard me, or else they came to understand you can't make lemonade out of avocados. Either way, my young brain wasn't equipped to psychoanalyse their decision. Nor could it figure out what might have frustrated a nun so much as to berate a child in such a manner. All I cared about was that I'd escaped from the not so passive-aggressive corporal punishment.

By the time I was twelve, and got to listen to my sister Máire play the piano well, I began to regret my lack of ability to elicit a tune, but I wasn't about to let anyone know. By then, my brother, Aonghus, was an accomplished musician in a rock band called *Mushroom*, and he introduced me to the guitar. The three- or four-chord folk songs of the 1970s were fun, relevant, and easy to learn. I would spend hours in my teenage bedroom "strumming my pain" and "killing me softly". I began tinkering with lyrics, making up words to go with well-known melodies. One day, my dad overheard me play and became excited.

"Look how well Aonghus plays lead guitar and he only began a year or two ago. If you practise now, you could be the first famous female guitarist by the time you are his age."

I nodded, but put down the guitar.

And as I gripped the pole in Fiji that day, I saw where my pattern had begun. I hadn't wanted to be the first famous female guitarist. I'd just wanted to be a girl who played the guitar, but I felt that would have disappointed my dad. So, from then on, I believed I had to be all-in or not-in-at-all. If I couldn't be the best, I wasn't going to try.

Now, here I was, stuck, three-quarters of the way up a pole. I couldn't have given a damn about reaching the top of it right then. It was insurmountable. My arms were tired and my legs had quit. What annoyed me was that my instinct for all-or-nothing had failed me. I had made the attempt instead of an excuse. Why had I not opted out? Oh, that's right, because I had signed up for *Life Mastery* and this was on the agenda. As I clung there, questioning what "mastering life" meant to me, Alexandra changed tack and yelled:

"Niamh, what would it mean to you to get to the rung above you?"

What indeed.

It would mean mediocrity; it would mean *so what?* I feared the so-whats. So what if I got three-quarters of the way up? That wasn't the objective, was it? No, it was to climb to the top, stand up, and jump to a trapeze that dared me.

I could hear the waning shouts of those below me – their chanting had grown weak and unenthused. I guess they were getting bored with this inaction, not realising that, for me, it was akin to sitting in a doctor's waiting office, flicking through the pages of my life: a magazine filled with patterns that had held me back and patterns that had propelled me forward. To those below, the only outward clue to my quandary was the incessant trembling of my leg. In the quiet of their impatience, I heard Alexandra more clearly:

"What about the next rung, Niamh?"

In the midst of panic, how often have you been told to take a deep breath? It sounds so clichéd, but when you actually do it, you draw an abundance of air into the lower lobes of your lungs, which then magically oxygenates your brain and calms your senses. I told myself to slow my breath, to take my time, to discard the noise and seek clarity. I focused on what she *actually* said: What about the next rung? If I could make it to the next rung it would mean the pressure would be on the other leg and this one would stop shaking. Simple as that. No need to worry about getting to the top; I just had to shift my weight and get to the next rung. As I made that tiny movement, I heard the cries of one or two loyal supporters who were still watching and hadn't given up on me. Others noticed and joined the chant. Someone had figured out the phonetics of my name and I could hear a chorus singing up to me: *"Knee-if, Knee-if, Knee-if"*. My spirit was spurred on by calls of support from my new best friends and my ego remembered I was being video-taped. I continued up. I had a new rhythm. Right arm, left leg, breathe; left arm, right leg, breathe. Simple. I had no other life purpose in that moment than to pull with one arm and push with the opposite leg. It was merely a meditative movement that required no thought. Somehow, I got out of my own way.

But when I reached the second-to-last rung from the top, the sequence fell apart. I had one foot on each of the final two rungs, the flat top between my knees and nothing but fresh air above my waist. I wrapped my arms around the top of that pole like a stoned koala bear would hold onto a eucalyptus. Here I was, at the top, my knees under my chin, my ankles under my bum. All I had to do was unwrap my arms, use my quads to push myself into a standing position on the last two rungs, step onto the top, ignore the eighteen-metre drop, focus on the trapeze in front of me, and jump. Simple, right? So what do you think happened next?

Yes, I managed to get my first foot on top of the pole, and then brought up the second – for a second. My unbalanced weight took one look at the trapeze and faltered. In an instant, my view was filled with a swirl of palm trees, ground and faces, as I stumbled off the top. The falling sensation lasted an interminable nano-second before the jerk on my harness reassured me I was dangling at the end of the safety rope, circling back to earth. So close. So close to making it perfectly to the top, but I had failed in perfection. Everybody got one chance to climb the pole. There were no do-overs. When my feet touched the grass, I found myself in the centre of a rugby tackle as those unfamiliar friends surrounded me with hugs and congratulations for what I had achieved. I wanted to embrace their enthusiasm, but I felt like a fraud. How could they not see I had failed? I could have done better. I should have done better. If only I could have one more go, I could give them a real reason to celebrate. I unclipped my harness and handed it to the next nervous person waiting in line.

I watched another ten people, younger and older, climb the pole that day, including a woman who only had the use of one arm. How could she even get past the first rung? All she had to work with was her legs. She used her right arm to drag the other one along. We all chanted her name as she took on rung after rung. After thirty minutes she reached the summit – her summit, which was halfway up. There, she signalled the ground crew, who told her to lean back as they counter-balanced her controlled descent. When her feet touched the ground, she punched her good arm high in triumph and her delighted grin matched that of any world record-setting athlete. We crowded around her to lay a hand on the imaginary Olympic Gold medal she had just won.

Amid the noise and congratulations, I pondered the difference between her summit and my own. She was so pleased with her effort, but I was disappointed mine wasn't perfect. I had got twice as far as she had, and neither of us made the leap to the trapeze, but her joy and contentment was far superior to the feelings I was having. She was thrilled with her success. What had been her expectations, to climb two rungs, not thirty-two? Had I done my best, or had I fallen short? Was it OK to be less than perfect?

I was conscious of a girl called Kaye, who would become a lifelong friend, slapping me on the back and shouting:

"You did great, Niamh."

Had I?

When God was handing out small-framed Celtic bodies to Irish women, I had been standing in the wrong queue. I got the big-boned Viking one instead. Over the years I added substantial padding. When I left school I also left behind my hockey stick, and with it any form of routine exercise. Dublin gyms were not as ubiquitous as potatoes back then. Nothing like mashed spuds with butter to warm you on a winter's day. As my twenties wore on, my fitness deteriorated, although I did become a dieting success, losing the same twenty kilos over and over again. I still hadn't figured out why. Why, when I would get within a dress size of my goal weight, or later in life my more realistic BMI, why would I turn around and self-sabotage my way back to fat? I admired anyone who physically achieved what I thought I could not. Watching athletes stand on the podium made me cry. I imagined how proud they must feel and I respected their resolve, their dedication, their commitment to their training and to themselves.

I was gathered up in a swell of movement as the group began heading towards the gate. It was over. Climbing the steps onto the bus, I looked back over my shoulder at the eighteen-metre pole. My lesson, that day, was not as simple as how far I could push my body physically. I needed to quit wallowing and start congratulating others. I was proud of everyone and what they had achieved. None of them felt like frauds to me. When I focused on others, my thought pattern shifted. I was kinder. Not only to them, but also to myself. I had actually done my best, and the moment in which my two feet touched the top of that pole was what my best looked like that day. Who was to say on another day my best wouldn't have included a leap for the trapeze or falling off on the seventh rung?

It was also time to live the life I was creating, not the one I thought was expected of me. I didn't need to seek my father's approval from beyond the grave. I knew he had been proud of me. I knew he had loved me. I could strive for perfection but not beat myself up if it eluded me. The top of the pole taught me the art of acceptance for what is. The tumble back to earth taught me the nature of self-forgiveness for what is not.

At the end of the week-long juice programme my body was cleansed, my brain defogged and I felt healthy. Refreshed. I had made friends, friends that shared a common bond. We'd supported each other through difficult days and rejoiced over personal growth. We'd helped repaint the outside of a church in one village, and donated toys and school supplies in another. The woman who had enticed me to come to Fiji went home so we never rented that house together. Luckily for me, however, Alexandra needed a volunteer to live on site and help with upcoming courses so I jumped at the chance to stay connected with the programme and be able to help new participants on their journey.

Living like a local in Fiji was delightful, its people, inspiring. The lush jungles, waterfalls and tropical flowers found on Vanua Levu perfumed the air. Random rain showers were intense but so too was the sun that evaporated their remnants. I loved to walk along the shore, on the way home from the market, bags filled with fresh fruits and cassava, dodging puddles and watching the rippled sea succumb to the wind.

On a calm day I treated myself with a trip to the outer reef with one of the local operators. How carefree it felt to dive for fun again and enjoy the abundant fish life, healthy corals and clear colourful waters without the responsibility of students or nervous divers. Although, on the way back to shore I realised just how much I missed working on a boat. I felt in tune with the sporadic spray from the bow wake and the feeling of infinite possibility.

Of course I couldn't live in Fiji without partaking in a kava ceremony, a cultural tradition of social gatherings and welcomes. I was delighted when a lady I'd met at the market invited me to spend an evening in her village. When I arrived, a group of men were sitting in a circle around a large wooden bowl, with several men forming a looser second circle behind them. The women were sitting in a line against the wall. I went to join them, but, as an honoured guest, I was ushered to the central circle. I presented the yaqona root (kava) I had been advised to bring. It was graciously accepted and put aside for future use as they had already crushed one for this evening. The powder was mixed with water and then, from the communal bowl, poured into half a coconut shell. Filled to the brim was considered "high tide". The chief clapped once, said "Bula", and drank it in one gulp. Then he clapped three times and passed the shell to be refilled. Having been warned that it was an acquired taste, akin to drinking a mixture of mud and dirty dish water (although who on earth would ever have drunk that to know?), that my mouth could tingle or go numb, it might put me to sleep, and since sipping was not allowed, I cowardly asked for a "low-tide" fill, half a shell. I clapped once, yelled "Bula" and surprisingly, for a woman who had managed thus far to avoid the peer pressure of downing a shot, I knocked it back in one go so that my taste buds wouldn't have time to catch up. Success.

Although, when I clapped three times and passed the shell, I hoped my Fijian friend was joking when she told me that meant I'd asked for three more cups.

Many of the families I met in Savusavu lived a meagre lifestyle by western standards, some living in small homes with tin roofs, nothing like the eloquently thatched *bures* found at the resorts. Yet they knew how to luxuriate in the simpler things in life. From one village I visited with a subsequent group on the juice fast, I have an image burned in my brain of a man laughing and waving at us while showering outdoors from a makeshift bucket strung on a tree above his head, his children dancing in delight chasing the suds forming bubbles in the air. When the kids then ran to greet us we laid a pile of gifts on the grass clearing. I noticed one little girl choosing fun sunglasses with pink plastic frames shaped in two hearts. She put them on, held out another pair for me and giggled. When I put mine on her entire face lit up and she hugged me fiercely. Such joy, such innocence and yet such connection – we were the same, she and I, both wearing silly sunglasses. As I looked at hers through mine I remember thinking *love is all around when you look through the window of your heart.*

Chapter 6
The Laugh List

Returning from Fiji was tough. Psychological jet lag. If you've ever taken a sabbatical leap of faith, you know it's not the packing up and taking off that is scary, it's the re-entry that causes anxiety. The trip will end. How do you re-establish yourself, find a new job, a new place to live, if you've had to let go of the old? How do you reconnect with longstanding friends who appear, to you, to have stood still, but in fact, have not? Change happens. Are the changes going to be so radical you lose the commonality that originally bonded your friendship? Can you return to your old life and still feel truly alive while queueing in the supermarket, if you've been off somewhere exotic, "*mastering your life*"? Could I?

Before I left the States, I'd been in limbo. Now that I was back I was still driving around the freeways trying to find my niche in America, this time in Los Angeles. I was also suffering from reverse culture shock. To me, motorists in adjacent lanes seemed oblivious to the extent of their wealth. The stark contrast between their opulent cars rolling past me, some with price tags of a hundred thousand dollars or more, and the living conditions of some Fijian families I'd met, was hard to reconcile.

It wasn't the flashy rims or discreet spoilers of the Californian sports cars that caught my attention, but rather the grimly set jaws of those behind the wheels. What were they thinking? Why weren't they happy? Was it simply impatience at the crawling speed of traffic, or was it a dissatisfaction with not yet having what they wanted in life, because the race had blinded them to the fortune they already had? Yet, in Fiji, I'd witnessed many a family living with substantially less but who seemed intrinsically happy. Whether they were farmers or fishermen, retailers or servers, no matter their task, they were always jovial. Their secret? They laughed – a lot. It seemed to me they laughed at everything and laughed at nothing. Their cackles were contagious. What a gift it would be to spread such joy. They inspired me to adopt a new purpose in life — to make someone laugh every day. And the greatest thing about such a mission? I couldn't fail. At bedtime I could review my "laugh list". If I hadn't made someone else laugh that day, I could always find something to laugh about myself. I could smile myself to sleep.

I also thought I could set a Hollywood trend by shouting the happy-go-lucky greeting of the Fijian people. If it had anything to do with the usual hoots of hysterics you would find bubbling up from a group of women sitting cross-legged on the earth weaving palm tree leaves, then maybe it could make the intense LA crowd happier too. It certainly made me smile every time I pedalled my bicycle along the Pacific Ocean, gaily waving my arms and shouting "Bula" to anyone who crossed my path. You might think this strange, or that I would be hauled off in a straitjacket, but this was Venice Beach after all, where *crazy* tends to fit in. However, despite my exuberance, it never caught on. Why not? How do trends actually start? What makes a society decide it is cool to wear jeans that look like they have been through a shredder, or black eyeliner so thick a raccoon might wonder if it has a two-legged cousin?

Years later, I found the piece of the puzzle I was missing. In his TED talk, entrepreneur Derek Sivers masterfully describes "How to start a movement" in three minutes. To demonstrate his theme, he shows a homemade video of people sitting on the side of a hill at what must have been an outdoor concert. It is a nice sunny day. Young people, lovers, and families are spread out across the grass, Woodstock-style. Slightly down the slope, with a spacious area to himself, one "shirtless guy" is dancing. When I say dancing, I'm not talking *Dancing With The Stars* or Britain's *Strictly Come Dancing*. No, this guy's uncoordinated boogying was from his own little world, which, in fairness, may have been influenced by a combination of recently ingested hops and afternoon sunshine. As the video unfolds, Sivers explains why a leader "needs the guts" to stand alone and look ridiculous, but be "easy to follow". That's when one other brave character stands up and joins him. What's key is for the leader to embrace his first follower "as an equal" so it is "not about the leader" or follower but about the two of them as a group. The follower then calls his friend to join in. The vast majority of the concert goers are still sitting on the grass but watching the three of them dance. Sivers points out that the first follower validates the initiator and the second follower creates the turning point. Now it's not just one crazy guy dancing, and it's not two, it's three, and "three is a crowd". As new frolickers participate, they follow the follower, not the original leader. The energy builds as more people get up to dance. The bigger the group, the less risk there is of looking ridiculous, so even more join in. Momentum creates the movement. Pretty soon, the people still sitting on the grass, who prefer to be part of the "in-crowd", get up and dance rather than be "ridiculed for *not* joining in". As Derek Sivers concludes his talk, he reminds us it was the first follower who transformed shirtless guy from "a lone nut into a leader".

Understandably then, along the bike path of the Pacific Coast Highway, without knowing I needed to attract a first and second follower, I was always only going to be a *Bula*-bellowing "lone nut". Ironically, a couple of weeks later, despite my "laugh list" I found my own jaw grimly set as I was stuck in heavy traffic on the Santa Monica Freeway, watching drivers cut me off in their efforts to move two spaces ahead. They say that, when two people meet, an emotional sale is always made. Either Mr Happy will uplift the grumpy person to his level, or Mr Grumpy will drag the happy one down to his. Was that what was happening to me? Was I buying into the ambient mood of LA – a culture that, to me, seemed to applaud accumulation of material wealth. Was I struggling to fit in when I knew, even though I had the sophistication to belong, I would never have the desire?

Another gem I'd learned from Tony Robbins was how to identify the source of discord in my life. We all have a notion of how our lives should be, what they should look like, and how we should live them. This, Tony suggests, is our "blueprint". When we are living our blueprint, we are happy. However, according to Robbins, it's almost impossible to maintain a core happiness when our life conditions do not match our blueprint.

For me, the level of unhappiness I experience is directly proportional to the intensity of disharmony I feel. I can ignore the issue, but it never resolves itself. Something has to change – either my blueprint or my life conditions – and *I* have to be the one to make those changes.

A blueprint is simply a set of beliefs. When it became clear that I was not going to have children, there was nothing I could do to change the condition. I had to change my thoughts instead. My only choice was to reconcile with what was and transform the way I felt about it. I had to radically change my blueprint.

The discord I was feeling while driving in LA, therefore, was fixable. I'd been flailing in the water, trying to swim against a current of consumerism, when all I had to do was turn around and drift downstream to a simpler style of living – back to my comfort zone of minimalism. That meant changing my life conditions. I needed to leave Los Angeles. But go where?

My marital home in Florida had not yet sold. I tied my kayak to the roof rack, drove cross-country again, and moved back into the empty house. I still had a sleeping bag, an air mattress, and a Swiss Army knife. My friends invited me to stay with them but I declined. When I'm feeling depressed, the last thing I want is people trying to cheer me up. Nor do I want to bring them down. I needed to be by myself. When they accepted I was determined to forgo creature comforts while I figured my life out, they reluctantly lent me a bowl and a chopping board and wished me well.

But my powers of reasoning had left me. Something about living on the floor in a house that used to be my "grown-up" home, absently catching wood chips under my fingernails as I repeatedly rubbed the back of my hand against the textured wallpaper, made me fall into the depths of despair. How could I be so high one minute and so low the next? Hadn't I just climbed a pole in Fiji? I felt lost.

I thought if I could just be by the ocean everything would be OK. The water would soothe my soul. I could begin again. I drove the three miles to the closest small beach on Florida's gulf coast. I sat on the tiny strip of sand

and waited for solace, for the uplifting, for a glimmer of gratitude. I expected the ocean to bring me back to joy, but it didn't. That made it worse. The one thing I could always rely on to raise my spirits – water – couldn't. What now? What's left? When I thought I had finished crying, it was only a ten-second reprieve. The tears were exploding from deep within my cells. I got back in the car, saw the blur of the red traffic light in time to stop, parked the car in the garage and shut the door on the world.

Down I went. Fast. For three days, I didn't leave my old guest bedroom except to make a snack and go to the toilet. Sunlight never had a chance to shine past the closed curtains. The frustrating part was that I knew what needed to be done. Had it been someone else lying on the floor, I would have helped them pull out of the nose dive, turn their thinking around. But I couldn't raise my spirits enough to do it for myself. I was in a self-perpetuating corkscrew of negativity. Absolute apathy. The more emotionally empty I became the more "'like'" attracted "like". Mentally, I got to the point where I couldn't see the point in living.

"Take me now," I said to the empty room.

It was one o'clock in the morning. By some divine intervention of gigahertz frequency my laptop connected itself to the internet. A message from Simon in Australia, one of the enlightened friends I'd met along my travels, asked me how I was. How could I answer that? I was down, and almost out. But I had just enough left to let him in. It was he who asked me the better question.

"What is the one thing that you have always wanted to do, and never done ... yet?"

"Easy!" I replied. "I've always wanted to work at sea."

"What qualifications do you need to have to be employable?"

"I don't know."

"Well, my dear, why don't you find out?"

I closed my eyes, knowing I had something to do tomorrow.

Action. I woke up the next day. I found out that I needed to take STCW95 (Standards of Training, Certification and Watchkeeping for Seafarers) and the first available course started in Fort Lauderdale in two days' time. Better yet, the Boat Show was the week after – an important event since it attracted captains of the mega yachts looking to hire crew.

After five days, some spent in class, others firefighting in a controlled environment, or pool drills, climbing into upturned life rafts, I proudly emerged with my certificate in hand. But, mingling with other hopeful crew at one of the social gatherings I was advised to attend, captain after captain turned me down. Towards the end of the evening one of the older captains approached me and said:

"Do you know why you're not getting hired?"

"No."

"Three reasons," he said.

"Oh?"

"Number one, you're over twenty. Number two, you're over twenty and—"

"Number three, I'm over twenty?"

"Now you're catching on."

Chapter 7
Islands without Cars

I'd studied hard, spent a lot of my savings on the course, and ended up with what? To those who classified it as another false start after my divorce – nothing. To me, it had been a lifeline that kept me breathing.

My mind opened and a new thought wandered in. If I couldn't work at sea, maybe I could work on an island surrounded by it. Better yet, what if I could find a rustic island without even cars?

I booked a dinner date with Google. The first three islands I found, all claiming to have a dearth of automobiles, were on the European side of the Atlantic: Hydra in Greece, and Herm and Sark in the Channel Islands, lying between England and France. What was this? Had my computer somehow tapped into my subconscious and extrapolated a desire to reconnect with my roots? Did it know that my mother was aging and that moving closer to home would become a need?

My love of sunshine and warm water notwithstanding, I couldn't bring myself to choose Hydra. Even if I could have learned the language, I felt it would have been wrong to take a job while many Greek families were struggling with unemployment.

The Channel Islands were the obvious choice. Herm, a tiny island off the coast of Guernsey, looked like the perfect spot for me to take a six-month seasonal job as a hotel receptionist and the employers confirmed food and accommodation would be included. I would be able to see the sea from every corner as the topography offered cliff walks to the south and beach strolls to the north. Not only were there no cars, bicycles were also banned. It was close enough to catch a quick flight to Ireland, but far enough away to maintain the independence I had attained.

So that was it; decision made. Time to get reacquainted with Craig and his List and start selling again. It's all just stuff, isn't it? Is it? Perhaps sometimes we do have inanimate objects in our lives that hold more meaning than other possessions. Why else would I cry when I watched a pleasant couple drive off with my seventeen-year-old kayak on *their* roof. That yellow boat had been my ticket to float. Miles of paddling amid alligators and dolphins in Florida, sea lions and kelp in California, and there she was – gone. Parting with her was maybe as hard for me as someone else having to put down their dog. Oh well, moving on.

I booked a one-way ticket, via a two-week stopover in Dublin, to Guernsey, purged the rest of my stuff and sold my car. At the airport, I checked in for my overnight flight, opened my laptop and logged in. As I waited for my email account to load, I paused to reflect. The flurry of activity it had taken to pack up and go had distracted me from the realisation that this was it. After eighteen years, and a failed marriage, life in America was over. Time to look forward, not back.

I scanned the list of emails and clicked on the one from Herm Hotel. What? What now? Instead of final details of my specific position and start date, I read, in stunned silence, that they had no job for me after all. What did they mean they had no job for me? During the phone interview they'd said my experience in the hospitality industry – a year as a front-desk supervisor for the Sheraton in Key Largo, three as a Director of Front Office for the Hilton in Monterey – would more than meet any of their requirements. With ninety seasonal jobs on offer, they would certainly find one for me. This must be a mistake. Perhaps they had sent me a *Dear John* letter meant for someone else. But, they hadn't. As I read it through for the fourth time, it was clear they had turned me down. What could have happened between that conversation and my selling my stuff?

"Ladies and gentlemen, we are now ready to board our flight to Dublin..."

There I sat, with a one-way ticket out of the US and nowhere to go but home to see my mam. Good Lord. Was I going to have to move back in with the mammy? I wouldn't be the first adult child in the world to do so, but it didn't concur with my ideal blueprint.

"Now boarding rows twenty-five and above..."

It reminded me of when I *was* twenty-five and had gone to my father with a problem. I'd already spent several years working in the theatre, but more recently had been employed as a production assistant for my brother's TV company. I'd been debating whether to take up Conor's offer to go on an eight-week course to become a multi-camera, live studio television director. My dad, whose philosophy of coping with the uncertainty of life as an actor was to "take the next job", couldn't understand my hesitation.

"Well," I'd said, remembering the newspaper clipping I'd found as a child in my mother's dresser, "I don't know if I'm going to look back and realise this was the day I chose career over marriage and children.

"Let me see if I understand this," my dad said. "Conor believes in you enough to have you trained as a director?"

"Yes."

"And you're worried about taking the course in case you'll miss out on marriage?"

"Sort of."

"Well, daughter, with the greatest of respect, I haven't seen anyone beating a path to my door asking for your hand, now have I?"

"No."

"So, what's your dilemma?"

It was the first time I understood critical thinking. I'd been creating a debate where there was none. I hadn't had a choice to make. There'd been only one offer on the table anyway.

At the airport gate, the seats beside me had been vacated.

In a journey "around the mind", I analysed my new situation. What was real, what was imagined? The reality was I had no house, no car and no job in the United States. Nothing to turn back for, and no one to begging me to stay. What did I actually have? I had a flight to Dublin and an onward ticket to Guernsey, two weeks hence. I had two bags, presumably already in the cargo hold, so if I didn't want them to be destroyed, it would make sense to get on the plane.

And yet...

"This is the final boarding call for..."

I came to a conclusion. I needed to invoke another law I had read about, this one via Deepak Chopra, the *Law of Detachment*. I had set the intention to find a simpler life, but I also needed to detach from the outcome. If I didn't, the violin concerto the universe was orchestrating on my behalf would screech out of tune. I would be deaf to the symphony of opportunities.

"Would the last remaining passengers..."

The plane wouldn't wait for me, and I couldn't wait for hindsight. I needed to let go of Herm. For some reason, one I did not yet understand, or might never come to understand, it must not have been the right opportunity for me.

"The doors are now cl..."

I stood up.

My mam would be disappointed.

My mam was indeed disappointed for me, but delighted I'd got on the plane. I remember feeling the whoosh of air as they'd closed the door behind me. I'd taken my seat and buckled up. I stared out the window, schooling my brain to relax, to let go of the anxiety and hold firm to the belief that in the next fourteen days anything was possible. The next chapter of my life would reveal itself when I was ready to see it.

My mother led a very active life, both professionally and socially, although she never dated another soul after she and my dad split up. Since I'd moved out, twenty-nine years earlier, she'd lived alone, so she revelled in the chance to feed me up and put hot water bottles in my bed. I took the time to stoke the turf fire and listen to her stories. Most of them were about my father; many I'd heard before. The night the Abbey Theatre burned to the ground, she and Dad had only been forty-two days married, living in

Granny's house, waiting for their own to be finished. Earlier that evening, my dad, in his role as a British soldier in The Plough and the Stars, had been the last actor to speak on that stage. Ironically, the line he sang as the curtain fell was:

Keep the home fires burning.

"I'll never forget the smell of the smoke," Mam said. "A group of us spent the next day rummaging through the smouldering wreckage, trying to salvage as many costumes as we could because ..."

"... *the show must go on*." I finished for her. That expression had been drilled into us from an early age.

"And we did go on," she said with pride, "the very next night in the Peacock. That's what a theatre company did in those days. But the smoke, it clung to everything."

Her favourite part of the story was about the papal blessing of their marriage. She'd brought the scroll to the theatre so fellow actor and artist, Geoff Golden, could inscribe their names in calligraphy. It had been in a drawer backstage. They found it, almost intact.

"Ray and I couldn't believe it," she said, tears in her eyes, "only the edges were scorched."

A lucky omen, most would think, but unfortunately, it couldn't stop their marriage going up in flames. My dad had been dead twenty-one years but I could see her love for him had never left her heart. Even after they separated, it was she who took care of him during his convalescence following heart surgery.

We also reminisced about our days together in that two-bedroomed house in Bayside, how she and I had shared one bedroom while Aonghus had the other for a couple of months before he got married. To celebrate my Leaving Cert results, she'd taken me on a youth hostelling trip around Italy. We laughed all over again at how shocked we were to see a German woman walking back from the communal showers with only Birkenstocks on her feet and a towel draped over her arm.

I loved the evening we talked about the times we acted on stage together, in the Eblana and Peacock Theatres.

"What about the role you turned down on Broadway?" I asked her.

"How do you know about that?"

"Remember one day, I was about nine or ten, I gave you a hug and said I'd tell you why when I was twenty?"

She looked at me blankly.

"I'd found the newspaper clipping."

"Oh."

"Did you ever regret that decision?"

"It wasn't a decision," she said without hesitation. "You and Máire were babies. It was flattering to be asked but I couldn't leave you."

I felt humbled. She too could have been as great a star as my dad but she'd stood back to let *him* shine, stayed home to nurture *our* light. My mother had chosen everyone but herself.

"Thank you, mam. For everything you've done for us, for me, for the family."

"It's what a mother does," she said, picking up the remote to turn on the telly, a clear sign that the conversation made her uncomfortable.

While she watched her favourite TV programme, I scoured the internet for jobs within a commute of Guernsey airport. If the boyfriend had been the vessel to get me to America, perhaps Herm had been the catalyst to bring me back. The two weeks had passed quickly and my flight was only twenty-four hours away.

"Any luck?" mam asked during the commercial break.

"Not yet."

"You know you always have a home here, love, you can stay as long or as short as you like."

"I know, mam, thank you, I know."

And I did. No matter what, I knew I had a home base, I knew she had always been there for me, and always would. I went back to the computer.

"Whoa!"

"What is it?" she asked.

"I can't believe I almost missed it."

"What?"

"I just checked my junk folder. Remember the application I sent off for a full-time position as an Assistant Manager on Sark, the other Channel Island without cars?"

"Yes?"

"They want me to come."

"Oh, that's fantastic, darling. Well done!"

We hugged and did a little dance. I showed her an aerial shot of the island.

"I'm so happy for you. Looks just like your kind of place. When?"

"As soon as possible."

"You deserve some good luck for a change."

I emailed the hotel to say I'd booked a flight to Guernsey for the following day. It was true. No need to tell them I'd bought it weeks before.

Mam drove me to the airport the next morning. We chatted all the way, as though talking could postpone the inevitable. I knew she was thrilled for me, but I could also see she'd grown accustomed to having me in the house. She was going to miss me all over again. At the entrance to security we hugged goodbye.

"Mind yourself, love."

"I will."

She was just shy of her eighty-fourth birthday, and I desperately hoped this was not the last time I would see her. But every time I left, I knew it was always a possibility. I went through the glass doors, turned and waved. She looked so forlorn standing there in her beige spring coat, belted at the waist, a silk scarf tucked around her neck. Then she turned away, and I knew it was because she didn't want me to see her cry. I stuffed my own tears down and busied myself with my laptop and liquids. As I approached the scanner, I stepped out of my youngest-daughter-shoes and put them through. When they came out the other side, I knew it was time to lace up my professional persona. I boarded the plane and went to the Channel Islands for what originally would have been six months, and stayed five years.

Chapter 8
Another Rock

We'd barely exited the quaint harbour of St Peter's Port on Guernsey when the ferry started to roll in the shallows of low tide. I'd opted for a seat on the starboard side, hoping the spring sun would burn its way through the low grey clouds but rather than seeing the sun, the view out my window was grey water one minute, and grey sky the next. Each time the boat rolled my bum would slide across the vinyl-covered seat and I'd be plonked first against the cold steel hull, then back to the aisle. Gallons of salt water slid down the windows as waves crashed over the superstructure.

After about twenty minutes, we passed to the south of two other islands. From my research on Google Earth, I recognised the small conical private island of Jethou and the elusive shores of Herm beyond that. A fresh breeze, at least Force 5, caused white caps to dance on the waves. Ahead, rising ninety metres out of the ocean, I could see the rugged cliff-rimmed island of Sark. While only 5.5 km long, and 2.5 km wide, all its coves and inlets give it a coastline of 64 km. As we approached the converging waters off the northern tip of Bec du Nez, the real bronco ride began. The fifteen other souls onboard that morning ignored the washing machine effect, seeming well used to the lurching creaks of the hardy ship. Once around the corner, the four-way rolling subsided but we still hobby-horsed our way down the eastern side. Halfway up the cliff face, a black and white lighthouse warned mariners of treacheries below and the wet boulders at sea level confirmed the tidal change to be a whopping ten metres. Islanders hoping for high water on return from a shopping trip to Guernsey would be disappointed. Once we were docked, it became clear they'd have to lug their bags up thirty or more slippery steps to the quay wall above.

When I put my foot on those stone steps for the first time I felt like I was home. There was a magic about the place that reminded me of remote fishing villages in Ireland. On the pier, locals clad in wellington boots, parkas and woolly hats, formed a chain to offload the Royal Mail and supplies. Attached to their tractors were all sorts of trailers and box cars used to haul goods up the hill to the main plateau of the island. They also handled visitors' suitcases. Today, mine were the only two. All the other disembarking passengers seemed to know everyone and where they were going. I heard one of them ask the harbour-master if Keith was driving the bus today. A bus? I thought this was an island without cars.

I followed them towards a tunnel in the rock face. The March wind howled through the arch and bit down on us with razor-sharp teeth. On the other side, the "bus", a metal welded box with bench seats and a covered roof, was attached by ball and hitch to another tractor. I climbed aboard the aptly nicknamed "toast-rack" along with everyone else. In a futile attempt to heat her hands, one small lady, wearing an old-fashioned headscarf, blew into her gloves and joked about closing the non-existent windows. The contraption was open on all sides and the cold crashed in from the sea. Waves, two metres high, broke and reverberated on the craggy harbour wall. Had it been a clear day, I would have been able to see past them to the Normandy coast of France.

Keith, the busman, did not discriminate against visitors. Like myself, residents, and even his own relatives all handed over a pound for the luxury of being hauled up the quarter-mile steep incline to the top. The large tractor tyres dug deep into the mud of the unpaved road as we chugged our way up. On either side, deciduous trees still hadn't sprouted any springtime buds, and on the ground lay last autumn's leaves, sodden from recent rain. We rounded one more bend and the tractor came to a stop. The fifteen locals stepped down off the bus and instantly dispersed. Some walked further up the hill to the one-road village, home to most of the 432 residents, others crossed a set of concrete tiles to the thatched-roofed white-washed pub.

My gaze fell on a fenced field and I nodded at the two horses looking my way. They seemed oblivious to the seagulls that hopped around their hooves. Another field to the right enclosed sheep with thick and enviable coats. Behind me stood a striking, stone-grey, granite building with castle-like turrets. This was the hotel where I would work; this would be my new home. Francesca, the receptionist, a local girl in a tidy uniform and sensible shoes, gave me a hearty greeting. My dinner had been set aside for me and Iris, an employee from Spain, showed me to staff accommodation. People smiled despite the cold and no-one cared that the uniform they gave me was not a size six. Life seemed simple again, and, at last, despite the weather, I felt that sense of belonging I had so desperately craved in Los Angeles.

As spring gave way to summer, daffodils and white-blossomed garlic were replaced by the bluebells of May. Girls and boys as young as five were safe to wander the streets alone, and many a dog could be seen taking himself for a walk along the undulating cliffs. The island's six hotels and countless guest houses soon swelled with visitors. Horses were taken out of the fields to pull sightseeing carriages across the island. The most popular destination was always the dramatic location of La Coupée: an extremely narrow isthmus joining Little Sark from the south to the main island. Measuring less than three metres wide, its cliffs fall dramatically down ninety metres to spectacular beaches on either side. In blustery days gone by, school-bound children from Little Sark would crawl on their hands and knees across the tiny rocky trail to avoid being blown down the sheer drop to their inevitable deaths. Built in 1945 by German prisoners of war under the directorship of the Royal Engineers, today's cement path is wide and sturdy enough to carry tractors and provisions across.

Work was hectic but fun. No two days were the same. I learned the ropes from Helen, the outgoing assistant manager. Between us we also managed the fine dining restaurant. While most of the ingredients were grown, raised, or caught on and around the island, including hand-dived scallops and pot-caught lobsters, many of the dry goods were shipped in. Managing orders meant also keeping an eye on the weather. Unfavourable seas would keep the cargo boat tied to the dock in Guernsey so we had to anticipate our dry goods and laundered linen needs accordingly.

In June, in the midst of the season, the general manager who'd hired me gave notice to the owners. She would be gone in sixty days; so too would the assistant manager. Now what? I could either wait to see who the owners might bring in from the UK to run the place or I could step up and apply for the job myself. I stepped up. A couple of weeks later I found myself in court – or rather the old school house that served as a court room. The island had only recently relinquished feudal law, but I still had to apply to the court to be granted the liquor/pub licence for the hotel. 'Landlady' status prevented my being off-island for more than seven consecutive nights without the court approving my temporary replacement. Not that that mattered for now. Although someone was hired to run the restaurant, the assistant manager was not replaced. I was so busy I didn't leave the island for the first five months at all, not even for a day trip to Guernsey.

One evening in September, I was about to leave my office and head home when I got a call from the restaurant. The supervisor had a cold. We were fully booked. While many a sniffler has martyred their way through a desk job, our food safety protocols recommended I send him home and run the dinner service myself. I took a moment to review the evening's menu with the head chef and briefed the waiting staff on the suggested wine pairings. Guests arrived and the evening began.

Fine dining service reminds me of a swan – all graceful and elegant above the water but paddling like mad beneath. We would march through the brightly lit, hectic, noisy kitchen, dropping off dirty plates and picking up the next course from the pass, but as soon as we'd get to the door into the restaurant we'd stop, and then amble into that soothing environment of soft music and romantic candlelight as though we had all the time in the world. Chefs work diligently to create exceptional food but the front of house staff need to combine it with the right atmosphere to create the fine dining experience. On smooth services like this evening, with the *amuse bouche* tantalising the palate and steaks cooked perfectly to temperature, both guests and staff leave on a high.

I closed the hotel front door behind me and walked up the hill. The night was black. Not expecting to be late, I hadn't brought a torch. Thankfully! Otherwise I would not have experienced the marvel that is another of Sark's claims to fame. With no light pollution from street lamps or industry, it has since been declared the first Dark Sky island in the world. I sat down on a bench and looked up in wonder at the celestial masterpiece above me. Some artist. Despite a sixteen-hour day, I sat awhile taking it all in. It was such a clear moonless night the Milky Way seemed to bubble with light. Either that or someone up there had dropped a glass of champagne into a perfectly good pint of Guinness. Restaurant analogies? I probably needed a day off. Cassiopeia reminded me of the cold months I'd spent outdoors earning my girl guides' astronomy badge. Some nights my dad would come outside with me and I'd follow his finger pointing out the invisible lines that made up the W. It's the first constellation I always look for, as though it is showing me The Way. Tonight Jupiter burned bright and The Plough lit the way to the North Star. The vast expanse was full of possibilities. I felt privileged to observe its beauty.

The variety of my work, and the uniqueness of the island, held me captive well beyond that first season. Where else in the world could I expect such a pollution-free, invigorating five-minute commute on foot? Or spend a July weekend placing bets on a teddy bear riding a sheep while being chased over bales of hay by a sheep dog at the annual fundraiser for the local medical centre? Or work with employees who travelled from economically depressed countries from eastern Europe in search of a sterling wage?

It was because of those same workers I found the middle of my fourth year to be my most challenging. The company, which owned four of the six hotels on the island, made a business decision to convert from year-round hotels to seasonal. By this time, besides managing one hotel, I was also human resources director of the group. We were about to lay off one hundred employees at the end of the summer.

My concerns were twofold: how could I help these people, whom I had come to regard as family, get jobs elsewhere, and how could I find a whole new team in the spring. It was hard enough to recruit a trustworthy, efficient, personable young workforce for seasonal jobs, never mind attracting them to an island without cars, shopping or nightlife. Not everyone prefers the quiet life. If only I could find a way to keep the existing trained staff housed and occupied in the winter until we were ready to re-open at Easter. My thoughts turned to volunteering.

In recent years a whole new sector of the leisure travel industry has erupted in the form of ecotourism and voluntourism. Traditionally, NGOs in developing countries attracted skilled workers in areas such as medicine or maybe engineering, but nowadays there are opportunities for non-skilled labour too. A plethora of websites offer short-term, long-term, and Gap Year Volunteer Travel. Some are hosted by non-profit organisations whose fees cover costs, others are intern and low-income overseas job placements (usually providing you take their course). Many are for-profit businesses offering once-in-a-lifetime exotic opportunities to wealthier clients, but you can still find a few that are merely the portal through which a volunteer and host connect.

My research led me to one such website, www.workaway.info a platform where hosts, be they families or organisations, offer food and lodging in exchange for five hours' work per day, five days a week, from the would-be volunteer traveller. This seemed like an excellent solution. The employees could spend the winter housed and fed, incurring zero expenses except the airfare to get there.

As the light faded in the early evenings of that 2013 autumn, I spent hours travelling the sunshine world through the window of my laptop. Projects were as diverse as trail-guiding in New Zealand, organic gardening in Cyprus, teaching English in Thailand, baby-sitting in Italy, building in Croatia, and farming in Australia – 174 countries with thousands of ventures to choose from, even some close to home. It had been twenty years since I had volunteered in Belize and it was thrilling to see how the internet had brought world-wide travel from the agents' desk to every home with a computer since then. I was so excited about the projects that I was almost sorry I had a year-round job and couldn't take off myself. But, there is always a way – and I found a project that could be squeezed into a three-week winter vacation.

Chapter 9
Knowing the Difference

I worked until the last minute, threw my gear in my backpack and ran down to the harbour to take the ferry to Guernsey. There, I caught a plane to Gatwick, transferred to Heathrow and flew thirteen hours to Kuala Lumpur, where I caught the last flight to an island off the coast of Malaysia. To say I was hot, tired, and thirsty when I arrived was like saying a Welshman likes to sing. Streams of sweat ran into rivers flowing down my back. The airport was hot and noisy. As arranged with the host, I waited underneath the information sign but no one came to greet me. I waited and waited. The project I'd chosen combined my love of the water and working in restaurants. An expat ran a charter business offering day trips and sunset dinner cruises.

I'd been waiting almost an hour. I had no Malaysian money to buy a drink, so I hung like a dehydrated dog around those tourists who held a coveted bottle of water, hoping they might offer me a sip. A woman in her sixties approached me and asked if I was Nigh-am-h. I was. I followed her out of the airport into the humid bathtub of the great outdoors. She said something about driving across town to the water. Water? Fabulous. I was going to get some. As we neared her beat-up car, it became clear I would have to sit in the back among the debris of rags, plastic bags, and goodness knows what fast-food takeaway rubbish, because the passenger seat was already occupied by a large and fully alert Alsatian. Alrighty then. I squeezed myself, my backpack and camera bag into the cramped space behind the driver's seat.

No matter what country I've travelled in, most routes from the airport to the city seem to pass through the seedier part of town and this one appeared to be no different. However, it was still more pleasant to look out the slobber-filled back windows than to concentrate on the tips of the canine's pointed ears or the woman's scabbed shoulders.

"Do you think we could stop for water?"

"Yes."

After what seemed an eternity, we pulled up at a local warehouse. The woman got out and said "Stay!"

It wasn't clear if she was talking to me or the dog, so I didn't dare budge. Time ticked slowly. By now, the one thing the Alsatian and I had in common was that both our tongues were hanging out. The woman reappeared fifteen minutes later with five large bags which she squashed into the boot. Not a drop of H_2O in sight. I was considering taking off my trousers to wring out some drops. I'm sure that's got to be in a survivor manual somewhere.

At the next stop she added a bag of crabs to the now highly polluted car. Maybe a spot of meditation could convince my brain that my body wasn't in a state of desiccation. If I could only relax, we would probably be at the accommodation in no time, and there, the taps would be flowing. We took a couple more turns which yielded to a prettier area of town. I almost saw a tourist. Then the ocean came into view and a myriad of boats swayed softly in the welcoming breeze.

"Here we are, at the water" the woman announced. "You can leave your stuff in the office. Hurry, the captain and others are waiting for you on-board."

"I don't underst—"

No use continuing the conversation because she and the Alsatian had already taken off.

I headed down the wharf in the direction she'd pointed. Apart from an hour or two of muzzy sleep on the plane, I'd been up for thirty hours already. I mustered my best smile for the man at the office.

"Hi, I'm Niamh, the new volunteer."

"Hello." He said, not looking up. "You can leave your stuff by the wall – they're waiting for you on the dock. It's a big group today, so we're taking two boats. The captain is on the one on the west side of the dock. Check in there first." Then he left, telling me to lock the door on the way out.

I was about to slide down the wall and curl up on the floor when I spied a water cooler. Or was it a mirage? No, actual water, just not so cool. I drank in sips at first, as I'd learned from a Clive Cussler action thriller. Never gulp, despite the dehydration. I stripped out of my long pants and into my shorts. Oh, what freedom to take off my socks.

Somewhat refreshed, I walked down the dock, found the boat and asked permission to climb aboard. A few of the workers nodded in my direction and when I asked for the captain, one of them pointed below. I descended the companionway and found another hive of activity through an acrid cloud of smoke. Two volunteers were crammed into the galley, chopping cabbage, and another one sat on the adjacent bed, spreading cooked rice out on a tray. A tall man, cigarette perched between his lips, looked up and mumbled "Welcome".

I nodded. It seemed the most prudent thing to do because the words that wanted to come out would not have been my finest.

"Hope you had a nice trip," he said. "We have guests coming soon so we will make formal introductions later. If you could help with the coleslaw. Cindy and Peter have it ready. Take the mayonnaise and mix it in."

I moved towards the sink to wash my hands but was abruptly stopped because we couldn't waste water.

I looked for a spoon with a long handle and began to mix.

"No, do it like this," he demonstrated, as he put both his un-gloved hands directly into the mayo and began mixing it through the cabbage, the burning cigarette still dangling.

A commotion on the dock suggested the tourists had arrived and the captain made a hasty exit to greet them. He called down and asked if anyone spoke French. Only I did, which gave me the envied excuse to climb back up into the fresh air. The Francophiles were not expecting to find a French-speaking Irish woman in Malaysia, much less an experienced bartender able to mix Blue Russians. I'd come a long way from my first job as an eighteen-year-old, pulling pints of Guinness for auld codgers in a Dublin pub. My new French buddies and I boarded the second boat which gave me a chance to meet the other volunteers. The surfer guy said it was a cool gig, but the hours were longer than five a day. One couple had been there three weeks and still had not had a day off; they were planning to quit. Another girl, who'd arrived at the weekend, seemed too young to question authority.

No matter how tired I was, however, I still delighted in being on the water. When the sunset cruise got underway I was enthralled by the view. It felt good to gaze over the waves. The deep blue water looked clean, fresh and inviting, albeit out of my reach. Perhaps on my first day off I could go for a swim.

One guest interrupted my thoughts. "Une autre, s'il vous plait."

"Oui, Monsieur." Another beer coming up.

He hung around the bar area a while and, unlike the rest of the party, seemed to think it wasn't beneath him to chat with the hired help. I guess it wasn't my place to tell him the business used unpaid volunteers instead.

The food, which had been prepared below decks, was artistically arranged on the cockpit table. Guests started helping themselves, savouring the crab legs and other seafood concoctions served over the bed of rice. They ate their fill, oblivious to the fact it had all been made *on* an actual bed. When we got to a cove, the skipper dropped anchor and guests soon started splashing about in the water.

"Should I bring the food below now?" I asked the skipper.

"No leave it there, they may want some when they come back on-board."

As well as not wasting water, apparently we couldn't waste ice either, because the food lay there, baking in the heat. Unfazed by the dishevelled design of leftovers, flies were now taking their pickings. Another ninety minutes passed and the guests who had dried off from their swim, started eyeing the food.

Having taught food safety at the hotel for so many years, I could practically see the *bacillus cereus* spores re-germinating in the lukewarm rice. I made one more valiant attempt.

"Could I wrap up the buffet now? Perhaps it's been in the heat long enough?"

"They've paid for the food; they will want it," the skipper said. "Besides, they're French – they eat snails, you know!"

I gave up.

As we set sail for home, the shellfish and rice was finally brought down to the galley, where the rest of the volunteers ate it for dinner. As hungry as I was, and, as much as I wanted to fit in, I passed. My second wind died along with the evening breeze, and the setting sun told me I had been on the go for forty-two hours. By the time we tied up at the dock, it was dark.

"We're going for a drink; would you like to join us?" Cindy asked me.

"Thanks so much, but no, I need to sleep. I'll go back to the accommodation."

"How are you getting there?"

"How do you mean?"

"It's too far to walk."

"How far is it?"

"About five miles."

"So how do you get there?" I asked.

"Scooters. After we got here, we were told we would need to rent one."

Well, that would have been something to consider in the budget.

"From where?" I asked.

"Over there." Cindy pointed at a kiosk at the side of the main square. "But they're closed now."

Terrific.

"Maybe the captain's brother can give you a lift?"

"Thank you."

"Oh, by the way," Cindy said, "I don't think there is a bed for you yet, until one of the other volunteers leave, but you are welcome to use my yoga mat."

"Thank you."

The captain's brother drove up and offered me a ride to the accommodation.

"Do you have any hotels nearby?" I asked.

He looked somewhat perplexed. "Oh yes, we have hotels, but you cannot go there."

"Why not?"

"Too much money."

Thankfully, I wasn't an eighteen-year-old kid without a couple of debit cards but I didn't want to insult him so I asked:

"Could we drive to one and just see?"

A list formed in my head: dump my bags, linger in a long hot shower, descend on the lobby for a cold, crisp glass of Pinot Grigio, then collapse. When we arrived at a hotel, I thanked the brother profusely and said I would call the captain in the morning. The receptionist asked for the fee up front, and then gave me my key. The room was not five star by any means, but nor was it a yoga mat on the floor. I know, I know, I was supposed to be a volunteer, ready to rough it, but was it too much to ask for at least one decent night's sleep before my "volunteer vacation" began?

The funny-looking hot water tap needed a little wrestling. We won't go so far as to call it a spa treatment but at least I was showered and clean. Almost bedtime. Halfway through my list.

Back down in the lobby area I went in search of that cold crisp white. Perhaps the restaurant was tucked away, or had a separate entrance?

"Yes, madam, how can I help you?" The receptionist asked.

"I'm looking for the bar."

I was moments away from a thirst-quenching pleasure that would soothe me to sleep.

"No madam, we are a Muslim hotel. We do not serve alcohol."

A better woman than me would have laughed.

I slept for twelve hours and awoke with clarity. To my mind, the charter company, a fully-fledged tourist business, was violating the spirit of the programme and abusing the willingness of unpaid labour, in the name of volunteer travel. Worse, in my opinion, they were denying any unemployed locals the opportunity to work. Morally, I wanted to stay; ethically, I could not. As with many tough decisions, I was guided by Reinhold Niebuhr's well-known prayer:

God, grant me the serenity to accept the things I cannot change,
Courage to change the things I can,
And wisdom to know the difference.

"Knowing the difference" is key. I knew I had the courage and knowledge to influence a change in how the food side of the business was run, but I also accepted that the brevity of my planned trip would not allow enough time to do so. Since I knew I couldn't follow their procedures, I felt I had no option but to walk away. They seemed to have plenty of people coming and going and had more volunteers on the way. I made my apologies and politely withdrew. With time to fill, I travelled up the coast. Sun, sand, and sea, I granted myself an actual vacation and only felt guilty about not feeling guilty.

Note: Upon my return to Sark, I sent a letter to the captain offering help in the area of food hygiene and safety, including some pamphlets that could help future volunteers and crew understand the importance of hand-washing when preparing food. Alas, I received no response.

Chapter 10
Mama Sesilia

Although the Malaysian trip turned out to be the wrong project for me, I still believed in volunteer travel. I knew I just had to find the right fit. Since I love being on, in, or under the sea, and small islands particularly excite me, for my spring break before the 2013 season on Sark began, I searched for marine conservation programmes in the most exotic of oceans – the South Pacific. There, I found an ideal project – turtle conservation in Vanuatu.

One of the major turtle nesting beaches is found on Moso, an island off the coast of Vanuatu's capital, Port Villa. It had no electricity, no running water and certainly no Wi-Fi or cell service. It sounded idyllic to me. The more people I'd met who'd never heard of this eighty-island Melanesian country, the more I'd wanted to go there. Something about my friends and family learning geography vicariously through my travels appealed to my sense of exploration.

A local theatrical troupe known as *Wan Smolbag* (because they originally operated out of 'one small bag') had been funded in 1995, the Year of the Turtle, to develop a play to raise awareness about turtle conservation. The play had such an impact that over 150 villages began participating in the project. Knowledgeable locals were appointed as turtle monitors and tasked with advising the village chiefs and elders on sustainable management practices.

Since then Wan Smolbag had aligned itself with one of the foremost players in today's volunteer travel arena: Global Visions International (GVI), which is how I and seven other travellers discovered the project — Olivia, an Australian on a break from college; Janine, a teacher from Canada on sabbatical; Jesse, an experienced volunteer also from Canada; Ben and Hannah, a couple travelling from the UK; and two other Europeans on extended vacations, Eva from Sweden and another Janine, this one from Switzerland. The eight of us had all opted to "pay to volunteer" to help conserve the hawksbill turtles.

We could probably have found many free instructional videos on the history and evolution of these ocean-faring creatures on the internet, but something about watching one in a dark and dusty playhouse that first afternoon, within a few kilometres of their birthplace, added value.

When the lights came back on after the film, we gathered our own less than *smolbags*, and were bussed to the northwest of the island of Efate. After tramping across a couple of fields to the mangrove-lined water's edge, we waited for the ferry to Moso. Conversation was hesitant. We were all competent individuals, but still a tentative group.

Shaded beneath its hundred-year-old branches, two local women sat on the exposed roots of a large tree. Clad in roomy dresses, reminiscent of the brightly coloured Muumuus from Hawaii, they chatted gaily, casually swatting mosquitoes. I sat down beside the woman in the more flowery dress and introduced myself.

"Are you the leader of your group?" she asked me.

"No, no, just another one of the volunteers." I explained.

Why, no matter where I travelled, did someone always assume I was in charge?

Her name was Sesilia and she had come to Efate to pick up supplies. She knew who we were and why we were there. We would all be going to the same village; there was only one. Sesilia told me that, during our month's stay, each of us would be adopted by a local "mama" and her family. When we weren't working with the turtles, our mamas would teach us about their culture and way of life.

"When you get off the boat," she said, "you will be lined up on the little beach. The mamas, who are selected by the chief, will choose who they want to adopt and will form another line facing yours."

Wow, we were to be chosen by sight. I wondered if we would need to have our teeth and hooves examined before we were decreed fit for purpose.

"It is a privilege for the mamas to be selected to adopt you."

"How does the chief decide?" I asked.

"Oh, he is fair, he makes sure everyone who wants to, gets a turn."

"Have you ever been picked?"

"Yes," she beamed, "this month it is my turn."

Although I didn't have a watch, I could tell we'd been sitting under the tree for a while, because the mosquitoes orbiting my ankles seemed to be getting full. Fresh meat. Would they ignore me after a month? Mama Sesilia looked at my rising welts and cackled.

"You'll be mine," she said.

"Sorry?"

"I will not wait until we get to the beach, I have already chosen to adopt you."

What could I say? There I was, sitting like a local under a tree, shooting the breeze with my new ni-Vanuatu mother. I reached over and gave her a double hug – one for her and one for my own mam back in Ireland.

The ferry arrived. When I say "ferry", I'm not talking about a metallic hull with a captain aloft. From under the overhanging mangroves emerged the silhouette of a young boy driving a wooden skiff. As the boat drifted towards us, the boy raised the outboard engine onto the transom, hopped out, and held the boat abeam some mangrove roots. Mama Sesilia, flip-flops in hand, strolled into the water and threw her shopping up under the covered bow. She beckoned for the rest of us to follow.

We were all dressed in our mostly new expedition trekking gear, so we first had to untie our Gore-Tex hiking boots, pull off our REI socks and roll up our L.L. Bean khakis before we could wade into the muddy water. It was cool, brackish, and the silty bottom soon squished its way between our toes. With much lugging of gear and balancing of weight, we managed to squeeze onto the boat without tipping it over. The seats were just wide enough to carry two abreast without the gunwales impregnating our hips with splinters. Once we began putt-putting our way across the glass-like sea to Moso, any discomfort was overwhelmed by the inspiring stillness of the evening. No one spoke. Either everyone was lost in their own thoughts or simply tuned into the magnificence of the natural world. The sun slanted its way towards bed and the orange glow danced on the foam of the small bow wake we created.

I heard splashing and high-pitched squeaks in the distance. Could it be dolphins? Could my absolute favourite sea creatures be welcoming us to the island? How exciting! No. As we rounded an outcropping of mangroves, the delightful sound was soon accompanied by visions of children, many naked, frolicking in the water just off the island. As soon as they spotted us, they began waving and shouting, and started swimming furiously after the boat. The smallest child, who looked no older than four, had a hard time keeping up. An older boy returned for him, sculling him back to the group, much like a dog corralling a flock of sheep. Our engine was cut and the bow of the skiff disappeared into the mangroves. We floated over the final metre of ankle-deep water towards a hidden beach. As the shallow keel glided to a stop in soggy sand, the singing began. Voices of the villagers infused the setting sun with a welcome fit for royalty. No question we were in the South Pacific.

Lined along the sandy path were seven women, all dressed in the same design of floral printed frock. The colours were bold and varied: pink, purple, yellow, green and blue. Every dress sported the same puff sleeves, the same ruffles along the hemline, and two intriguing pieces of material hanging from each side of the waist. I thought about the runways of Paris, New York and Milan, and the models who have to maintain svelte figures in order to fit into those hip-hugging outfits. Yet, here on the other side of the world, body shape or dimensions didn't seem to matter. There was one dress, one pattern, and maybe for once, one size that actually did fit all.

Matching the colourful dresses were the women's smiles. They grinned and hooted as they looked each one of us over. I noticed one woman catch my eye. She stood fourth in line, as did I in the line of volunteers. But not for long. No sooner had Mama Sesilia embraced two of the younger children than she made her way to the greeting line, expertly manoeuvring her ample hips in beside mama three, manipulating mama four into becoming mama five. Yes, Sesilia fully intended to be my mama. I didn't dare move my position.

The chief beckoned Olivia, the first in our line and the youngest of our group, to advance. As we passed in front of our respective mamas they reached out and bestowed leis on us, followed by hearty hugs and peals of laughter. They were so excited, chatting among themselves in their own dialect and conversing in heavily accented English with us. Holding our hands, they led us down the sandy path to a large thatched open-air hut, where a rice dish was laid out on recently plucked banana leaves. The rest of the village crowded in behind us and watched us eat. The women were taking a particular interest in our appetites, so, although none of us could recognise the meat used in the dish, we cleared our plates to many nods of approval.

The chief spoke. His words were short. He welcomed us as guests of his village and thanked us for visiting.

Next, we were led out of the "dining hall" to two smaller thatched huts adjacent to the mangrove beach. The waist-high walls were caked in a dry mud which supported the mesh windows. Long dried palm leaves covered the roofs of what were to become our sleeping quarters. Inside each hut, a bamboo wall separated the space into two rooms, each containing two single beds which had been constructed with imported two-by-fours and some precious nails.

I've never been to boarding school or been escorted off to college by my parents, but this felt like the closest thing. Mama Sesilia unsnapped the clips on my bag and started unpacking for me. Despite my polite protests, she unashamedly dug through all my belongings. Out came my camera, notebooks, bug-spray and tee-shirts. She was a no-nonsense mother on a mission. She flung my underwear, toiletries and medications out of her way, in her quest to unload my sheets. Satisfied she had found her prize at the bottom of the pack, I stood back and watched her flap, flap, flap my linens onto the thin mattress. I was a grown woman who had tended to my survival in many an obscure situation, but had never stood by while someone I'd only known two hours made my bed. I was her temporarily adopted daughter, and she ran her family *her* way. With her task complete, Sesilia wiped her hands in one of those material flaps at the side of her dress and declared I would sleep well tonight.

I dreamed of mosquitoes biting, rats running in the eaves and land crabs crawling up the walls, until I realised I wasn't dreaming, but wide awake listening to the sounds of my new home. In moments, or rather long nights like this, wonky thoughts wander in. *What is so terrible about staying in an air-conditioned hotel? Why does contribution have to come with hardship? Good grief, what was that under my bed?*

In those dark hours, I tried to focus my brain on why I travel. Even though YouTube is flooded with videos of everywhere I might plan on going – a couple of clicks and I can see Mary Jane's recording of the Taj Mahal in spring, or Billy Bob's trackside view of Formula One cars racing through Monaco – I travel because it tingles. Certain words make me tingle, "travel" being one of them. Add in "voyage", "expedition" or "pioneering" and the tingling becomes electric. I may never climb Mount Everest or trek across the Antarctic, but if I can journey to places like Moso, places that are so different from my culture, stay awhile, and learn the customs, then I feel a sense of living a global life.

I rolled over; comforted by the allure of adventure, gladdened by the goal of giving, and reassured in my sense of purpose. All was well until, right outside my window, the premature rooster screeched away the edge of slumber.

Chapter 11
Turtle Beach

Our first morning on the job was exciting. I pulled on my expedition clothes, laced up my hiking boots and even donned the wickedly ugly hat designed to protect my ears and neck from the searing sun. At seventeen-degrees south latitude we were as close to the equator as Guatemala or Vietnam. With my fair Irish skin, the only colours I would turn would be from white to red to crispy and then back to white again. As much as I would love to achieve a golden honey hue, the only way I would ever get a tan was if my freckles all joined hands and sang "Kum-by-yah".

A new group of ladies from the village brought us breakfast – half a banana, two pieces of papaya and a slice of bread. Lots of people love papaya. I do not. The texture and flavour of this sub-tropical fruit reminds me of used socks lying forgotten in the bottom of a gym bag and warmed all day in the back seat of a car. But when I'm living off-grid, at the mercy of local cuisine, I devour all foods with relish. Happily, I washed it down with what my friends like to scrunch up their noses and call my "swamp juice". I don't care. Since drinking a glass of powdered greens every morning for the last ten years, I've fought off every cold or flu that tried to get their clammy hands on me. Moreover, in remote locations where there's little chance of getting my daily dose of fresh leafy vegetables, it's invaluable. Mind you, even the concoction of water, spirulina, wheat grass and pulverised broccoli would taste a whole lot better if it could be served chilled, or at least twenty degrees below hut temperature.

Jacob, the locally appointed turtle monitor, arrived, wearing a bright red tee-shirt, jeans, and a New York Yankees' baseball cap.

"Follow me," he said.

We were off. As we paced out, Jacob's friend, David, hung back, bringing up the rear. The first part of the trail led us away from the mangrove beach and across dead, sharp, coral rock. I was glad of my thick-soled boots. I marvelled at how easily Jacob covered ground in his worn out flip-flops. Not a bead of perspiration crossed his brow, yet, at nine in the morning, we volunteers were already sweating up an inland sea. We crossed an area of sandy mud, rife with holes, none of them large enough to fall through, but perfectly shaped to twist an ankle. These were the homes of the nocturnal land crabs. Luckily, they were sleeping now.

As we turned inland, the foliage became dense. The terrain rose, gently at first, but then the incline became steep enough to necessitate frequent stops to rehydrate and admire the view. It's amazing how long you can look out at nothing when you are trying to disguise catching your breath. My companions, at least twenty years my junior, recovered quickly. Had I, regardless of all my pre-planning and organizational skills, forgotten to pack my fitness? But muscles have memory and the athleticism of my youth met the commitment in my heart, and kept me going. Next came the rolling ridge, a relief to the calf muscles but not to body temperature as the trees here thinned out. Despite the lack of shade, we welcomed another rest stop.

Even though we were still not quite halfway there, the rest of the trek became an easier slow descent to sea level on the western side of the island, our boots trudging again across a dark sandy earth. We could hear the breaking waves of the wide-open ocean.

It had been quite the sweltering ninety-minute hike but as we came through the last of the trees we were rewarded with a view that merited our sense of achievement. The exposed bay of royal blue water was dotted with volcanic islands to the north and a golden strand that stretched for a kilometre to a rocky point to the south. Jacob seemed set to continue down the beach, but we had grown roots, mesmerised by the feral beauty.

Strangled weed marked last night's high tide. Unbroken shells lay scattered about. This beach had never seen a deck chair nor an umbrella. It was untamed, uncultivated, and it sang *pioneer* in my head. No wonder the mama turtles had chosen this as their safe place to dig holes in the sand to bury their eggs.

It was February and we were on the cusp of change in the turtle projects. The egg-laying season was coming to an end and the hatching would soon begin. Although most of the turtle nesting happens at night, and we risked being too late in the year to see one, I was glad we'd made this first trip across the island in daylight. The panorama was already locked in my visual memory. I knew I could, and would, revisit it frequently in the years to come.

Jacob rallied us again and we headed south along the beach. It was slow going. Most of us wore the recommended gaiters on top of our boots but they did little to keep the sand out of our socks. My right hip tired from walking on the soft slope. It was arid, and although the sea was less than three metres away, the only moisture we enjoyed came from the torrents of sweat raining down our faces. My hat may have kept the mid-morning sun off my head, but I longed for a facecloth or bandana to dry my forehead.

The next time you are perusing Tinder, Match.com or any other online dating site and your prospective soul mate says he loves "long walks on the beach", let me weigh in and tell you he is full of it. Bikini- and Speedo-clad beach bods strolling hand in hand at the water's edge, occasionally cooling off in the shallows, are not the same thing as wearing full hiking gear going for an *actual* long walk on the beach.

We arrived at the rocky point, but what I thought was the end of the beach wasn't. We climbed over those rocks and around the corner. Before us lay another expanse of sand stretching another kilometre. In the distance, I could vaguely make out some thin poles where the sand met the edge of the trees. These were nest markers. The first one Jacob pointed to was nest number two. Great, except the one we had come to check was number eighteen.

Before we got to the first pole, Jacob got excited. He stopped and pointed out a pattern in the sand that looked like bizarre tyre marks.

"This is new, this is last night," he said.

We peered more closely at the indentations and saw that the flat space in the middle of these markings came from the underbelly of a large turtle. The tyre-like tracks were the sweeping motion she would have made with her flippers as she dragged herself out of the water and up the sandy slope to the treeline. Wow. How cool. And we had missed it.

David, who had been walking behind us, barefoot, looked around for a suitable pole-like stick while Jacob took a clipboard out of his pack and noted this new nest – the date it might have been laid and the date it might likely hatch. Our mission, they told us, was to observe, to document and not interfere. Most nests, we learned, took about sixty to seventy days to hatch and could contain anywhere from 80 to 120 eggs. When the mother has dug the hole, she begins to push them out. The first several drop to the sand and the next ones are laid on top of them. It may take up to an hour and a half for her to deposit all her eggs in the hole. She then uses her flippers to pile sand on top of them. When she is satisfied they are well covered and safe from predators, she makes her way back to the water, exhausted. Interestingly, the temperature of the nest during the incubation period, which can be influenced by several factors including sunshine, rain, and even sand colour and grain size, and the position of the egg within the nest, play a vital role in determining the sex of the babies. Warmer temperatures produce more female hatchlings while males result from the cooler ones.

The unexpected break was over. It was time to trudge on. Nest eighteen was supposed to be ready to hatch any day now. If it was possible, the sun had become hotter. We were two poles away, our goal in sight, when we heard a shout from David. He was at least three hundred metres behind, wildly waving us back. We turned and started in his direction, but, at the sight of his frenetic arms, we somehow gathered momentum enough to run. As we reached him, we saw the sand beneath him move. Crawling over his right foot was a tiny baby turtle. Damn it, where was my camera? Then another one emerged, and another.

"Start counting," Jacob said.

Easy at first, *one, two, three, four*, but then the sand appeared to boil, and within a minute there were twenty to thirty purpose-driven baby turtles climbing out of the nest and making a run for the sea. How did they know where they were going? I sat down on the beach halfway between the nest and the water trying to keep tabs on the little ones scrambling along. It was astonishing, like a *National Geographic* film reel, and I was there, sitting right there on the sand, feeling so privileged to witness their birth and migration to the sea. Some of them were racers, some took their time, others seemed disoriented, occasionally bumping into a shell or divot. The waves were only four inches high but when the turtles reached the water they were tossed about. These little triers swung those minute flippers and tried to right themselves in the surf. Some made it easily, others flipped over on their backs, the next wave righting them again. Hard as I tried, somewhere around eighty-five I lost count. The movement slowed as the main body of hatchlings was already in the water. Only the stragglers and runts were still en route. I noticed one with a deformed back flipper that was having a rough time. I watched as it made progress, then made a three-point turn, and found itself back where it started.

"What about this one?" I asked Jacob.

"Oh, that one won't make it."

He was probably right. Out of every nest only a certain percentage make it to the sea; many are snatched up by birds. Those that do make it must survive a day or two of frenzied swimming before they can find safety in a clump of floating seaweed. Known as the "lost years", from then on they swim in ocean currents until their beautiful shells become as large as a frying pan and they come back towards the coastal reefs. As the years go on, they say only one in a thousand make it to sexual maturity. So, the likelihood of this baby girl, if it was a female, making it back to this same beach in thirty years' time to lay her own eggs, was about as likely as my getting a ticket on Virgin Galactic.

Still, sentimentality took over. I asked if I could do anything. Jacob said I could pick it up and bring it to the water if I wanted. He was probably placating me, believing that, no matter what I did, the poor creature would be dead by sunset anyway. The other volunteers clicked their cameras as I reached down, my forefinger and thumb taking hold of either side of her shell. The poor mite, now suspended in air, kept on flapping with her three good flippers. I rested her two-inch frame down on the inside of my palm and covered her body with my other. The last thing I wanted was a damn gull to swoop in for a tasty morsel. As we approached the water I didn't care about getting my boots wet. They were already drenched from the inside out and I wanted to make sure I put her at least the far side of the breaking waves. Then I let go.

It reminded me of the story of a young girl who was seen on a beach full of stranded starfish, dying in the sun. She bent down and started picking them up and throwing them back into the water. A passer-by looked at the sand carpeted in starfish and said to the girl:

"Why are you bothering to throw them into the water? Can't you see there are so many thousands of them it won't make a difference?"

The young girl looked at him, picked up another starfish, threw it into the water and said, "it makes a difference to that one."

A myriad of thoughts rambled through my brain by nightfall. Had I made a difference to that little turtle or had I interfered with the law of the jungle; the survival of the fittest? One reason you shouldn't usually pick up a hatchling, especially if it *is* a female, is that you may deprive her of the sensory ability to find the same beach when she needs to return to lay her own eggs. So what was my real motivation? Was it to give a fighting chance to one more of this endangered species or was I surreptitiously creating a photo op: *"Look mam, here I am in the South Pacific, holding a baby turtle."* If I am honest, it was probably a mixture of both. Regardless, without my "help", the baby hawksbill would be dead for sure. Another thought struck me – had I interfered with the natural order? In saving the turtle, had I deprived a bird of its dinner? Given the number of the times my seaside picnics had been ruined by a shrieking seagull swiping my sandwich, that thought didn't keep me awake for long.

So if, on your next snorkelling trip, you come across a hawksbill turtle with a deformed back right flipper, I'd like you to think maybe, just maybe, it was the one I carried into the water that day.

Chapter 12
Breaking Bread

On Saturday, we took time off from turtle conservation and spent the day with our mamas and their families. Mama Sesilia lived on the outskirts of the village. It was a meandering walk along the sometimes rocky, sometimes sandy path. Her home was a collection of small huts spread about an area of dirt cleared of leaves. Compared to the other mamas' homes, it was quite the compound. Whittled poles supported sheets of corrugated iron and some even had wooden doors on hinges. The first time I visited she greeted me with a hug befitting a bear and invited me to sit on a wooden plank attached to the six- by four-foot table she called her outdoor kitchen, like a homemade picnic bench.

My three-and-a-half-year-old baby "sister", Favianna, ran out to greet me. Completely uninhibited, she climbed up on my lap, stared quizzically at my blue eyes and started twirling her fingers through my unfamiliar blonde, straight hair.

"Today, you will stay with us for lunch," Mama Sesilia announced.

"Oh, lovely. What are we having?"

She smiled and told Favianna not to dirty my hair with her sticky hands. Many of the chickens that roamed around the area trotted over. Sesilia threw flour directly onto the wooden table. As she spread it out with her hands, I wondered how she didn't get a palm full of splinters. On top of this, she thwopped six handfuls of dough and began to knead. It reminded me of all the times I used to sit up on the kitchen counter, watching my own mother kneading her famous brown bread. Worlds apart, from different cultures and economic backgrounds, they were still the same, these two women, the heart of the family. But never did my mother have to beat down the yeast with one hand while mindlessly shooing curious chickens off the table with the other. I wondered if the Western obsession with germs was merely a phobia. The whole cleaning products industry was redundant in a place like this and yet not one of Sesilia's family ever seemed to have got sick.

As she worked the dough, she asked me about my life, where I got my sunglasses, and how come I didn't have a husband. How do you answer that? Here was a woman who lived a modest, humble way of life. Her husband was out fishing and she was home making bread and minding the children. The family unit was sacred, and a given. Women grew up, married, had children, grandchildren, and tended to their family and neighbours. Water, food and shelter were the main concerns of daily living. Stress? What caused stress in her world? Real anxieties: crop failure and hungry bellies, a distant earthquake and ensuing tsunami — not slow Wi-Fi or whether there would be traffic on the commute home. I couldn't help but ponder the disparity between the privileges I and my mother enjoyed in the western world compared to the complexities Favianna and Sesilia had to deal with. There, but for an accident of birth went I. But I had to accept that neither of us had a choice in how and where we came into this world. Our jobs were to embrace the next breath, live the best life we could with what we were given, and offer love and support to those around us. I only hoped that had we swapped lives, I would have been just as jovial.

"Well, I *was* married," I told her, "but not anymore."

"Your husband died?"

"No, we got divorced."

She seemed to consider this, then said: "How will you find a new husband?"

How indeed.

She slapped the six pieces of dough into three metal pans, then handed them to me and said, "Come."

I followed her through a low wooden door to her indoor kitchen. It was dark and shafts of smoke were illuminated by the contrasting bright streaks of sunlight coming through the cracks. In the corner, on the dry mud floor, a ring of stones contained a burning fire. She used a large stick to manipulate the embers, took the pans from me and positioned them in the centre of the fire. Next, she placed a large metal lid on top, and then with her bare hands put the hot stones on top of that. This would heat the mixture from above and below, she explained. No knobs to turn to the correct temperature for forty minutes. She knew the heat of the fire and how long everything would take to cook. An hour later we were sitting down to pulled chicken and warm crusty bread.

As I was leaving later that afternoon, Mama Sesilia handed me one of her best flowery frocks. It was pink, white and black. Sewn by her own hand, it mimicked the same pattern as all the island dresses.

"You'll wear this tomorrow for church," she decreed.

When I got back to our base by the mangrove beach, I noticed that all the other female volunteers, returning from spending the day with their own mamas, also had dresses under their arms, and the two guys carried equally loud shirts.

Religious or not, we dutifully turned up for church the next morning wearing our gifted island clothing. In all my travels, especially in areas that have been called "third world", it fascinates me that even the poorest communities have extraordinarily elaborate churches.

We knew the population of Vanuatu was predominately Christian, but we weren't exactly sure whether this island followed the majority in being Presbyterian. The other choices would have been Roman Catholic, Anglican or Seventh Day Adventist. Judging by the enthusiastic singing, waving of arms, and a generally vociferous congregation, my money was on Seventh Day. Everybody from the village was there, in all their finest. Even the children were scrubbed, noses perfectly clean, ribbons adorning their hair. I thought about the warnings we got back in Ireland when my granny's and later my dad's death was announced in the newspapers. We were cautioned to have someone babysit the home while everyone went to the funeral, such was the level to which opportunistic thieves would descend.

Here, we had no worries about the meagre possessions left in our huts. Only the dogs, chickens, and lizards roamed outside. Every living human on the island of Moso was in the Church too.

Although much of the service was in the local dialect, the preacher broke into occasional English, welcoming us, as we took our places next to our mamas. A grinning Favianna clambered up my leg and attached herself to my hip. Her twinkle opened my heart, releasing all those maternal instincts I'd buried long ago. For the length of the two-hour service I felt like a mother holding her child, the love just pouring out of me. I knew it was temporary but I cemented the emotion by "living in the now". This was my community, this was my family, and this was where I belonged – today.

Over the days that followed, we fell into a routine. We awoke with the six a.m. rooster, unless of course we were already still awake from the three a.m. rooster, the four a.m. barking dogs, or the five a.m. mooing wild cows. Before breakfast, two of us trekked up to the well in the grassy clearing of the village and hauled pails of water down to a bin beside our "facilities". There was one small hut designed to add a modicum of privacy to the cylindrical cement toilet bowl. The trick was to tip as much water in, with as much speed as possible, without spilling over, in order to leave it ready for the next person. It wasn't uncommon to be queuing outside and hear a scream from one of us girls. It meant the rather fat, indigenous spider was hiding in the toilet roll, again.

After breakfast we made the hike to the nesting beaches, but little was stirring after that first exciting morning. One day we found one vacant nest, the exodus having happened the night before. To document the size of it, we counted the empty leathery shells from which each hatchling had broken through, using their caruncle, or temporary egg "tooth". By the end of the week we recognised how lucky we had been to have witnessed the hatching that first morning.

On the night of the high spring tide, Jacob thought there might be one last chance to see a turtle coming ashore to lay a nest, so we hiked across the island in the dark. Unfortunately, this spring tide was on the new moon, not the full, so it was pitch black, making the trek more daring. Our torches illuminated land crabs scurrying away from our feet, annoyed that their nocturnal foraging was being interrupted by tromping humans. Despite the dark, the pace was faster than in daytime. Maybe it was because of the cooler air, or familiarity with the route, but more likely it was just plain fear of not wanting to get left behind. As we neared the beach, Jacob stopped.

"Did you hear that?"

He stood, still as a statue, and cocked an ear.

"There!" Jacob said.

This time we heard it – a wild strangled sound, much like a cross between an elephant's yawn, a tiger's growl and the wail of a violin being played by a four-year-old student.

David, who had been walking ahead of us, came running back, the whites of his eyes lighting his way.

"The trees, the trees," he shouted. "Hide!"

"What is it?" Jesse asked.

"Cow."

"Oh, is that all?"

None of us "travelled folk" were scared of a cow until Jacob ushered us into the trees and we saw David was seriously afraid.

Years ago, someone had tried to cultivate and farm the island. The first animals introduced were cows. Ultimately, the project failed, the people left, but the cows remained. Over the years the hungry cows were neither milked nor fed. They lived in the wild and became somewhat aggressive. However, they seemed to have come to an arrangement with the locals. The cows kept to the hills and south side of the island, the villagers to the west and lowlands.

Generally.

But, tonight, one of them had wandered onto the turtle beach. Judging by the reactions of David and Jacob, this was a rare but frightening experience. They didn't speak. Jacob pushed us further off the path and into the foliage. Olivia almost giggled but the look Jacob gave her soon stifled any humour. David motioned us to be quiet. Fear is like an overpowering perfume that infiltrates the nostrils of innocent bystanders. Within minutes, this entire gang of seasoned adventurers had been infected with trepidation. Our anxious minds posed ridiculous questions. How big are the horns on a wild cow? Could the cow smell us? If it charged, what would be the best direction to run away? I reckoned any route would do, so long as my legs moved faster than the others'. Minutes ticked, maybe even thirty. After what seemed like hours, David poked his nose out and sniffed the air. As if by magic, he pronounced the path was safe, the cow was gone. If there had been one last turtle nesting that night, we never saw it. We were too anxious to hike back and tell the tale of the night we escaped the wrath of the "killer cow".

"It's not like any other volunteer project I've ever been on!" said Jesse, our young Canadian. "We're hardly working, are we?"

We were hanging out on the beach waiting for dinner. The month was half over and the eight of us had formed quite the team, streamlining our system for chores. One of our tasks was to fill the water bins, but on this, as on several other days, the tubs had already been filled by local families.

"They are treating us like guests, not volunteers," said Eva. "They do everything for us, even cook our meals."

"Agreed," said Swiss Janine. "I feel we should do more to help them."

"But they seem so focused on making sure we're happy and having a good time," added Hannah, "they're such sweet people, I'd hate to upset them."

"So what should we do?" Jesse asked.

"Maybe because we paid to be here, they feel obligated?" said Janine, the teacher, who was closer in age to me than the others.

"Where does the money go anyways?" asked Olivia, "We paid more than the price of three meals a day, and it's not like we're sleeping on memory foam."

I'd been scratching a drawing in the sand with an old mangrove root, wondering exactly that – where does the money go in this industry? Paying to volunteer seems like an oxymoron. Surely the definition of volunteering is to offer one's time, skills and labour for free?

Is the volunteer travel business satisfying a shift in human consciousness, our need to "do good" in the world. Or has the plethora of excursions on offer been engineered by clever marketers appealing to the egos of the enlightened or the wallets of the wealthy?

Remember Derek Sivers' talk: it takes the first and second followers to start a movement. The first time I saw a hotel invite guests to reuse a hand towel, I thought it would never catch on. The second hotel upped the ante with edifying packaging. Little tent cards appeared on the tops of toilets and by mirrored sinks, explaining how we could save the planet by reducing the amount of laundry we incurred. The big chains joined in, educating us in how many pounds of detergent and gallons of water we could save each day, each month, each year, if we hung up our towels rather than throwing them in the bath. By the time the movement was in full swing, I wondered how many were in it on behalf of "global warming" and how many had conveniently jumped on the socially trending crusade because it virtuously increased their profit margins and boosted their bottom line.

"So what should we do?" Jesse repeated.

I looked up from my musings and found all seven volunteers eyeballing me. Oh, here we go again, I thought. Why me? Why now? I had done everything I knew how to hide in this crowd, to be just one of the group. But I could see that was no longer possible. Something needed to be done and someone had to do it. Who cares whether leaders are conceived in the uterus or nurtured in the cradle? When you are one, you are one. And when you need to step up, you step up.

"Well," I said, resignedly accepting the role, "the first thing to do is ask the Chief what they actually need."

It was a delicate meeting. The Chief, David, Jacob, and the elders of the village, stood in the dining hut, with tension in their shoulders and wariness in their eyes. This was the first time any volunteers had asked for an assembly. I chose my words carefully, using the "sandwich approach" – start with something positive for the first layer of bread, introduce the meat of the discussion, and top it off with an accolade. It worked. No one got offended. They agreed to let us do more. The girls were taught to thatch, and the guys learned to whittle. It may no longer have been still standing after the next cyclone blew through, but, before the project was over, we'd helped construct a wooden hut at the top of the hill, so that future volunteers and monitors alike, could rest in shade along their heated hike to the nesting beach.

More importantly, we reconciled our questions about where the money goes. The Chief explained the many ways our volunteered money helped his small community thrive. From farming, to fishing, to building supplies, every cent of the portion of our money they received was cherished and shared. In gratitude, they wanted to provide us with the most rewarding experience we could have, teaching us about their culture and having us share with them about ours. As I watched the villagers nod their heads in agreement, I understood. Over the years, we've all probably donated money to a cause close to our hearts, and we've definitely given freely of our time. With paying to volunteer, we just do both at the same time.

However, to change things up, I decided that, for my next spring break in 2014, I wanted to find a project that did not ask for money, or help, something unadvertised, that would gladly avail of my offered services and something that would make my heart sing. It took months of research, but eventually I found it off the coast of Kenya.

Chapter 13
Dolphins

"Dolphins! I see dolphins!"

My favourite creatures had made an appearance; it was going to be a wonderful day. The sky was blue, the ocean calm, and a dolphin calf had just breached the surface along the shores of Kenya.

"Good spotting," said Jane who worked with the Watamu Marine Association (WMA).

I have an affinity with dolphins. For some reason, I can sense these mammals and know where to look before they surface. Jane was sitting on the port-side of the wooden box-like boat, clipboard in hand, noting the time of day and the location of the sighting.

"Are you getting this, Mike?" she asked.

Mike was a local Kenyan. His job on this conservation project was to photograph the dorsal fins of the dolphins as they came up for air. From this, a database of the pod was established and each dolphin was given a photo ID which helped monitor their numbers, behaviour and how, within the Malindi-Watamu Marine National Park and Reserve, they were being impacted by the threats they faced.

I was both excited and somewhat anxious as I bent over the side of the boat. My toes were straining to keep contact with the deck, my bruised belly was flattened over the four-inch wooden gunwale, my head skimmed the waterline, while my arms grasped the video camera below the surface. We were hoping for a live shot underwater as the dolphins passed nearby. Mike may well have been viewing them through his long lens, but I believe it was the playful Kahindi who thought it would be much more beneficial to the project if he snapped photos of what was directly in front of him – my suited glutes and naked hams! Modesty aside, at least it provided a chuckle for the crew, and made my "laugh list" for the day.

What is it about dolphins that make us smile? It doesn't matter whether they are bottle-nosed, spinner, spotted or striped, the minute they come up for air our joy goes up the scale. There is nothing more exhilarating than being out on the water watching a pod of dolphins underway. It's a special privilege to observe. We cherish every moment because they are with us as long as they want to be and when they don't, they aren't.

Did we always feel that way? Or was it the result of a TV show we saw as children? A fairy-tale that followed the adventures of two kids and their pet dolphin, who lived in the lagoon at the end of their dock. Following the popularity of *Flipper*, the industry that holds dolphins in captivity exploded. People the world over now want to pet them, feed them and hang out of their dorsal fins. With hundreds of dolphinariums worldwide, are these programmes educational or are dolphin tricks just big business?

The single most determined activist, who has made it his life's mission to free dolphins in captivity, has got to be the man who believes he created the problem in the first place: Ric O'Barry. As the trainer on the TV show, he was not only responsible for capturing the five dolphins that played Flipper, but for teaching them to jump, twirl and tail-walk on cue.

In the Oscar-winning documentary *The Cove*, Ric explains how he spent ten years contributing to the building of this industry and the rest of his life trying to tear it down. Most of the dolphins people kiss and stroke in what O'Barry refers to as the "Abusement Parks" throughout the world, are captured during an annual hunt in Taiji, Japan. Those not chosen to be shipped to seaquariums are slaughtered, out of sight. Barbed wire, guards and angry fishermen, protect the cove from outsiders. In order to capture the images of what happens there, it took the ingenuity and stealth of the documentary's producers to disguise their cameras to look like rocks, and hide them along the cliffs. Once you watch the movie, the blood red water of the scenic cove is a sight you can never un-see.

What causes a man who makes a lucrative living as an animal trainer to undergo such a radical shift? The show had wrapped up, the props returned into storage, and the dolphins back to the tank. Dolphins are sonic beings. On any given day, depending on their food supply, they can travel forty to fifty nautical miles. They socialise in groups. A concrete tank or artificial lagoon is not the open water in which they were born. Sunburned and depressed, Cathy, the primary dolphin who'd played Flipper, died. Unlike humans, whose subconscious takes care of breathing, dolphins inhale on purpose. Ric said he was right beside her when she took her final breath and sank to the bottom of the tank.

He called it suicide.

From that moment on, he vowed to spend the rest of his life freeing as many captive dolphins as he could, much of his effort being centred around that one cove in Japan.

Bottlenose are the first to be chosen, maybe because of that infectious smile. But according to Ric, "a dolphin's smile is nature's greatest deception, it creates the illusion they are always happy". Yet, in a tank devoid of life, surrounded by the noise from the filtration system, the loud music, and the screaming crowd, what chance of happiness do these sonic creatures have? What if an accident of birth kept your face frozen in a permanent grin? Would anyone see your tears?

Once they are captured and shipped, that's when you and I, unknowingly, play our part. I've done it. Maybe you've done it, or you know someone who has. We purchase a ticket to the dolphin experience, thereby creating the demand.

But what about the other side of this controversial issue? What about the parks, the zoos, the habitats of research, conservation and rescue? What about the folks like Jack Hanna, Director Emeritus of Columbus Zoo and Aquarium, who believes that, unlike himself or Ric, ninety-nine per cent of the world's population would not have the opportunity to see animals in the wild and therefore people benefit from the industry. An animal lover as well, Jack Hanna is committed "to protecting and preserving species; educating young people about the risks that animals face in the natural world; and inspiring the next generation of conservationists, marine biologists, scientists, and animal enthusiasts". He is another man proud of his work and holds a firm belief in his cause.

Whichever side of the argument you lean towards, when you know something, you can't not know it anymore. According to the World Society for the Protection of Animals (WSPA) one of the ways to conscientiously "commune with dolphins is from the deck of a dolphin-watching operation that follows a responsible code of conduct."

For these reasons, having forgiven myself for the small part I had previously played in keeping dolphins in captivity through buying tickets for the shows, I had come to Watamu Marine Association to volunteer my time and learn about their work.

Communities and countries tap into their natural resources to produce a living for their people. What drew me to WMA was that they recognised the Watamu economy was directly and indirectly reliant on the marine environment. Dolphin watching was an already established eco-tourism activity in the area. Popular with tourists, it provided an important source of income for the local community. Rather than trying to solely highlight the threat this might pose to the dolphins, WMA set about training local guides and tour boats operators in "best practices" when bringing visitors to the dolphin sites.

"Stay this side," said Jane.

We were on a different boat from yesterday. WMA did not have their own vessels, preferring to hire local boat owners for survey work. Jane was teaching today's captain how to maintain a safe distance parallel to the pod. There were already two tour boats in the area and it was important to keep all boats on the same side so as not to surround the dolphins, making them feel trapped.

"You never want to approach them from behind," Jane continued, "as they will feel chased, nor head-on as it will create a barrier forcing them to either change direction, split up or dive deep."

It was the last day of my week on dolphin survey. Besides photographing, our job this morning was to monitor the behaviour of the dolphins and the tour boats. Were the dolphins feeding, travelling, resting or socialising? Were they making abrupt changes in speed and direction or taking prolonged dives to shake off the boats? We were watching out for tail slaps.

"A mistake people make," Jane told me, jotting down the names of the boats, "is in thinking a dolphin is saying hello when he slaps his tail on the surface. He's not. That's a sign to back off. The dolphin doesn't want you there." She discarded the third pencil with a broken point and reached in the bag for another.

"Ever think of a pencil sharpener?" I asked.

"No point," she said, "they rust."

We both laughed at the unintended pun.

The tour that had been there before us left the area as another two arrived. Jane made a note of its good practice. The captain was a man she'd trained during a previous survey and he knew what he was doing. He'd peeled off slowly, making sure he was well away from the pod before gently increasing his speed.

"I've got a new-born," said Mike, click, click, clicking away.

"Where? Where?"

"Ten o'clock" he said, without lifting his eyes from the viewfinder.

We all turned in excitement to look off the port bow. Even Kahindi lost interest in my posterior and Jane grabbed the binoculars.

"You're right, Mike!" she said. "I can see the stripes."

Sure enough, when she passed the binoculars to me, I was able to see the tiny dark dolphin with three or four white stripes running vertically down its sides. He swam alongside his mother, thrusting his head high out of the water.

"They're known as neo-natal folds." Jane explained. "They are caused by the way the baby is shaped when it's still inside the mother."

"How long do they have them?" I asked.

"Not long, maybe days, maybe weeks," said Jane. "Mike, can you get a shot of the mother, is she one of the pod?"

"I've got her dorsal," Mike said, "but I'm not sure."

Back at the office, we were eager to see if the mother had been identified previously. Comparing shapes, sizes, indentations, scarring, and colour, it took a few minutes to cross-check the photographs of dorsal fins with the ones Mike had taken this morning. It sure looked like the mother could be dolphin number twenty-seven. Mike uploaded his photos of the new-born and added them to the database.

I was impatient to see my underwater footage. Perhaps, after a week of trying, I finally had shots of dolphins swimming. Alas, what I had was forty-three minutes of nothing. Well, that's not strictly accurate; I did capture one murky shadow and a few clumps of seaweed floating by.

As the afternoon took hold, we set about our various tasks. Mike cycled off to the local school to a give a presentation. Kahindi went to Mida Creek, where he also worked as a bird-spotting guide. I was finalising the format for the training manual while Jane was trying to post a photo of the new-born online. The internet was intermittent and slow.

"C'mon," she said, giving up in frustration, "let's call a tuk-tuk and go into Malindi to get these pages laminated."

About three hours and the equivalent of three-euros-a-page later, we had double-sided waterproof instruction sheets listing the "Do's and Don'ts" for the tour boat captains. A time-consuming exercise, but every step of this project was organic.

My time with WMA had been short, and I wondered if, and how, I'd helped. It had been an enlightening week on survey, an uplifting time with dolphins, but when I thought about my purpose, I felt I had gained more than given. It was then I remembered my discoveries in Vanuatu. Not all volunteering has to be with time; some of it can be with money.

"Asante, asante. Thank you so much," an excited Jane called me three months after I had returned home. "We got your package."

"You're welcome." I said, imagining Mike and Kahindi's surprise when they opened the box and discovered a portable laminator and several boxes of mechanical pencils.

Chapter 14
The Other Safari

Every one of my muscles ached. As well as the dolphins, the other reason that had brought me to Kenya was my lifelong challenge to attain a fit and healthy body. The internet led me to *Wildfitness* founded by Tara Wood. Growing up, she'd noticed that people who came from cities to visit her family home on the white sandy beaches of Watamu invariably left feeling happier and healthier. "Being outdoors in nature, eating real natural foods, and moving with purpose allowed them the chance to live like our ancestors." As a result, Tara designed fitness courses in the wild.

For the last nine days, alongside eleven other participants making up my newly formed tribe, I had kick-boxed at dawn, lifted tree trunks before lunch and crawled along the beach like an alligator at sunset. We'd used our body weight to move like crabs, bears, chimps and frogs. We climbed trees, swam in the creek, balanced on slack lines, heaved rocks and generally learned the value of intense, short, sharp workouts with plenty of rest and sleep in between. We ate leafy green vegetables and fresh juicy mangoes. We ran barefoot on the beach. Dispensing with electronics, we soothed our senses with the swaying of the leaves. We were re-wilding. The kick-start course was over. On my three-day break before the longer transformation course began, I joined a safari to Tsavo's National Park.

It was the jeep-driver who explained that *safari* was the Swahili word for *journey*. Standing on the back seats of his vehicle, the three of us on the trip could pop our heads through the roof and appreciate nature in the raw. The terrain was vast. Animals I'd only seen in zoos as a kid, were free to roam. Here, they were in the wild and we were the ones in cages. Giraffes picked at tree-top foliage as a zeal of zebras cantered by. On a rock in the middle of a small river, a lion tore at the side of an antelope. A herd of elephants, about twenty-five including calves, strolled across the road in front of us. We watched them traipse along, nudging young ones with their trunks. A larger male, near the back of the line, paused and turned his head toward us. His ears flared out, a sign for us to be wary. Ready for a quick retreat, our driver's hands never left the wheel. The elephant held his stance. I'd seen videos of elephants upturning jeeps larger than ours. I watched his eyes and felt his challenge. He would protect his herd. As the last of the stragglers crossed in front of him, he relaxed his ears. The threat was over, for him, and for us. He took one last look at us before turning to follow the rest.

Back in my tent that evening, I rolled up the side walls. Through the dusk and the mosquito-repellent screens, I could vaguely make out the savannah. Twilight was enveloped by a heavy darkness and night time fell on the reserve. My own private safari continued. A parade of animal sounds played in an orchestra of their kingdom. I could hear the wheezing grunts of hippos as they cooled off in the river. The reed frogs clinked like ice in a glass and the call of the leopard sounded like sawing wood. The buzzing mosquitoes didn't bother me but the eerie *whoo-oops* of the spotted hyenas were nothing to laugh about.

Growing accustomed to the sounds, I was drifting asleep when I was startled by a bird. Schrrrrp-schrrrrp, schrrrrp-schrrrrp. The strident shrill was constant; like no other bird I had heard before. It took me several moments to comprehend it wasn't a bird at all, but the ring of an old flip phone I kept for emergencies, buried in my pack. I knew. I just knew. I was in the vast wilderness of the African savannah, a three-hour jeep-ride from an airport, and I knew this was going to be the call.

"She's gone," my sister said.

Three months earlier, to the day, my mother had taken a bath, a bath which grew cold. For some reason she forgot to get out. As her chilled body turned blue, hypothermia trapped her brain in confusion. In hospital, she thought the pieces of toast they gave her to eat were playing cards and she wondered whether she should produce the Ace of Spades or Jack of Hearts. It was the unofficial start, the broken hip, as it were, so many of our seniors find to be the beginning of their end. She never went home.

That was, until tonight. I had just learned my mother had made her own safari that day and crossed over to the non-physical world. For that single second, acceptance came before grief. I spoke to her, rejoiced with her, cheered for her clarity. The haziness that had been creeping around the edges of her mind would never now grab hold. She had taken the shortcut on the long goodbye. She was at peace and I was strangely serene, although I couldn't sleep.

"Ladies and gentlemen, we apologise for the inconvenience."

Malindi Airport had come to a standstill. The plane that was supposed to take me to Nairobi was "delayed". That was the sanctioned word. It didn't take a genius to look out the window of the tiny terminal to see the wheel on the left side had a flat. How long to change a tyre, I wondered? Was I going to make my connection to London and on to Dublin? Would I be late for my own mother's funeral?

Anxiety released the dam. Tears flowed as I searched in frustration for a solution to my plight. Didn't they understand? I had to get home. Home to see my mam. In the years I'd lived on Sark, I'd come home three or four times a year to see her. Each time I left I feared it might be the last time I'd hug her. So I started planning the next trip before I said goodbye. It felt like some weird insurance policy; if she knew I was coming back in a couple of months, she'd be alive. She'd wait for me. We had planned that I would visit her after my trip to Kenya. In ten days' time, we were supposed to look at my photos together. She was supposed to share my adventures through my images. She was supposed to wait.

The lady in the side office was sympathetic but she couldn't change the fact that, although the airport had a mechanic, no one had a spare wheel.

The gate became an overcrowded sweatbox, housing stranded passengers and relatives who didn't want to wait with them any longer. Announcements were few, and information was lacking. Snack machines were abundantly absent.

I had to take action.

I left my bag unattended and walked across the car park to the hangar with private planes. Perhaps some businessman could give me a ride? No one was flying today, the receptionist told me, but I could charter a plane if I liked. An elegant English couple had a similar enquiry but, even if the three of us shared the costs, there were still too many zeroes on the price tag. Deflated, much like the tyre that had caused it all, I dragged myself back towards the terminal. Locking the door of a red Honda Accord was a tall man dressed in uniform: black pants, white shirt, and yes, he had wings on his lapel. I hurried over.

"Are you a pilot?"

"Yes, I am."

"My mother died, can you take me to Nairobi?"

Whether it was the Irish accent, the womanly tears, or because I was tugging on his sleeve like a five-year-old, the man put his hand on my shoulder and said: "Come with me."

Why is it that, when you need to make things happen, you can hold yourself together, be pragmatic in your pain and sensible amidst your sorrow, but the moment someone is kind to you, emotion wins the war and the breakdown begins in earnest? He told me to take a seat; he would be back in a moment.

She was gone. My mother, my mammy, my mam was gone. No amount of wishing would bring her back. There was none of the denial I'd experienced when my dad died. This was real. Once you experience the death of the first parent, and lived with their absence, it's no longer a question of *if*, but a knowing that it's only a matter of *when* the second will die. She was dead. Both my parents were dead. Overnight, my siblings and I had become our family's elders. But they all had homes and families of their own. I had none and no-one. Since my divorce, my mother's house had been my permanent address. The more I travelled, the more she became my magnetic north, her home my bolthole. No matter what befell me, I knew she would always be there, at the airport or on the end of a phone. My steadfast cheerleader. If my father had been a spring tide in my life, my mother was a neap – low highs and high lows. But no matter my dilemma, she never gave me advice. She'd listen, and when my words were spent, she'd simply say: "May God direct you."

I felt as if a part of my centre had dropped out.

My phone rang. Aonghus and Máire were in a meeting with the priest. They needed a decision. Did I want to do a reading at the funeral? Or write a prayer of the faithful? Aonghus was going to sing. Conor, who was on his way from America, and Máire were going to read. I could hardly hear them above the airport noise and at that moment I was too upset to know if I could pull myself together to be coherent at the church. Couldn't they wait till I got there?

Where had he gone, this kind pilot-man? Was that him coming now with news?

"Nigh-ammey?"

"Knee-if," I spluttered, wondering if my mother knew when she chose an Irish name for her baby girl that I would spend half my life telling people to think of their *knee* and then say *if*. Perhaps she never thought I would have travelled so far from my Celtic home or that the day after she died I would be sitting in an African airport trying to get back to my roots.

"There is a plane with no one on it coming from Nairobi. I think it's your best chance," the kind man suggested.

I wondered if he truly meant there was no one on it. Hopefully it had at least one human pilot.

"OK," I said. "So this plane-with-no-one-on-it, it's taking off right away, yes?"

"Yes, it's going to Mombasa."

"But Mombasa is in the wrong direction."

"Listen to me now," he said. "The plane-with-no-one-on-it is going to Mombasa to pick up its passengers for Nairobi, but, first, it is going to stop here in Malindi to drop off a new wheel. I think you should get on it."

"But," I said, still resisting the idea of doubling back to Mombasa, "with the new wheel they can fix my plane?"

"Yes, but it will take one mechanic some time. You will most definitely miss your flight to London."

Years later, when I could see through the blur, this man stood out as the only one I had met that day who knew how to colour outside the lines.

"Ladies and gentlemen, thank you for your patience. The new wheel has arrived," announced the young woman at the gate. "We expect to have you in the air shortly."

Funny old word, *shortly*, isn't it? It can mean anything from minutes to months, but somehow it seems to satisfy those willing to wait. Not me, not today. My pilot-man gave me a nod and walked me across the tarmac to the plane that had delivered the wheel. For one glorious moment I thought he was going to fly us there himself, but when we reached the bottom of the steps, he stopped and shook my hand.

"It's going to be close."

"Thank you." I said, returning the shake.

"When it lands in Mombasa, stay on the plane, OK?"

"OK."

He looked at his watch. "It's going to be close."

As soon as I boarded the plane-with-no-one-on-it, the flight attendant sealed the door, and we pushed back. She took her seat, clipped herself in, and delivered probably the shortest safety speech in aviation history:

"Buckle up."

The thirty-eight-minute flight took thirty-two. Great. We were on the ground. But then engineers came on board and told me to leave.

"I was instructed to stay on the plane," I said. "I have to get to Nairobi."

"Yes, we are going to Nairobi, but first we must take on fuel."

The flight attendant escorted me down the steps and we stood one hundred metres away. The six minutes we had gained were swallowed up in fumes. When the hose was finally disconnected, people slowly emerged from the terminal and wandered towards the plane. *Hurry up*, I silently screamed at them. *Hurry, hurry up*. I climbed back on-board and sat back down.

Please, please, please, let's go, I thought.

The attendant was busy with the pilots when the first few passengers boarded. Those who thought they were first in the queue seemed surprised to see me already there. One man waved his ticket at me.

"You're in my seat," he proclaimed.

"It's open seating," I lied. "Just pick a row, we've gotta go." He was about to say something else when the attendant guided him to the seat behind.

We were in the air, but the kind pilot-man was right; it was going to be close.

Thirty-six hours after leaving Mombasa, I stood on the altar of our local church in Dublin, reading words I had written on that flight: a daughter's perspective of the woman who gave her life:

She would stand in the rain to watch me play hockey,
And cook mashed potato whenever I'd a toothache.
In my seventeenth year, we toured Italy together,
And took snaps of each other holding up Pisa.
She would visit the new places I chose to call home,
And tell all her friends of my crazy adventures.
She would listen when I cried,
And laugh when I triumphed.
She would tell me to take it... one day at a time.
I'd celebrate Mother's day on the fourth day of August,
Because that's when she gave me this life I now have.
She has passed through the gates to her new life hereafter,
Now she stands in the sunshine to watch over me still.

In many a Hollywood movie the weather underlines the graveside scene. There may not have been any cameras rolling in the cemetery that day, but the elements sure played their part as we laid this actress down. Umbrellas were ripped inside out by the twenty-five knot winds from the west. Driving rain pockmarked our faces and the priest trundled through the dying prayers in his best speed-reading style. I worried about the elderly few who had bravely walked the five hundred metres from where their cars were parked.

How many of them would catch their death of cold today despite their woolly hats?

As for me? I looked like a roaming banshee and felt like a bike that had been left out to rust. Having arrived from sunny shores, south of the Equator, I didn't have a coat. The only thing between my borrowed suit and the dark grey sky was the in-flight blanket Emirates Airlines had kindly let me take.

Hours later, after the condolences had left the building, my siblings and I stood in the house my father had built. You wouldn't think four kids, only ten years apart in age, would have such different memories of growing up. Items of value and the value of items were different for each of us. Like anyone else who hasn't moved house in thirty years, my mother had a plethora of *stuff*. Should we keep it, should we sell it, should we give it away? Minimalist that I am, I wasn't the one to ask. Yet, with only Aonghus and Máire still living in Ireland, we couldn't leave the onerous task of clearing the house to just the two of them.

"Did you guys hear that?" I asked.

We were standing around her bed. The house had been empty for quite a while but water had just gurgled in her en-suite bath. It didn't matter what any of us thought. Whether we believed it was a coincidence or a message from the other side, it helped us take a breath. What would mam want?

"How about this?" Conor said. "The most important thing we have left is our relationship with each other. We need to protect it at all costs, so maybe now is not the time for this. Why don't we close the door and walk away, and in six months' time come back?"

The plan was genius.

Although, that left me with another *what's next?* I had three choices. I could finish out my vacation time in Ireland, but cumulonimbus clouds push down on my heart and rain corrodes my spirit. Dublin in February can be dark, cold and wet. If you're sad, and suffer from SAD, it's not the month to stay. Having worked seventy-plus-hour weeks for the previous four years on Sark, going back to work early seemed silly. Therefore, releasing endorphins and getting fit beneath the blue skies and sunshine of the

Kenyan coast made more sense. Besides, my travel insurance covered the cost, and I owed the airline a blanket.

The time I spent at Wildfitness in Kenya – before and after my mother's funeral – had shown me how to exercise outdoors. I was so enthused with this new way of living that I signed up for a top-up weekend in April on the Isle of Wight, a small island just off the south coast of England. While the food and exercises were similar to those in Kenya, the weather was not. Friday night was chilly and the early morning session on Saturday was conducted in pouring rain. Since the workouts always produced enough sweat to saturate our clothes, being wet was not new. Being cold and wet, however, was. I shivered.

By lunchtime the wind had blown out most of the rain, but also most of my enthusiasm. We were driven to the cliffs above the island's south-western coast. The scene was dramatic. The North Atlantic squeezed its way up the English Channel, past the three distinctive sea stacks known as The Needles. The clouds boiled, each one threatening to dump a fresh shower before speeding across the sky. Grey and white waves, pregnant with kelp, delivered their fury on the rocky shore and underfoot, the grass was muddy, drenched by the morning's rain. We climbed down at least a hundred wooden steps to a beach that stretched for kilometres. The renowned chalky cliffs, similar to the White Cliffs of Dover, did little to shelter our backs from the sudden gusts of wind.

Uju, who had also been my coach in Kenya, gathered us around to explain today's "game". She drew a line in the sand, which we stood behind. In front of us were cobbles, stones and all things heavy. In what would have been considered a weight-lifting session in a gym, we had to raise those rocks above our heads and then heave them down the beach. I felt particularly unmotivated. I was too cold to see the point. As I squatted, deeply, to pick up an especially heavy boulder, my mind went off on a wander. Between the chatter in my head and the chatter of my teeth, I never heard the rip as the meniscus cartilage in my right knee tore. I carried on. I only noticed the soreness on Sunday morning but thought little of it. My whole body needed a massage.

Back on Sark, our hotels and restaurants were filling up. The strain of working on my feet twelve to fourteen hours a day highlighted the niggle in my knee. I ignored it. Work was work and it had to be done. *The show must go on.* Taking time off in the height of the season was not an option. Except, of course, on my birthday!

I have four rules about my birthday.

Number one: I never work on my birthday. Regardless of how many holidays there are on the calendar, I believe we should reserve at least one day per year to celebrate the self. It is the least we can do to nurture body, mind and spirit.

Number two: it has to be celebrated *on the day*, not the Saturday before or the Saturday after, just to accommodate those folks wanting a party.

Rule number three, and probably the most important one, is that I have to do something I have never done before. That could be as challenging as jumping out of an airplane, riding in a hot-air balloon or swimming among sharks, or as gentle as a hike in a newly found forest, a picnic on a deserted beach or cooking a celebratory dinner with friends.

That year, even though a limp had snuck up on me, I set about creating my own mini-version of Wildfitness by inviting Uju, my Kenyan coach, the chefs from the Isle of Wight, and my friends, to a spend the weekend in a log cabin on Sark. By the time my August birthday arrived, I had adopted a hobble to ease the pain that had now taken hold of my knee. Uju cautioned me to have an MRI but in the meantime strapped it in ugly blue tape so that I could still run, skip and jump along with the rest of the tribe. Weight-bearing "fun" was off the table, however. The only thing I picked up and threw that day was a bouquet of flowers off the edge of the cliff – satisfying the fourth birthday rule, to celebrate Mother's Day and Father's Day on that day rather than whatever Sunday the greeting card companies chose because that's the day they became my parents. Today was my first birthday since my mother had died, but she was getting her flowers nonetheless, even if the ocean below the cliffs had to be the vase to show them off.

The MRI confirmed a horizontal tear of the cartilage between my femur and tibia, which required an arthroscopic repair. Then, five weeks after knee surgery I lost my job. My hotel chain, which had gone from year-round to seasonal, decided not to open at all in 2015.

I felt the crossroads more acutely this time. For a freelance-minded woman, I sure had slipped into the comfort of a full-time job over the last five years. Having lived in staff accommodation, on an island without cars, meant that redundancy had a triple impact. In the length of a day I became jobless, homeless, and the only transportation I owned was my feet. And yet, it had been five years spent working sixty- to eighty-hour weeks, chained to a Blackberry that couldn't go unanswered. I was tired.

My siblings and I had already cleared out my mother's house and listed it for sale. My base, my permanent address, was gone. I was a single, childless woman of no fixed abode. Where did I fit in society? I thought about my own mortality. With no heirs to carry my DNA, what would be my legacy? Would anyone even notice that I'd lived?

I wanted to matter. My life had to be about more than just the sum total of being me. I wanted to make a difference. And so, the idea of taking a year out to circumnavigate the globe as a volunteer was born.

But, I am not a Mother, and you know my name is not Teresa, so I'm not saying I chose to spend a year in service purely for the altruistic joy of it. I knew if I found projects in countries I wanted to visit and volunteered five hours a day, five days a week, I would be housed and fed, which meant I could afford side trips along the way. The families and organisations I chose to work for would benefit from the skills I could contribute and I could fulfil my original dream of world travel. It was a win-win.

I love writing lists, but had never written one for my bucket. Instead, my method of identifying things I wanted to do during my lifetime had been to create a visual representation of them. I didn't have an elaborate "vision board" or digitised "dream screen", but what I had worked. On the side of the metal filing cabinet facing my desk in the office, I'd taped two pictures. One was a shot of the Aurora Borealis, the Northern Lights; the other, an aerial photograph of Bora Bora in French Polynesia. I would look at them every day and they would make me smile. From the greens and pinks of the aurora to the turquoise waters of Bora Bora, their colours brought me joy. Even though it had been my desire to experience both "someday", I was able to enjoy their beauty right then, right in the moment I was looking at them. I felt like I was there, and I knew, because of that, and the Law of Attraction, that one day I would be.

On my last day of work, I peeled the photos of Bora Bora and the aurora off the cabinet and put them in my pocket. "Someday" had come.

PART TWO
Around the World

Chapter 15
Overture

In less than ninety-six hours I was sitting in a wheelchair. Behind me, a tall, able, blonde Swedish woman was pushing me through the corridors and hallways of Stockholm airport. She was strong. Concorde had long since left the flying skies but, with her strength, she may have just broken the sound barrier. Shops blurred past me; I couldn't understand their names anyway. By the time we got to the gate, I could have been pronounced dizzy at the scene. People stared as I was wheeled to the front of the queue. I wanted to assure these folks it wasn't my idea to cut wilfully in front of them, especially when I appeared to be Lazarus incarnate, took up my pack and walked. I wasn't disabled, but it had only been six weeks since the knee surgery and Charlotte, my travel coordinator from Arctic Direct, wasn't taking any chances with the large airport and tight transfer time between flights. I was too excited to let any judgement bother me. I was starting my year of volunteer travel with a side trip to number two on my bucket list – Lapland. I was off to see the Northern Lights.

In much the same way as I had found *the guy* for an arthroscopic visit inside my knee – a Mister Moran of Santry's Sport Surgery Clinic in Dublin, a surgeon who put Bon Jovi back on stage a week after his operation – I had wanted to find *the place* to see the Aurora Borealis. Should it be Iceland, Canada, Alaska, or Scandinavia? No matter where I went, there was always a chance they wouldn't show, or the weather would cloud over their dance. I had heard of several people who had brought home a suitcase full of disappointment wrapped in expensive arctic clothing they'd never wear again. The black night had stayed black and they'd never seen a flicker. It doesn't matter how many money-back policies we demand in commerce, natural phenomena don't come with guarantees. If the weatherman says there's a seventy per cent chance of rain today, you don't put up seven-tenths of your umbrella. When it rains, it rains at a hundred per cent.

What was the solution? When planning a trip of this nature, I've found it best to centre the focal point around something I can control and turn the unknown element into an additional benefit instead. So an expedition to see the aurora had to be about more than waiting around to watch the splendour. I needed to find an activity that would be satisfying in and of itself, making the trip worthwhile. If the lights showed, they would be a heavenly bonus. The answer had come once I identified what I wanted from the experience. It was to stand in wonder and capture the moment. I found a five-day on-site photography course, led by Peter Rosén, of Lapland Media, the man who "wrote the book" on how to photograph the Northern Lights – *Aurora Borealis in Lapland*. What sealed the deal was that there were no one-off, trip-specific purchases to be made. Peter supplied all the camera equipment, and the local tour operator would supply all the outer gear to prevent death-by-freezing.

We landed at Kiruna airport, in the far, far north of Sweden and disembarked in the cold blue light. It was the middle of December, in the middle of the day, but nobody had told the sun. It was hibernating somewhere beneath the horizon and was refusing to get up till New Year.

"Welcome, welcome! My name is Klara," said the young woman with long blonde braids. "I am from Nutti Sámi Siida. We are waiting for two more guests to arrive."

Having been whisked past the restaurants by my chair-pusher in Stockholm, I was famished. Klara directed me to a window in a wall, behind which a mono-lingual native pointed to the two sandwiches I could buy. One looked like a beef salad in mayonnaise, and the other one its twin. I chose the one on the left and began to devour it before I had collected my change.

"How are you enjoying the reindeer?" Klara asked.

"I haven't seen any yet."

"No, I meant the one you are eating."

"Really?"

Why had that not occurred to me?

"Yes, we are very grateful for our reindeer, we use every part." Klara explained. "They provide transport, food and clothing."

Hoping Santa wouldn't put me on the naughty list for eating his reindeer, I swallowed the last of my sandwich.

"There they are," said Klara.

Walking towards us were two men. Carlos turned out to be a skilled amateur photographer from Portugal, now living in Sweden. David was a professional photographer from Australia, who shot for *Lonely Planet*. Since there were only going to be three of us, I was embarrassed to tell them I had the infamous PhD in photography (Press Here, Dummy), but at least I made them laugh.

The airport was emptying. Klara encouraged us to make haste across the car park. We legged it to her van before Celsius himself got word we were out there. Reindeer noses, I was to learn, are specially adapted so they can warm the air before they draw it into their lungs. Sadly, I hadn't ingested the red one when I gulped down Rudolph for lunch. Ice cubes formed in my nostrils.

Thankfully, that was the only time we would wear actual street clothes on the street. In a wooden hut, somewhere near Jukkasjärvi, Klara kitted us in outfits the Abominable Snowman might have turned inside out and shed. Climbing into the one-piece ensemble was akin to squeezing into a wetsuit. I wanted it to fit snugly, but perhaps not cut off my circulation. In contrast, the fur-lined hood swallowed my head, and the Eskimo mitts could have doubled as surfboards. Back outside, my polar boots left such enormous prints a Yeti might think he'd found his eccentric aunt.

Not much further down the road we entered the grounds of Reindeer Lodge, home of the Nutti family and a herd of antlered deer. Set in the forest by a near-frozen river, the fairy tale unfolded. Our individual log cabins, circling the main house, were swaddled in a foot of snow. Chopped firewood framed each colourfully painted door. Lights from within promised cosy warmth, while the snow crunched crisply underfoot. It was magical, direct from a childhood imagining. Even Hollywood couldn't have captured this enchanting scene.

After a dinner of reindeer fillet (of course), I sweated every drop of chill from my body in the wood-burning sauna down the lane. To run from one building to the next, without taking the fifteen minutes required to pull on all the gear, was tempting, but foolish. We'd been warned not to leave the door to the toilet cabin even slightly ajar, as it would freeze the water in the pipes. Suitably scared, I wasn't going to play roulette with my bloodstream, so I donned it all to come home. However, I ignored the warnings that I might get too hot if I lit the fire inside my cabin. I snuggled down between a sleeping bag and reindeer hide and slept the night away. Darkness never gave way to dawn, so I was almost late for breakfast.

We were heading out for a walk when another van pulled up, and out hopped our delightful tour guide, Peter Rosén. How he could look so debonair in his polar gear was beyond our tubby frames. He seemed excited; earth was approaching a fast-moving stream of solar wind, so it would be a good week to see the Aurora. We nipped back inside to learn more.

"It's the geomagnetic activity we're after," Peter explained, "which is measured by an index called Kp. Ranging from zero to nine, the numbers indicate the strength of the Aurora, which lets us know our chances of seeing it. Right now we are showing a Kp index of three, which means there is activity going on right now, but it is too bright outside for us to see."

Bright? Was the man daft? Granted, the light had lifted a wee bit, but it was about as bright as a child's muddy soccer shirt before it got stuffed into the laundry. God help him if he ever saw the sun again; blinded he would be.

"Let's go shoot reindeer," Peter said.

This was turning into quite the experience. First, I had to eat Rudolph, and now I had to gun down his brother? A week before Christmas, this hardly seemed fair. Of course the back of Peter's van revealed that our weapons of choice were an extensive array of camera equipment. While

David had brought his own gear, I couldn't help but notice how he ogled all the toys Peter had on display. Carlos jumped at the chance to use the professional kit on offer. Tempted as I was, I chose the high-end amateur camera body instead, figuring that, when I chose to buy one later on, it was more useful to learn how to use something in my price range than a fancy one outside my budget.

"Don't worry too much about the body," Peter told me. "When you are ready to make a purchase the place to spend the real money is on the lens." He uncovered one as big as a mini-telescope. It was so impressive, no one made a single reference to size.

Out back, behind the cabins, reindeer of all shapes and sizes roamed the frozen ground. As we crossed into their area of forest, they seemed unfazed – here was another bunch of fur-wrapped travellers willing to stretch out on the icy ground to take their picture.

"The secret to animal photography," Peter said, "is to make sure the eye is in focus. Even the nose can be soft if the eye is sharp."

With fluffy snow beginning to fall against the blue light of midday, these splendid creatures posed for our cameras – the quintessential image of Lapland. Saint Nick must have been hiding around the corner.

As the evening wore on, clouds rolled in over Reindeer Lodge. By dinner, the window to the night sky was closed. Despite the exciting Kp index of six, our chance of seeing the aurora was extremely slim. The show was going on, but we weren't invited to the performance. We couldn't complain; we knew the score. Still, it was disappointing. The three of us wandered back indoors. No point in freezing without the glory. I was pulling off my boots when Peter strode into the dining room and said, "It's still a six up north, let's go."

Grabbing my camera bag and renewed energy, I scrambled out behind the boys.

"It's simple," Peter said, opening the doors of the van, "we'll go track it down, find it where it can be seen."

Of course. Mohammed must go to the mountain. Chatting excitedly, we all piled into the van. The chase was on. We were eager, we were daring, we were now *The Aurora Hunters!* Peter drove on the snow-covered two-lane roads with the certainty of a local. To him, the conditions were normal, to us, the headlights illuminated nothing but potential snowy disasters. After an hour, he slowed and pulled the van off to the side. What had he seen? As he opened the door and stepped out, the blast of cold air that invaded the vehicle brought water to my eyes. He looked skyward. We seemed to have driven to the edge of the clouds. There was a glimmer, a pale green glimmer ahead. Was this it? While it was not something I had witnessed before, it wasn't exactly the spectacular scenes I'd hoped we'd see.

"It's starting," was all Peter said, buckling himself back in the driver's seat.

We drove a few more minutes down a side road and parked. Carrying tripods over our shoulders, camera bags on our backs and anticipation in our bellies, we followed Peter's flashlight, single file, down through a valley of pristine snow. Only our tracks disturbed the drifts; no one had passed this way recently. Peter marched confidently ahead, but without a discernible path, I marvelled at how he could tell where we were. When the terrain hardened and flattened out, we found ourselves standing on the partly frozen rim of the Torne river. It was early in the season; the smooth black water could be heard lapping under the ice beneath our feet. It was not all that thick, but Peter seemed unperturbed. We set up our tripods, screwed on our cameras and lined up our shots. In the foreground, a couple of wooden-planked fishing boats were embedded in the ice, the rest of our frames were filled with a cold empty sky. Waiting. We were ready, we would wait.

Celsius was having a laugh though. The temperature was minus twenty-two degrees. I exhaled downward, so the water vapour escaping from my breath wouldn't freeze my eyebrows, and to keep blood flowing through my veins I shifted from foot to foot. Within minutes, a faint glow of green light illuminated the lower horizon, but then it was gone. I wondered if I'd imagined it. But there it was on camera playback – an eerie green light, more vibrant than what I'd seen. Disappointment tried to creep up on me. While I was thrilled to have the shot, I wondered if the hype was contrived. Maybe all the incredible pictures I'd seen over the years had been enhanced in the camera lens. Perhaps this was one phenomenon better seen from an indoor chair with arms, by the warmth of a spitting log fire.

Then I was slapped by the flash of illumination that followed. The cold was forgotten as the sky burst into song. Above the wooden boats, a swirl of green laced its way through the sparkling stars. It flowed across the heavens like a curtain blowing in the wind. Sometimes the edges ruffled into pink and then to green again. Another band flashed, more violently than the last. It streaked across the water past the mountains to the south. Just like the tapping toes of Irish dance, this was building layer by layer. The geomagnetic storm was on. The black river lit up, reflecting back the riot. There wasn't a sound to be heard. It was a kaleidoscope of colours without the mirrors, a lightning show without the thunder. Our ears could not perceive the clapping sounds it made and our eyes could not believe the expanse of its domain.

I stood there, staring at an energy capable of creating worlds, feeling significantly insignificant. Who was I amid this cosmic chaos? A mere mortal in random greatness? But how could I not believe that I was somehow connected to this source, a source I shared with my family of friends, strangers I had yet to meet and life forms beyond my knowing. We're connected. Fumbling in the dark is futile, when we can tap into the light guiding our way. It's within us all, to share and to shine.

My fellow photographers and I captured this celestial celebration, knowing these images would be forever retained in the retinas of our minds. And when the sky had spat her last, we walked back to the van in silence.

Little did we know that what we had witnessed was just the overture. The opus had yet to begin.

Chapter 16
Symphony of Light

The next morning, we felt like we had stepped through the wardrobe to the fantasy world of Narnia. Nils, the leader of the Nutti family, and his assistant, Nila, dressed in traditional Sami red and blue tunics, with leggings and boots of fur, had harnessed reindeers to sleighs for each of us to ride. This was the element of the trip my travel coordinator and I had discussed at length. After my recent surgery, would I be fit enough to attempt it? There was no tourist allowance. These reindeer were the real deal. No sign of stabilisers on the wooden slats on which we would stand and steer. If I went off the rails, literally, I could end up buried in snow. But Nils, assuming I was going to drive one by myself, sized me up and picked out a handsome male, with antlers tall and wide. I called him Bob, because Klara had told us they never named a reindeer they were going to eat. Bob and I followed the group, he, hauling my camera gear, me, hollering in delight.

We sleighed through the most magical of landscapes. The tiny hollowed pathways through the forest of snow-laden trees were barely wide enough to pass. Snowbanks on either side were bitten in frost. The quiet was broken only by the crunching hooves of reindeer and the echoes of Nils' lilting call. The ride was thrilling. Not too fast to be scary, but nerve-wracking enough to have me clinging tightly to the reins. I knew that if I steered too close to the edge of the trail, a swinging branch filled with snow would kindly smack me back. The air was crisp, my cheeks inflamed with blood. As we cleared the woods and approached the river, the horizon blushed in a rosy and tangerine hue, but the sun still hid her face. When we came to the final incline, I stepped off one rail, scooting my foot along the ground, like I was shown. Bob seemed remarkably relieved with the lightened load and pulled us up the hill. His heart was beating fast, as was mine, not from effort like his, but from the excitement of such an expedition. If I'd never come to see the lights, I'd never have experienced one of greatest rides of my life.

It wasn't on our agenda, but before we left Jukkasjärvi, en route to Abisko, we *had* to stop at the Ice Hotel, an extraordinary feat of engineering and design. Apart from the two wooden doors in front, it's constructed entirely out of ice. Every winter they start from scratch, as the previous one melts in spring. Each unique room, designed by an original artist, is carved with an intricacy akin to cut crystal. Guests can sleep on beds of ice, at a balmy −5 degrees. There's even a bar serving Absolut in glasses made of ice. We stood at the entrance, but like many a country club, you can't just wander in. Proceeding through the icy halls requires a reservation. However, I just *had* to go in. Perhaps I could pretend I was lost and at least get to look at the foyer. The last the team saw of me was my body slipping through the Gothic doors. I didn't get very far before being stopped by an employee, but I was inside the grand entrance long enough to see the funniest thing I've ever seen. Apart from lighting, and the pale blue translucent ice, the only other thing of colour was bright red. It was placed on a shelf carved out of ice, surrounded by a wall of ice, a ceiling of ice, and a floor of ice. It even had a sign to tell you what it was. A fire extinguisher! Seriously? In a structure made entirely of frozen water, where were they going with a fire extinguisher? Even Adele can't *really* "set fire to the rain".

"Oh, Mammy!" was all I could think to say. We were swinging, suspended in mid-air. I am not a skier, so never had I sat on a chairlift, heading up the side of a mountain, at night. This was not a cable car. There was nothing but a foggy cloud between my boots and the earth sixty metres below. Only three things were holding me in place: the bar across my lap, Peter's body, squashed in beside me and an unapologetic terror. Why had I not comprehended that the Abisko Aurora Sky Station was so named because it is actually *in the sky*. I could see David and Carlos dangle and sway in the chair up ahead which made it even worse. Peter, the perfect gentleman, did his best to keep me calm and his amusement hidden. He was saying something about the eleven-year solar cycle, Mount Nuolja, rain shadows, cloud free skies and why *Lonely Planet* deemed Abisko one of the best places in the world to see the lights.

After our chairs reached the Sky Station, we regrouped. Peter led us on foot, away from the other photographers, further up the craggy mountain. When he'd found the perfect spot, we pierced our tripods in the snow, claiming it. Peter then pitched an orange igloo tent, the kind manufacturers label as three-man, but realistically it only sleeps two. I was scared. Not only were there four of us, but I hadn't brought a toothbrush. Happily, the tent turned out to be a prop. Peter placed a light inside and zipped it up. The orange dome glowed in the foreground of what would become our spectacular images of the ethereal sky.

If last night had been a six on the Kp scale, tonight was a seven for sure. The swirling curtains of green, pink and orange light reached down to touch the mountain and swept back up again. Spears of neon light rose up from behind the hilltop as if heralding us to a première. Instruments of light, playing here, then there, created an orchestra in the sky. The symphony went on for hours. There was time to photograph and time to watch. We weren't cold; we were ecstatic.

I reached for words to describe what I was seeing but couldn't find one with the radiance required to give it justice. We've used them all up, I thought, bandied the good ones around so that their meaning has been diluted. *Fabulous, Fantastic, Brilliant*, weren't enough. No word had been exclusively reserved for a spectacle like this. The only one I could think of, the only one appropriate, the one that should be held in reverence, is so misused. It now describes things as random as a pretty dress, an interesting comic or a charbroiled meal. I've got to bring it back, I thought. We need that word. We need it now. What could I do about it in this frozen wilderness? I set my camera on a time-delayed twenty-second exposure, and stepped in front of it, into the shot. With my head raised to the heavens and my body silhouetted against the raging sky, the lens sucked in an image I later entitled: "Putting the Awe back into Awesome".

On our way to the airport the next day, Peter made a quick stop by a ravine at the edge of the road so we could get a couple of final photos. It was easy to climb down through the drifts to the black pond below. Climbing back up was not difficult; it was impossible. The guys had gone ahead. Every time I took a step I disappeared knee-deep in the newly fallen snow. I looked for tree limbs, rocks, anything protruding from the white, which I might grab and use to pull myself up, but if they were there, they were covered from view. I felt lost inside the polar suit, jailed in a garment that restricted my flexibility. I found it difficult to bend my knee and lift it out of the snow. It was growing darker, but I couldn't move. Were it not for my buddies, there I might have stayed. Carlos shouted encouragement from the road above, and David and Peter climbed back down to get me. Each of them placed a hand under one of my mine, which gave me something solid to push against. I pulled my right leg out of the snow and pushed down to release the left. Gaining momentum, and some footing, the next I felt was their hands under my bum, pushing me up the embankment. Another step, and another whoosh up the rear. The guard rail of the road was now in sight. I was going to make it.

And in that comforting thought, I took a moment to cherish the absurdity. Here was Peter, the master behind Lapland Media, and David, who, with a shot he had taken minutes before, would go on to win Australia's Landscape Photographer of the Year Award, both shoving my ass up a snowy hill in Sweden. A humbling start to my trip around the globe.

Chapter 17
Taking the Plunge

Were we going to the beach or coming in to land? Both. If you've ever flown onto the island of Sint Maarten, also known as Saint Martin, in the Caribbean, you will be familiar with the approach that sees it permanently ranked in the Top Ten lists of most dangerous airports in the world. From my window seat I could see young children playing in the sand, and bikini-clad women desperately holding on to their triangles of lycra in the downdraft. I wondered whether their tans were from the sun or from jet fuel exhausts. We were coming in so low I could even tell who hadn't bothered to shave that morning.

It's an interesting island, split between two European nations, with Dutch settlers on the honky-tonk side, and French on the rural north. From the tourist beaches of Philipsburg, you can see the volcanic island of Saba, another Dutch colony. With rocky cliffs and deep ocean on either end of the shortest commercial runway in the world, Saba's airport also merits a spot on the list of most dangerous. To the south-southeast, on a clear day, the Federation of St Kitts and Nevis come into view. Stunning scenery notwithstanding, the party life of Philipsburg drove me across the border to Oyster Pond on the quieter French side, where I relaxed in the pool and swam in the bay. After two days decompressing, I was ready to start my first volunteer project of this sabbatical year on the nearby French island of Saint Barthélemy (St Barth's).

The ferry-ride to Gustavia Harbour took only an hour. Upon arrival, I was amused to note the absence of the normal excited greetings you'd expect. Visitor welcomes were muffled in discretion. This is an upscale playground for the mostly rich and famous, after all. Along the pier, the wooden fence corralled us into the queue for customs. It wasn't long, just slow. Waiting cars, taxis and courtesy vans, eventually rolled away with friends, family and passengers. Departing tourists boarded the ferry and the hardworking deck hands cast off. The sun was shining, and without a breeze, only the wake of the ship rippled the seas. A quietness descended and I stood alone on the dock. I had been instructed to wait by the water's edge for Birdy.

Bertrand Caizergues, or Birdy, as he liked to be called, is a French man who left France in the 1980s and settled on this small Caribbean island. He had one adult son, Thibault, who lived with him, and he ran a dive business based from his boat docked somewhere around here in Gustavia Harbour. It was Sunday morning and he would be working. I waited, watching the ferry become a speck in the distance. I was about to admonish myself for not getting a phone number, when I saw a small dive boat approaching from the west side of the harbour.

"Bonjour!" the captain yelled as a young man threw a loop of line around a dock cleat near my feet.

"C'est vous, n'est-ce-pas?" he asked.

"Oui, c'est moi!"

When everyone seemed satisfied that I was me, I threw my backpack over the gunwale and climbed aboard. Four men were getting ready to dive. A loud sharp hiss signalled that one of them was checking his air tank. I made my way forward to greet Captain Birdy, the owner of Island Diving and the man who was to be my host for the next month.

"'Allo, how are you?" he asked in his best English. "Ready to dive?"

Despite, or possibly because of, being an ex-scuba instructor, I declined his offer. My gear was at the bottom of my pack and I didn't fancy having to unearth my year's supply of toothpaste, underwear, solar chargers, and sunscreen, in order to get it out. Besides, I like to be calmly prepared and have researched the dive site before jumping in. Instead, I spent an hour trying to chat with the dive master, his son Thibault, while the others plunged below. My French was rusty, his English broken. Apparently, I was to share his bed, but not until tonight.

"Do not worry," he said. "The sheets *were* clean."

Did I look worried?

Luckily, it wasn't long before Birdy and the rest of the divers surfaced and I learned Thibault was leaving that afternoon on vacation. Before he left, he did indeed see that the sheets were clean.

The two-storey house where I was to live stood on a high terrace on the eastern side of the island, overlooking the famous Eden Rock resort. The beach area, to the left, marked the end of another short Caribbean island runway, this one named Gustaf III after the King of Sweden, in deference, I guess, to the ninety-four years in the eighteenth and nineteenth centuries when France had sold it to that Scandinavian country. Through the downstairs window of my room (that is, Thibault's), I could see the small Twin Otter planes taking off, banking sharply to the left before reaching the mountains across the cove. To the right, the hill continued to climb up the valley to where the four winds collided at La Barrière des Quatres Vents. With all these picturesque ocean views, my new home was a secluded property worthy of any celebrity looking for privacy, and I revelled in it with gratitude. My room was spacious, with good internet, and the furry thing that just caressed my legs was only a cat. Here I was, with nothing standing between me and paradise save a few hours' work a day.

Birdy was happy that I was settling in, but concerned about where he would put me once his son came back, but two weeks seemed such a long way off that I chose not to worry.

My work began the next day. In the mornings I would go with Birdy and help on the dive boat, sometimes diving with him and his clients, sometimes staying on board. Since it is a volcanic island surrounded by shallow reefs, the dive sites are only a short distance from the harbour and can be reached within thirty minutes. This allowed plenty of time for the customers to enjoy two separate scuba-dives before we brought them back at midday.

Birdy and I would then return to the house where I would prepare a healthy lunch.

The first time we drove home, I was startled by the sudden noise when we got to the roundabout at the top of the hill. It seemed like there were only three metres or so between us and the landing gear of a plane in mid-descent. As it passed overhead to our left, I could see the white of the pilot's teeth. More a grimace than a smile, I would think, as he flew down the side of the mountain onto the landing strip below. We too descended, albeit on the road. The aircraft came to a stop just shy of the start of the beach. I bet those tourists wondered if their holidays would start with a swim. Another successful landing on another from the Most Hazardous list. Excitement over, we pulled into the parking lot of the supermarket where Birdy liked to shop for fresh organic foods.

"*Ooo là là!* What is this?" Birdy asked half an hour later, when I put a *Salade Niçoise* on the table in front of him. Unlike the Irish, who wouldn't be caught dead saying "top of the morning", French people do say "Ooo là là"!

"Lunch?" I tentatively replied, worrying if something was wrong with it. The tuna looked rare, the salad neatly plated, and, as he preferred, the dressing was on the side.

"*Un moment,*" he mumbled in French and disappeared.

I wondered what he was up to until he came back with his phone. Perhaps he was going to look up a translation? *Mais, non!* He started taking photographs of the dish.

"Is very good" he said. "I make a photo and send it to my Papa."

Phew!

I guess all my time working around restaurants in the hotel industry had paid off and I had picked up a thing or two about making a meal look, as well as taste, appetising.

So what was the deal with his Papa? Was he trying to make him jealous? Perhaps his father had no one to cook for him, or maybe Birdy wanted his family to know I was doing a good job. Each meal I prepared, Birdy would nod his approval, take a photo and send it to his Papa.

Have you ever pondered the cause and effect of people raising their game? Praise encourages and congratulations satisfy. The more photos Birdy took, the more I challenged myself to improve my cuisine. Each day I tried a new garnish, a new presentation. It was fun and helped me forget that the dreaded hairy floor-mop was among my other daily chores.

Birdy was a man of rituals and habits. Routines and punctuality were the norm. In the evenings we went back down to Gustavia Harbour and walked the docks where the various multi-million-dollar mega-yachts would tie up for a night or two. Impeccably uniformed staff would sweep monogrammed mats or tidy sparkly flip-flops in wicker baskets near the stern. A smart businessman, Birdy would hand his card to these deckhands, welcoming them to invite the owners to a diving adventure.

One day, a man in his mid-seventies came aboard to dive. The seas were rough and he seemed flustered putting on his gear. To me, this has always been an early warning sign. When I see someone fiddling with their equipment, continually checking their air gauges, or sighing deeply, I see nerves. An appropriate degree of pre-dive nervousness is healthy and keeps you alert; an excessive amount is not. What seems *minor* on the surface can become *major* underwater. All three of us were kitted up and ready to dive. On the way to the stern, the man slipped and fell. We caught him as he went down and helped him regain his balance. However, I was now more nervous than he was and chose to stay aboard, thinking it would be better to have someone on the surface helping him out of the water than returning to an empty boat. That was what I told myself anyway.

We had tied the boat to a mooring ball to prevent our anchor vandalising the coral reefs below. Birdy had planned to swim in a loop, against the current at the start of the dive so they could drift back with the flow at the end. My concern was that the older, nervous man might breathe more rapidly and use up his air too soon. If the dive needed to be cut short, then they would be forced to surface further away from the boat.

In Ireland, we rarely, if ever, tied up to a mooring ball. From our inflatable dinghies we dropped divers in the water, watched for them and then picked them up. Trained as a coxswain, I was well able to drive a boat to a tired diver on the surface. But here, in unfamiliar waters, in an unfamiliar boat, as my eyes continually scanned the water for their bubbles, I wondered what I would do if the older man surfaced in the distance. It was a long forty-minute wait but eventually I was rewarded with a large spreading circle of smaller bubbles nearby – a sign that they were surfacing right beside the boat. From a shaky beginning, the man had settled himself and enjoyed his dive after all.

The older I get the more cautious I become. I wondered if my sense of safety had been over-conservative. In hindsight, perhaps it was that day, but, by the end of the month I was going to wish I had been on-board when disaster struck.

Chapter 18
A Crushing End

"*Bonjour! Tu as bien dormi*? You slept well?" Birdy greeted me as always, three days before I was due to leave.

By this stage, I'd settled into the routine of working the dive boat in the mornings, preparing lunch upon our return and cleaning the house in the afternoons. Thibault, having arrived back from his two-week vacation, had graciously moved to a friend's house down the road confirming my belief in not wasting time worrying about something that may or may not happen.

"*Oui, merci, je suis prête à partir*. I am ready to go."

"*Pas nécessaire, ce matin.*"

I wondered why he didn't think it was necessary for me to accompany him on the boat this morning.

"It's only a one-tank dive," he said. "Please, if you could stay here and take care of the garden. I will be back at one o'clock for lunch."

While Birdy left to take the divers out by himself, I set about clearing the scrub in the yard. They say gardening is therapeutic. I've never fully understood what criteria apply for an activity to be described as therapy, but if it provides a natural environment in which to perform a repetitive action while leaving the mind free to wander or think about nothing at all, then yes, gardening can be satisfyingly relaxing. Pulling on a rake that morning provided such a movement. I was in a rhythm and progress was being made.

The pile of brush behind me was getting larger than the pile in front. I bent down to extricate dead fronds from beneath a palm tree, when along came a spider. Seriously, it was very long, and definitely a spider. Decorated in yellow and black bands, colours I normally associate with poison in the wild, it hung in the centre of an elaborate web, right in front of my face. Who cares if scientific measurements for insects and arachnids do not include the legs, to my mind it was about ten centimetres long. I didn't wait around for Google to confirm this was an *Argiope Argentata*. It was time to go make lunch.

One o'clock came and went. The Mediterranean salad I had prepared was wilting. Unusually for him, Birdy was running late. I was hungry, but being polite, the cat and I chose to wait. When there was still no sign of him by two o'clock, I answered the rumbles. I killed another twenty minutes washing up.

I went out to the patio; a couple of sit-ups would pass the time. But it was such a lovely sunny day, albeit windy, I rolled over on to my side and elbow so I could look down the valley. Without thinking, I started to do a side-leg raise, an exercise I'd subconsciously deleted from my repertoire long ago. The second my foot was in the air my body went cold. Every cell in my leg had trapped the memory of the last time I had performed this drill and I was catapulted back to the moment I had been lying on a shaggy rug when the phone rang and I found out that my dad was dead. My emotions had been entombed in my muscles. I couldn't believe the simple act of repeating the same physical movement all these years later not only brought back the memory, but the actual feelings as well. I stood up and jumped in the pool, wanting the water to wash away the moment and soothe my senses. I didn't want to relive the rawness, feel the pain again. That was then, this is now. Now, I just wanted the memory of the good times, moments of his life I could cherish. I went back inside to dry off.

By three o'clock, still no Birdy. I was schooling my brain not to jump to conclusions. Everything was fine; no need to fear the worst. Maybe his car broke down; maybe his clients had invited him out to eat instead. Maybe...

The sliding glass door was swept open and an agitated Thibault rushed in.

"*Papa! Accident! L'hôpital!*" He ran up the stairs to his father's room. Within a couple of minutes, he was back down carrying a folder and a wallet.

"What happened?" I asked.

Thibault shook his head. Unsure whether he didn't understand or couldn't speak, I tried again in French.

"*Qu'est-il arrivé?*"

A flurry of words flew out his mouth as he flew out the door. I got the gist of it. It wasn't an accident in the car, but with the boat.

From what I could ascertain, the accident occurred when Birdy tried to tie off to a mooring ball over the dive site. He had driven the boat as close to the ball as possible as usual, without running it over. Normally, it was my job to hook the pennant attached to the ball and run a line through it and secure it to a cleat on the bow. With two people, good teamwork and fair conditions, the task is relatively easy. By yourself, with a strong wind and current, it can be quite the challenge. It was a blustery day. Birdy had missed catching the ball but the wind had caught the boat blowing it towards the rocks. In a quick decision (that should never be repeated), Birdy jumped into the water and tried to push the ten-metre boat to safety. Nature won. The wind and boat pinned his body against the rocks, breaking many bones, including his pelvis.

I walked over the hill and down the town to the hospital the following day. In my best French, I asked directions to Birdy's room. It wasn't difficult; there were only two floors. The door to his was open. I crept in. Birdy lay prone in the bed and had been advised not to move from that position for at least six weeks. His arms and legs were lacerated and dark shadows underlined his eyes. He was dozing. I waited a while until he opened his eyes. After a weak smile, he spoke.

"I saved my boat." He paused. "Could you stay longer?"

I knew he didn't mean by his hospital bed, but to stay longer in St Barth's. My month was up. I was supposed to board a plane the day after tomorrow. My next host in my next country was waiting for me. Yet, once discharged, I knew Birdy would need help. How could I leave him like this? I stayed up most of the night trying to see what I could arrange.

Unfortunately, I had four pre-paid flights to catch. From St Barth's I needed to take the ferry back to Sint Maarten, from there a plane to Puerto Rico, then a change to Fort Lauderdale in Florida, another one to San Francisco, and a then a long haul to New Zealand. Regardless of how many people I spoke with, no one in the chain of transport wanted to refund a cancellation and I hadn't heard back from my new host.

I returned to the hospital the next day.

"I'm so sorry, Birdy, I can't stay."

"Is OK, *je comprends*."

"But what will you do?" I felt bad about leaving him.

"Thibault, he is a good boy, he will check the boat yard does good work."

Despite all Birdy's efforts, the hull had taken some scrapes.

"But when they release you from hospital, what then? How will you manage at home?

"Ah, my Papa is coming from France."

The famous Papa, the one to whom Birdy had been sending photos of my food. In times of trouble, support from family is certainly most comforting.

"Can he cook?" I asked.

He laughed. "*Mais, oui*. He is a Michelin Star chef."

Note: Thankfully, Birdy recovered well from his injuries and within six months he was back at the helm of his boat taking delighted divers to discover the reefs of St. Barth's. Sadly, I never got to see a photo of what his papa made for dinner.

Chapter 19
We Should Say Something

It wasn't just the four plane rides that made it a long journey to New Zealand. I had wanted to go there since the early 1990s. When things would get tough in the television studio in Dublin, I would often exclaim, "Oh, to be sheep-shearing in New Zealand instead!" Why I thought working with sheep would be less stressful than directing live TV shows was a mystery. I'd rarely been on a farm, and had no formal training in hair salons. Perhaps it had been an old Maori-carved chess set, which my parents had been given as a present, that brought *Aotearoa* or "land of the long white cloud" into my dictionary of exciting words.

Whatever it was, it wasn't because of reading any travel guide. I've long since given up on buying those spoiler-filled books. Satellite imagery stirs my imagination. Guidebooks do not. They mock me with someone else's story. But once a place on earth makes it into my lexicon, I know that one day I will stand on that soil, even if I don't know much about it. It'll be there for me to discover. It makes me feel like a pioneer instead of a tourist on travel tip overload.

Out of the 700 volunteer projects on offer between the North and South Islands, I had come to help a young entrepreneurial family who had acquired a piece of land with a vision of creating a hospitality business in the countryside. They needed help setting it up and offered volunteers the chance to get in at the start.

The start, indeed. Shelly and Ryan, with their two-year-old toddler, were living in the barn. To keep funds flowing, they rented out the main house and two cottages to weekend guests from the city. When the place was unoccupied, volunteers could sleep in the main house; otherwise, in the old disused mobile home next to the road. It wouldn't have won any architectural awards, and water wasn't on tap, but there was a bed and a fridge, so it was fine. The work on this project was only four hours per day because food was not included. On the plus side, Shelly kindly lent volunteers one of her cars to go grocery shopping. The cost of living in New Zealand, I learned, is not cheap, so I was glad I had not committed to a long period of time there. My hospitality background had landed me this gig. Shelly needed direction in how best to market the resort. In the meantime, however, there was plenty of hands-on work to be done.

The main house was a large five-bedroomed log cabin home. Out back, the sun had split many of the planks on the south-facing deck, but, with a good sanding and a couple of coats of outdoor varnish, they could be restored to their natural beauty. No doubt many a weekend guest would sit out there and enjoy the pure air and panoramic vista.

I was pegging newly laundered bed linens to the outdoor line and admiring that view myself when a man of fair complexion arrived. Casually dressed, in shorts and tee-shirt, I guessed he was in his early sixties. He stretched out his hand to shake mine and introduced himself as a nomad who had also come to volunteer. We connected immediately. The remarkable thing about his suitcase was not that it weighed fifteen kilos, or that half of the interior was taken up with his pillow, but that it was the same case and contents he'd been carrying for the past seven years. For much of his working life, he told me, he'd been living on the top rung of the corporate ladder in India. One summer, he went to an Ashram to learn meditation and was so enthralled he gave up his capitalist ways. Since then, he had been travelling, sometimes staying in hotels, sometimes volunteering, but, mostly, sleeping on other people's sofas before "couch surfing" had been invented. He found my idioms charming, and I reckoned it was more likely to have been his Irish mother, rather than his English father, who had given him the name Seamus.

We became a good team. Some of the work was back-breaking, some of it less so, but tedious. My least favourite, was – you've guessed it – cleaning toilets. His was folding laundry. But no matter the task, we made each other laugh. Domestic chores seem so less mundane when you share a joke while you work. When Shelly gave us our jobs each morning, we would, between ourselves, work out who wanted to do what. Seamus enjoyed feeding farm animals, especially the pigs. I preferred to save my nose and offered to vacuum floors instead. When I made up the guest rooms, he would empty all the trash cans. If there was gardening to be done it'd be mine, but painting was usually his.

We were both "big picture" type people, but as the days progressed, we noticed Shelly liked to focus on minutiae. It was the first time I had to "punch a clock" while volunteering. Normally, I would work at a task until it was finished, but she would make us quit after the four hours were up. Conversely, if she came to check on us and spent two minutes chatting, she would expect us to stay late and make up the time. As far as work on the house was concerned, we pointed out the major things that needed to be done, but she concentrated on trivial stuff instead. In our opinion, the more we tried to help her, the more she resisted. She would have us clear brambles that were out of sight of the house, but ignore a hole in the deck in view.

On one particular sold-out weekend, we were expecting about thirty people for a stag and hen party. The guys had rented all the rooms in the main house, while all the girls would stay in the cottages. The day before their reservation, Shelly handed me a toothbrush and asked me to clean the grout between the terracotta tiles on the outside porch. While I'm in favour of a clean entryway, I felt the state of the grout underfoot would not be noticeable, unlike the dog slobber and sticky toddler handprints on the floor-to-ceiling glass doors I wanted to clean.

"I think she's nuts," said Seamus.

While I thought she might be a tad irrational, I didn't think she was crazy. If anyone was half-crazed it was me, down on my hands and knees scrubbing outdoor grout with an indoor toothbrush.

"We should say something to her," Seamus said.

"Like what?" I asked.

"That she is treating us like children."

"Hmm."

"You're so much more experienced at running guest houses and hotels than she is. You should say something," he said.

That was true, but how was it helpful? I didn't think she would listen to me, even though that was allegedly the reason she took me on.

"She only said you can't have the car today, because she knew you were planning on touring the area this afternoon. She doesn't need it," said Seamus. "I'm telling you, she's bonkers." He seemed convinced, but I didn't respond.

He tried again. "It's not fair she won't let us work five hours a day."

I kind of agreed with that. An extra hour a day would be nothing, but would give us a full day off instead, plenty of time to sightsee.

"We should say something," Seamus said again.

My four-hour grout work turned out beautifully, although I was still sure no one would notice. Despite Shelly's rules, I sneaked back later in the day to clean the glass doors before the guests arrived. It certainly made a difference. I was proud of my work and of helping her out, albeit on the sly.

Because the house was full, I slept in the trailer by the road, and Seamus was in a tent nearby. He grumbled about the camp bed and the cold.

"We should say something," he said.

I was beginning to agree. My mattress was also uncomfortable. I'd flipped it over and put my pillow at the opposite end. In changing things around, I found that the sheet, which had been near my feet, was hideously stained. It didn't take a Rorschach test to know it wasn't caused by an ink blot, but by fluid from someone else's body.

"You should say something," said Seamus.

Shelly stopped by the main house later that morning. She was in one of her distracted moods. She was carrying dirty laundry from the barn, her hair hadn't seen a brush, her two-year-old, Anabel, was running around half-dressed, and she had her phone stuck between her ear and shoulder. I was deep-cleaning the long island in the middle of the kitchen and Seamus was sweeping the floor. He nodded at me when we saw her come in. I didn't think the timing was quite right, but he kept looking at me and nodding in her direction. When she got off the phone I asked if we could talk.

"What's up?" she asked.

"Seamus and I wanted to talk to you about a couple of things including the work schedule."

"What about the schedule?" she asked.

"We wondered if we could work five hours a day instead of four, and have an extra day off to sightsee?"

"No, that's not going to work for me."

"Well, could we both take the same day off this week, when we have the car, so we could go for a drive around the countryside?"

"No, I need at least one of you here on Thursday."

Seamus hadn't stopped sweeping. I wondered if I should mention the sheets. Instead, I said: "Could we show you things around the house we feel need fixing?"

"I don't have time right now. Anything else?" she asked.

I paused, but decided to go for it.

"Well, I'm a little upset about the soiled sheets that had been put on my bed."

"They're not soiled, they were washed. It's just a stain," she said.

So she knew.

"I've got to go, anything else?" she asked as she pulled her daughter up onto her hip.

"No, that's it."

"Seamus?" she asked.

He finally spoke up. "Everything's fine," he said. "By the way, would you like if I take Anabel with me to feed the pigs?"

"Oh, would you? That would be a great help," she said. Then the three of them walked out the door together.

When Seamus came back an hour later, he prattled on about how sweet Anabel was, and how much she loved helping feed the pigs. I had no time for small talk.

"I see your game."

"What?" he asked in that ridiculous tone of feigned innocence. He knew damn well, and he knew I knew it too.

"*We should say something. She's bonkers. We should say something.*" I repeated his words back to him. "You had no intention of saying anything, did you? You wound me up so tight that I'd speak for you. Now, you're the hero and I am the troublemaker." He only answered with a smile.

I marched out back, more annoyed with myself than with him. How often did I need to get tangled in this type of situation before I would learn the lesson? I had, many times, ended up as the spokesperson for a bunch of disgruntled people, who all agreed *we* should say something, only to stand up front and speak, but be deafened by the silent group behind me. I had met those instigating cowards before and survived their chicken ways. So what just happened? This time I had encountered the manipulator, not the gutless. I forgave myself, but vowed not to fall for this ploy again.

Shelly wasn't away with the fairies; far from it. She was an enterprising young woman with a big dream. She was trying so hard to balance a fledgling business with a start-up marriage and young family, that she'd just been caught out on the ledge of multitasking. All that was needed to bring her in, was some organization and a solid plan. I went back inside, handed my cleaning cloth to Seamus, and set off in the direction of the barn to find her.

Chapter 20
Beyond the Shire

I spent the next few days teaching Shelly several strategies on running a hospitality business and managing volunteers. Together we brainstormed advertising ideas and laid out a marketing plan. I showed her several systems for organising work schedules so the volunteers could handle check-ins which would leave her more free time for herself and her family. Then it was time to move on. However, I couldn't leave the country without experiencing the landscapes so dramatically filmed for *The Lord of the Rings* trilogy. I needed to see those mirror scenes of blue lakes and snow-capped mountains for myself. Missing them would have been like going to France and missing the Eiffel Tower, or Rome and bypassing the Coliseum. So I granted myself a "side trip". But with only four days available, where exactly should I go? Ironically, it was to the seven-year nomadic Seamus I later expressed my gratitude for pointing me in the direction of Queenstown, the Adventure Capital of New Zealand.

The stunning scenery began as soon as I deplaned. The tarmac was surrounded by trees like Christmas and majestic mountains. The chatty cab driver made me laugh when he said he would take me to the hotel via the *scenic route*. All of it was a photographer's fantasy.

It was the height of the summer season. I had reserved what I thought was reasonably priced accommodation out of town, but when we ascended the canyon alongside Shotover River, and arrived at Nugget Point Hotel, I thought my computer must have swallowed a couple of zeroes. The lobby was elaborately decorated, the front desk agents flawlessly mannered and the background music tastefully accentuated the incredible views. This was definitely not the type of bed-and-breakfast to which someone on a yearlong world trip would normally allocate funds. I wished I'd asked the driver to wait. It was only eleven minutes back to the sold-out hostel – surely at least one person had called to cancel? But, I was here now; I might as well stay one night.

Surprisingly, the rate on my registration card did not reflect the ambience. Perhaps I'd been offered such an inexpensive tariff because they'd put me in a "last sell" room, some little corner in the basement that needed renovation. To my absolute astonishment the room was gorgeous, with sliding glass doors that led out to a patio just for me. Across the ravine, the mountain range caught every shade of the setting sun, the distant peaks shadowed in indigo, the closer ones tinted in gold. Hundreds of metres below, a red jet boat spun a dozen passengers around u-shaped river bends. Screams of delight made their way up the gorge as white-water spray filled the air. When the red and yellow stern disappeared from view, a quiet descended on the valley. I sat in the stillness, basking in gratitude, as the sun gradually slipped away and the trees around me fell into the black.

"I know where you are!" the message flashed.

"I'm in New Zealand." I typed back to Kaye, my Australian friend, whom I'd met in Fiji.

"I know, but I know *exactly where*."

I was enjoying a sumptuous breakfast in the hotel's dining room. My corner table was surround by glass walls on either side. I was suspended in the mountains overlooking the same view of the canyon I had enjoyed the night before; a scene I'd posted on Facebook only minutes before.

"There's only one place with that view," Kaye wrote back, "which means you must be close to Onsen Pools."

"Pools?" Much as I love to swim, I didn't want to waste a moment in this exquisite nature when I could douse myself in chlorine anywhere else in the world.

"Trust me, you *have* to go."

I'd planned a day downtown by Lake Wakatipu, walking the Queenstown Trail and photographing the gardens. With light streaming through the foliage, a child flinging his first Frisbee to his dad, and a couple of lovebirds floating beneath a parasail over the lake, everywhere I turned an eye-catching frame revealed itself. Capturing those sparkling moments sewed sequins on my memories. The quaint streets and shops demanded I wander rather than stride, while tourist kiosks boasted adventures of every kind. As serendipity would have it, I came across a brochure for the business right next door to my hotel. Kaye had been right, Onsen Pools shared the same magnificent view of the canyon and I simply *had* to find room in the budget to go there. But first, there was the matter of Milford.

There are many ways to get to the famous fjord of Milford Sound – by air, by land or on foot. To hike there was against my timeframe, which meant I didn't have to admit it was probably also against my stamina. The idea of skirting along the tops of these Southern Alps by light aircraft or helicopter seriously appealed to my sense of adventure, but the cost of the sixty-minute flight did not. That left the bus. Not the charming locals' bus, the type of bus that said *Endeavour,* but the big monster tour bus we "travellers" love to hate. I had to get over myself and my snobbery for the two-week vacationers who undoubtedly made up more than half of the fifty folks on-board. During the five-hour journey – including, of course, the mandatory stop at a souvenir shop – the lively driver kept us entertained with his mixture of landmarks and tales from days gone by. He was only short of stopping off to introduce us to The Hobbit.

Milford didn't dress up in clear blue skies that day. If anything, the threatening clouds suppressed the majesty of Mitre's Peak. Despite working overtime, my camera could do little to retain an interesting image of its seventeen hundred metres. Grandeur had left the Sound. If the tour bus had been packed, the tour boat was overloaded. Photographs of nature were bombed by elbows protruding from other shots, and audio tracks of the kea birds were voiced over by "Johnny, put that in the trash!" Any attempt to produce a shake-free video of Stirling Falls was vetoed by the "Excuse Me" bump. There were more people than mountains, and I got the distinct impression that the wildlife was watching us. I yearned for the nineteenth century, for the days before Captain Grono and his ships first found the fjord. What would have happened to this majestic place if he, like Captain Cook, had feared the mountains and sailed on by. The inlet breathes beauty down this valley of waves. It is a sight to see, but it is no longer the place of pioneers.

When it was time to get back on the bus, I remembered the inside scoop a local pilot had given me. If the plane wasn't filled on the return trip, the empty seats could be snapped up for less than full fare. How much less was determined by demand. Demand was determined by how well the bus driver could make the five-hour coach ride home sound interminable. A young couple, impatient to get back to their honeymoon, took two of the three empty seats. I vied for the remaining spot. But the bus driver had done his job well (presumably earning a decent commission), and the seat was sold before the discount could get deep enough to reach my purse.

As I scrunched my fleece against the bus window, I laid my head down to dream. A box had been ticked that day. Time to conjure a new one. When I opened my eyes, hours later, beads of mist had fouled the darkened window and the front windscreen wipers were in full swing.

Fog continued to seep its way through that night, setting the scene for an eerie dawn. I hadn't sat in a kayak since my yellow boat had disappeared down the road in the States. I wondered if my wrists and lats were up to it, but neither fog nor fitness could impede my desire to paddle up Lake Wakatipu towards Glenorchy. Including our guide, only four of us pushed off from the pebbly beach along the northern shore. I was delighted the two other explorers were experienced, so there were no squawks and squeals of newbies going round and round in circles. Instead, we serenely wove our way around Pigeon Island, blades dipping silently as we went. Through the gloom, we glimpsed a trek of horses heading towards Paradise, a nearby rural town. As the sun ignited the mist, the breath-taking mountains pierced the sky, and we were regaled with expansive views of what the world has come to think of as "Middle-earth". Cold dribbles slithered down the paddle's shaft and ran across my knuckles. I didn't care. The thrill of being a part of the watery lake warmed my being, and the push and pull of every stroke caressed my soul with purpose. I was where I wanted to be, doing what I wanted to do, and living in the absolute now.

Smart businesses know that offering a complimentary secondary service often entices people over the edge of decision. The same savvy marketing could be attributed to Onsen Pools.

Having spent my final day picnicking on the sports ground of the local school in Queenstown, watching the tandem skydivers coming in to land, I needed a ride back up the canyon. Onsen, situated four hundred metres beyond my hotel, sent their courtesy van to pick me up, which guaranteed my business.

Built into the side of the mountain, the architecture followed natural lines of the trees and the wooden building offered a feeling of calm. At reception, I was greeted with a smile and warm towels. These people knew how to unwind a guest.

Down the corridor, I found number four. I opened the door to a chamber made of wood. Before me, three steps led up to a deck surrounding a sunken cedar tub. Had my Japanese been better, I might have figured out *Onsen* meant "hot spring" or literally, a "bath house". The clear, aerated rain water invited me in. As soon as I was settled, I pushed a button on the side. The wall in front and the ceiling above, peeled back. As if by magic, my indoor hot tub was now in the great outdoors. The vast expanse of canyon lay before me. Poised on the edge of creation, with crisp mountain air tingling my exposed skin above the surface, swirling bubbles soothed every muscle ache below. This was New Zealand and this was *"taking relaxation to the summit"*.

Chapter 21
The Scary Ferry

In stark contrast to the mountainous skyline of southern New Zealand, I was en route to the flat land of Tongatapu, the main island in a string of 170 in the South Pacific that make up the Kingdom of Tonga.

It had been months since I had first communicated with the Sheens – an incredible Australian family living off-grid among the islands and waters of Tonga. Theirs was the volunteer project around which I had designed my entire year's trip. During the winter season they lived on their sixteen metre catamaran sailboat, *Wildlife*, operating *Whale Discoveries*, one of the few businesses licensed by the Tongan government to offer guided swims with humpback whales in the wild. Each year the whales would migrate from their cold-water feeding grounds of Antarctica, to give birth to their young in the warmer seas around Tonga. For the rest of the year, Dave, Tris and their two teenage children, Kai and Dior, were in the process of cultivating a land base on Nomuka, one of the more remote islands in the Ha'apai chain. I was excited about the opportunity to live on a secluded island with its own coral reef but had been a little concerned about the volunteer job itself: to tutor the children. I had plenty of certifications in "how to teach" but I wanted to make sure they knew I was not an *actual* teacher. Dave and Tris explained that because the children were enrolled in a distance learning programme back in Australia, their true teachers would be at the end of a computer. My job was to ensure their assignments were submitted on time.

They had also informed me the only way to make the six-hour journey from the main island northward to where I would be based on Nomuka was aboard the "scary ferry" which left once a week on a Tuesday, or maybe Monday, but could be Wednesday. So, having arrived on a steamy Saturday night in March – I had forgotten how draining tropical heat can be – I had a couple of days to explore the capital, Nuku'alofa.

Sunday, I discovered, is truly a day of church, food, and rest in the Kingdom. It was astonishing to walk through a veritable ghost town, nothing open and no one about. The only sign of life was the delightful singing emanating from the rather ornate church. As well as headstones, the neighbouring graveyard sported huge, larger-than-life photo billboards of deceased loved ones. I silently hoped my mam wasn't too disappointed with the couple of dates we'd recently etched onto the plain in-ground slab she shared with my dad. Further along the seafront, I saw a guard at the entrance to the port and one lone youth sauntering along. Other than that, streets were deserted until God let out. Then, like a volcano erupting from a long sleep, men in decorative shirts and cloth wrap skirts, women wearing fancy high-heeled shoes and brightly coloured dresses covered at the waist with traditional woven mats, paraded noisily by, as family after family headed homeward for *Umu,* the weekly feast.

The following afternoon, I arrived at the harbour clutching my ferry ticket for a Monday evening departure. Given Lonely Planet's description of Tongans as not being the greatest sailors, regardless of conditions, I was suitably apprehensive about the trip. Evidently, it was a pretty sure bet that someone would be ill five minutes out of port. While the ocean swell doesn't affect my equilibrium, the seasick-domino-effect certainly could.

The crew was busy on the dock, but unfortunately, casting off was no longer planned. Earlier this morning, half an hour after I had bought my ticket, I should have been listening to the radio (in Tongan) because that's how the rest of the passengers knew the ship wouldn't sail till Tuesday.

Time stands still while you are waiting. Time stands even stiller when you are waiting in the suffocating heat. It was so humid I could eat my own breath. The only thing pushing the clock forward in those twenty-four hours was knowing that these would be the last moments of internet connection with loved ones back home. Tris and Dave always had to sail to other islands to send and receive emails, or walk higher into the jungle to make a call. So, I cherished every dialogue with friends and family.

Tuesday eventually came and this time the hustle and bustle on the wharf led me to believe it would sail tonight. Men, women and children arrived at the outdoor concrete waiting area, many of them carrying large mats, bags and boxes. Some carried nothing at all. I thought I was going to be the only *Palangi* (outsider) travelling, until a young man with a blonde toddler sat beside me. As he chatted with a few locals, I incorrectly assumed he was an ex-pat. He told me he was visiting from Australia, having spent several weeks here before. Many of the people I'd met in the preceding days had asked me why on earth I was going to the non-tourist area of Nomuka, so I was curious if he knew the island. He looked at me and said,

"Ah, you must be the new schoolteacher."

So much for anonymity.

"Tutor," I explained. "Their teachers are at the end of a computer back in Australia."

His name was Lucas, his daughter's Ava, and along with his dad, would get off at the same spot. In fact, he was friends with my host family and would be staying with us for a week.

More and more people laden down with *stuff* arrived. All of them seemed to move in that soft, well-worn, dusty flip-flop shuffle. Children hung out of mothers' arms. Some were playing, some sat eating peanuts. About an hour passed as the crew loaded cargo. Large containers, gas tanks, boxes big enough to hold washing machines, and even cars, were strapped up and craned aboard. High on deck, the crew, cigarettes dangling from their mouths, guided load after load into position, not a hard hat among them.

Then, as if an inaudible bell had rung, the waiting crowd stood up and shuffled towards the chicken wire fence. The gate opened and the procession began. Across the dock and up the steep wooden gangway we went. Everyone seemed to be in a rush to claim a corner on the outer decks.

I dumped my gear inside and joined them by the railings. Down on the quay, those who'd arrived without luggage were, in fact, not travelling but were the "wavers-off". They patiently stood by the fence waiting for the gangway to be forklifted off, strapped up, and craned back on to the aft deck, so the final rope could be thrown ashore. And then, as the props churned the water white and we peeled away from the wall, the waving began. Children, running up and down along the inside of the chicken wire, shouted out to loved ones, women waved hankies in between their tears, men strolled with one hand in a pocket, the other raised in fond farewell. Those on-board waved and whistled back. I waved too, to no one in particular. The whole affair reminded me of the opening scene in the movie *Titanic* and I hoped it wasn't a premonition of another catastrophe at sea. Six years earlier this ferry's predecessor had left port on this same journey to the outer islands. Tragically, after only a few hours into the voyage, it had sunk and dozens of passengers, particularly those inside the ship, had lost their lives. That, plus the air conditioning below decks this evening being turned to arctic, probably explained why the majority were camped outside.

Darkness fell less than thirty minutes out. For those headed to the northernmost islands of Vava'u the trip would take twenty-four hours, which made the six-hour trip for me feel positively short. Thinking I wouldn't need it again until back in the Northern Hemisphere, I had to dig deep to find my fleece. Then I settled down to read the rest of the way.

Over the years I've disembarked many a ferry in various swells, but both the good and bad always had one thing in common – one side of the boat was tied to dry land. Not so on the wharf-less island of Nomuka. At midnight, the fifty-three-metre ferry stopped in what felt like the middle of the South Pacific. Announcements were only made in Tongan so I followed passengers who looked like they were getting off. We descended to the lowest deck where a hatch door opened to the black, boisterous sea. An aluminium skiff, with a lone coxswain hugging the outboard, bobbed alongside. Were we being boarded by pirates? No, this was the tender that they'd towed behind the ferry. Tonight, it rode the one-metre swell both up and down, as well as forward and aft. I was certain the clash of metal on metal could be heard on the distant shore.

There seemed no system to the transfer: off went a couple of boxes, then some people, then more boxes. I was being moved along by the procession of Tongans descending the metal stairs. When I found myself standing in the open hatch, I was thinking the doorway of a skydiving plane from adventures years ago seemed less daunting. But, with a line of passengers pressing behind me, I didn't have the luxury of debating my exit from the ship. I handed off my large rucksack, keeping the smaller one on my back. I took the first available moment and timed the jump down into the skiff, all the while praying that Mister Moran's surgical handiwork on my right knee would survive the impact. I stumbled, but at least I was in the boat and not the water.

At first, I crossed to the opposite side and leaned my bum on the gunwale. But with all my prized possessions in the knapsack on my back, I was in fear of a freak wave inviting me and my electronics over the side. I hurried to the centre and hooked my toes under someone's duffel, clinging to someone else's fridge-freezer. The chain continued, handing over boxes and children. Across the tender, I saw Lucas clutching Ava, his father also safely aboard. When I thought we were full of people and stuff, we weren't. There were always more. Becoming accustomed to the rhythm of the swell, I began to settle, until a mesh bag flew past my head, wriggling as it went. It wasn't until the bag squealed as it was caught by the man behind me I realised we were taking on pigs. Finally, the clash of metal stopped and, by torchlight, we proceeded to shore.

Twenty minutes later, having narrowly missed a couple of coral heads breaking through the surface at low tide, we reached dry land. Nomuka at last. A dozen or so people on the beach unloaded passengers and cargo. It wasn't hard to pick out the silhouette and accent of my Australian host, Dave. After months of pre-planning and anticipation, we made our introductions in the dark. Then along with Lucas, his father, little Ava, and all our gear, I piled into the truck Dave had borrowed. Bouncing down the dirt track, past the small and only village, we crossed to the western side of the island. Two of Dave's rescued dogs ran ahead in the high beams, showing us the way. When we passed through two iron gates I assumed we were arriving on the property but Dave told me those gates marked the edge of town and were normally closed to keep the pigs in. By Tongan custom, if a pig wandered onto your property, you had the right to kill and eat it. I wondered why the gates were open tonight. Shortly afterward, we stopped in a forest of trees but I could hear the waves lapping nearby. This was it. Lolofutu.

The beach barn and deck Dave and family had constructed was more sophisticated than I expected and housed a cooker, an American-style fridge freezer, a gravity-fed sink and enough shelving to store everything from peanut butter to school books. A two-hundred-yard walk north of the barn led to a path in the woods at the end of which was a tent. Standing inside, I was amazed to see a king-size mattress on top of a base Dave had constructed in wood. Within minutes I was asleep in my new home.

Chapter 22
Catching Rain

I stepped out of the tent the next morning onto a sandy trail that led me through a handful of trees out onto the beach. The tide was low again, exposing tips of the house reef. The sun had broken the eastern horizon behind me, but had not yet risen high enough over the trees to dazzle the sand beneath my feet. It was cool and damp. My footsteps would be immortalised – at least until the next high tide surfed in.

I retraced them back past the tent to the trail along which I had come the night before. I was close to the barn when I stopped. I could feel I was being watched. There was no one there, but the feeling was strong. I peered through the trees. Sunlight found its way between the leaves, dappling the sandy soil. When I quietened my breath, I heard another. Not mine, but that of a tranquil being standing behind the tree to my left. It had been there all along. Watching. A flurry of breeze parted the leaves and a greater splash of sunlight illuminated a magnificent chestnut horse. Her eyes were on mine. I nodded. She stood still. I was not a threat, but was she to me? I took a step closer but she didn't move. Feeling at peace in the morning's calm, I murmured a hello to the horse I would come to know as Taffy, and walked on by.

When I reached the barn, Dave, Lucas and his dad were sitting on the deck, drinking coffee. Ava played with cornflakes floating in a bowl of watery milk made from powder.

"So, how did you sleep?" Dave asked.

"Wonderful, thank you. I hope I'm not late."

"No. No rush." He took another mouthful of coffee. "There's been a change since we last wrote," he said. "Kai and Dior are still in Australia with Tris."

"Oh?"

"It was a last-minute opportunity that came up. Our friend is a vet and the kids were invited to spend a couple of weeks helping in the clinic. They will be back next week."

I was surprised. However, given how much effort it took to get here, and that I was due to stay several months, a week's delay hardly seemed relevant.

"So, what can I do to help in the meantime?" I asked.

"We reckoned you could get acclimatised. We brought back school books from Australia and Tris is picking up more now."

"Great, perhaps I can look at their assignment schedules."

"Yeah, about that," said Dave. "There's been a change in plans there, too."

"OK...?"

"Since we've been living on this island we've run into problems getting their assignments emailed on time. The closest internet is a day's sail away. So the system no longer works for us."

"I see."

"The school said the kids couldn't continue in distance learning if they couldn't keep up with assignments."

"So, what now?"

"Welcome to home schooling," he said with a grin.

They used to say that to teach you just have to be one chapter ahead. In this information age, with "How To" videos available on almost every subject on YouTube, anyone should be able to do it. How hard could it be to educate two teenagers. All I would have to do is look up each subject the day before.

Oh, wait now ... that's right, we were on a tropical beach without internet.

I looked through the text books the parents had brought from Australia and fretted about not being an actual teacher. The five core subjects were maths, science, geography, history and English. English would be easy, history and geography, manageable. Science? Well, I still remembered all the gas laws as they pertained to scuba diving, so that was probably a good start. But maths? Maths was my weakness, my nemesis. Painful memories of sitting in the back of my own maths class came flooding back. I liked to blame my awful teacher, who, in my opinion, had the full capacity of boring even herself to sleep. If I didn't understand it then, what hope did I have decades later.

Dejected, I flicked through the five-hundred-page text books. We weren't talking two plus two; thirteen-year old Dior was learning trigonometry and fifteen-year-old Kai, advanced algebra. But there, in the last pages, I found the answers to all the tests and quizzes. Now all I had to do was figure out how to arrive at them, and Dave kindly offered to help if I got stuck.

For electives, the kids had chosen art, music, health and the Tongan language. The text book for health was straightforward. Coupled with the outdoor physical activities I had learned at Wildfitness in Kenya, I reckoned we could add fun to those lessons. As for art and music, their mom was a beautiful artist and would teach them everything from water-coloured still life to making pots out of clay, and Dave was an accomplished musician, hence the guitars and ukuleles lying around. As for Tongan? There was neither book nor dictionary available, and, since it was my first time in the country, I wasn't exactly fluent in the language. I had a week.

During that week, I settled into living on the remote island. On the days the tide was in, I would wake myself up with a swim before breakfast. I'd spend the mornings setting up schedules and lesson plans that would allow me to "teach" two different grades at the same time. In the afternoons, stretched out in a hammock slung between two palm trees in front of my tent, I would review one of their text books.

The only source of water came from rain, so collecting and conserving it was crucial to survival. Dave was always seeking ways to increase the catchment area. During the days, Lucas and his dad would help Dave on the construction of a new shed. Once the upright tree limbs were pounded into the ground, they began installing a large corrugated tin roof, slanted so that the rainwater would run off through a gutter system into a holding tank. From there, another pipe would lead to the kitchen sink. When the water levels were high, gravity would assist the flow as soon as the tap was turned on. When they were low, a pedal below the sink was pumped to force the water through. Forgetting to turn off the tap, which was easily done when the levels were low, was about as mortal a sin as you could commit. If it rained when no one was around, the water would just flow out the tap and into the soil.

While the men toiled, Ava played in the sand nearby, the four rescued dogs constantly by her side. At night, we would all eat together. Life was simple, with nothing electronic to interrupt our evening chats after dinner.

The day came for Lucas and his family to return to Tongatapu and for Dave to pick up Tris and the kids from the airport. The ferry wasn't running for another few days so the four of them set off in *Tropic Bird*, Dave's rigid hulled boat with inflatable pontoons. The blue canvas top would shade them from direct sunlight but do little else to protect them from apparent wind or sea-spray. It was the size of a tender for a decent-sized yacht, more exposed than the ferry, but faster. Dave reckoned they could make it in about four or five hours. Once past the house reef, he kicked the outboard engines into high gear. The trail of white wake dissipated as the boat zoomed away. Finally, the tiny speck disappeared over the horizon.

I was alone. Alone on the beach. No other human graced this side of the island. I had no phone service and no internet. No one would come this way again for at least twenty-four hours, longer if the weather kicked up. Did anyone in the village know I was by myself? One half of me wished they did; the other half hoped they didn't. I made a dinner of manioke, that root vegetable from the South Pacific that wants to be a potato, and took my plate down to the shore. As the sun sank, I sat on the beach and watched the breaking waves. I was waiting for the turn. I'm not sure why, but one of life's puzzles, which I have tried to decipher on beaches the world over, is how to identify which wave is the last of the incoming tide and which is the first of the tide going out. It remains unsolved.

Clouds faded away and darkness came quickly. With no city lights to pollute the canvas, the night twinkled. Diamonds shook loose from the black velvet sky and fell across the heavens. I was here on a tiny beach, on a miniscule island, on a microscopic planet, in the middle of the Milky Way, only one of billions of galaxies. I was as infinitesimal in the universe as a single grain of sand and yet I felt I had a purpose, I had a part to play.

Change happens, we transition from one period of life to another, and, just like the tide, sometimes we can't pinpoint that moment of change, but there is always an exact moment. As Tony Robbins so eloquently said, "it is in the moment of your decision that your destiny is shaped". It was my destiny to sit on this particular beach, on this particular night, counting these particular waves. Why? Because I had made the decision to come. I had taken action and packed a bag. I had released the fear and embraced the outcome.

It was a long night of restless sleep, however. Every sound of the jungle was magnified. Land crabs scratched at the guy lines, chickens rustled leaves beneath their feet and wild hogs honked on the run. But my zipped-up tent would keep me as safe as an alarmed house inside a gated community. Wouldn't it?

Clouds covered the morning. I boiled an egg and waited. When there was no sign of anyone by early afternoon, I wondered if they would make it at all. Even though the wet season had been unseasonably dry, it looked dark enough to rain. By dusk there was a shift in the wind and I felt the first drops fall. I gathered all the pots, pans and coolers I could find and placed them around the uncovered sections of deck. Every drip captured would be used. I considered soaping up my body and rewarding myself with an unexpected shower. But before I danced naked in the rain I checked the shore once more.

From the south I saw an orange speck grow bigger. Soon I could hear its engine. They were coming. They must be frozen. I raced up to the barn, turned on the gas and heated the pumpkin soup I had found in the freezer. By the time I heard Dave throw out the anchor, the soup had come to the boil. I turned off the stove and went down to greet the rest of my new family.

The kids were shy at first. Their previous tutor had been a young man, closer to their age than mine, who'd lived with them for over eight months. Adapting to change would take its time. I said hello and gave them space. Tris was friendly but it seemed she, too, needed time to decompress from the trip. Dave was more used to me and delighted to hear there was something warm for dinner. Hours at the helm, bouncing over building waves, can take its toll. We all sat down and tucked into the pumpkin soup. The ice broke when Tris said:

"This isn't soup."

"It's not?"

"Where did you get it?"

"From the freezer." I replied.

"No, it's a bag of fresh mangoes we picked last month."

Oops. No wonder the lumps tasted sweet.

Chapter 23
The Natural Classroom

Miles from any structured society, it may have seemed silly, but we started school term on a Monday. Certification in TEFL (Teaching English as a Foreign Language) had taught me how to improvise in remote locations, where the learning environment might not include a desk and chalkboard. It certainly didn't in Lolofutu. We were sitting on a bench Dave had fashioned out of driftwood. The table was a disused wooden cable spool laying on its side. Our feet were planted in the sand. Since there's nothing more fun than ripping off a Band-Aid, I started with maths. Kai was keen, Dior less so. I'd had a week to study the lessons, so my help seemed well informed. The rest of the morning went well and then came the challenge of teaching them Tongan.

They say the easiest language to learn is the third one. Once your brain accepts there is a second word to describe something, it's not such a stretch to think there is a third or fourth or even a thousandth. But what if you have never heard the language you're supposed to teach to two mono-lingual young adults? With no access to books, videos or internet, how do you teach them?

How I taught them was not important, but how they learned was. The first step was to give them a VAK test: a simple quiz that would identify their preferred learning style, whether that be visual, auditory or kinaesthetic. I had an idea how the results would turn out based on their style of speech. I listened for the verbs they used – whether they said *I see*, *I hear you*, or *I get it*. Not surprisingly, given these children's lifestyle and the manner in which they had been raised, they were both a mixture of visual/kinaesthetic, with Dior being more visually dominant and Kai leaning more towards kinaesthetic. What a relief. The mix is also how I learn. I marvel at people who can absorb information just by listening, as many of us need to see things written down.

The children had been sailing around the islands of Tonga for over half of their young lives. During that time, they had picked up several isolated words of the language. Using strips of cardboard torn off old vegetable boxes, they'd written those words down and created the equivalent of flashcards. I could work with that. Instead of my studying these words, independently, I invited them to take turns teaching me what they already knew. Not only did it help catch me up, it gave them both the opportunity to reinforce their knowledge, and develop a self-confidence in public speaking at the same time. However, by the end of the second week, we had run out of lessons and neither they nor I knew how the language was structured. With no resources available, it was time to get resourceful.

A thirty-minute walk through the jungle trail brought me to the village. While there were several churches, there was only one school ground. The classrooms, which housed children ranging from kindergarten age to high-school graduate, were spread out around a field of grass. The older children were learning English but the younger ones were learning their native language. I went in search of the principal and offered him a trade. In exchange for my assisting the high school kids with English in my spare time, he would lend me a book from the junior classes. If the little ones were learning how to say *the cat is on the mat* in Tongan, so could we. Two things surprised me, however. Tongan had a unique structure compared with any romance or "Anglo-Germanic" language I had previously learned and grammar had not featured heavily in the Australian kids' education thus far. While Dior had a creative flair for writing, Kai was not in love with the subject of English. Nouns, verbs, conjugations held no relevance for him compared with the practicalities of learning how to panko-fry a fillet of Wahoo he'd speared himself.

It was then my two-fold plan came into being. I had Jerry Seinfeld's wife, Jessica, to thank for it. In her cookbook *Deceptively Delicious*, she had devised a way to "sneak healthy vegetables into traditional recipes that kids already love to eat." Although Kai had little interest in English grammar, what he had was an interest in a local girl. I reckoned his desire to communicate with her was why he paid particular attention during Tongan lessons. I'd found my way in. Instead of pushing English grammar on him, I hid the definitions of verbs, nouns and adjectives in my explanations of how the Tongan language worked.

"*Alu*, the verb *to go*, never changes." I told him. "Unlike English where the verb changes when the tense changes, in Tongan it stays the same."

"So the verb is the action word?" he asked.

Excellent; I had him on the hook. "Yes, in English, the word *go* is the verb and it changes to *went* in the past tense and *will go* in the future tense."

"So, in Tongan, how do you know if you *go* or already *went*?" he asked.

Time to reel him in. "It's easy," I said. "They put in a tense marker instead."

"Huh?"

"They put in a word before the verb to let you know whether it is past, present or future. So the verb *to go* in Tongan is always *Alu*. What changes is the word before it."

"Oh," he said. "So that's why we say *Oku* before *Alu* so we know it is happening now, right?"

"Exactly! <u>*Oku*</u> *ou alu* means *I go* and <u>*Na'a*</u> *ku alu* means *I went* and—"

"And <u>*Te*</u> *u alu* means *I will go*," he finished for me.

"Yes, well done. So you see, the verb changes in English but not in Tongan."

"That's simple," he said.

Simple indeed, although it seemed to me the Tongan people had a profound understanding of the human condition because unlike English, the pronoun *I* also changed with the tense: *ou* for present, *ku* for past and *u* for future. Had they somehow woven into the structure of their language their understanding of character development, how we change and grow from our past, to our present and into our future?

It was time for a break. We gathered our pencils and copy books and set off for the barn for lunch.

"So," Kai said, as we were walking up the sandy path, "how do I say *Are you going to swim after school, tomorrow?*"

Hook, line and sinker!

Observing Kai and Dior grow and learn, in the incredible environment their parents had created for them, was a lesson in life itself. Their activities of daily living provided them with a base of knowledge that no school kid seduced by a smartphone or video game could appreciate. Chores included washing their clothes in excess rain water, stringing lines in trees to dry them and emptying the compost toilet. They hunted, fished and cooked their catch. Behind the barn, they had cleared a space in the jungle where they grew vegetables and collected eggs from their free-range chickens. Together, the family created a NICE society (Nomuka Island Conservation Environment) whose first project was the development of a rubbish disposal programme. They weren't learning about sustainable lifestyles and protecting the environment; they were living it. What could I possibly bring from the western world to offer these young adults, except maybe the art of focus and self-discipline. I learned from them as much as they learned from me.

Kai was a doer. If they were casting a re-make of *Lord of the Flies*, he could play the lead without having to act. He could snorkel dive to fifteen metres, harpoon a fish and feed the family. If a wild pig ran through our "classroom", he could chase it through the jungle, spear it, clean it and roast it on a spit that he would have whittled by hand. If we were thirsty, he would scale a palm tree in bare feet and, with a handful of strikes from his machete, fashion a drink from a coconut. He had a talent for construction and a quest for knowledge in how things worked.

Dior was equally accomplished in survival skills. Two years younger than her brother, she was as graceful as a mermaid underwater. She could unwrap a fouled anchor chain ten metres below and still come up with air left in her lungs. She had an affinity with animals and hated to see them suffer. She preferred to swim alongside the sea creatures rather than hunt them but, if necessary, she was well capable of plunging a screwdriver through the brain of a fish jerking in its death throes on the bottom of the boat. In the kitchen, she baked bread and made pasta from scratch. In art, she inherited her mother's elegance and innate awareness of the natural world. On mornings before school she would ride Taffy bareback along the water's edge, such a beautiful sight to behold.

Tris had a mission to protect animals and it was her goal to bring vet services to the island. She would often care for stray dogs abandoned by their owners. One Saturday afternoon she returned from the village carrying a live, almost fully grown turtle. A fisherman had caught it intending to cook it for the Sunday *Umu*. Tris went to see his wife, to explain that turtles were endangered. The woman explained to Tris that she had to feed her family.

I've often wondered what makes an animal acceptable fodder in one culture but not in another? In India the cow is sacred, yet gets slapped on BBQs in the west. The French like to devour a horse; in Ireland we only ride them. Bugs are delicacies in Asian communities but stomped on in Lower Manhattan. Who's to say what's right or wrong, other than tradition and custom. I imagined the two mothers sitting in the woman's kitchen, one driven to protect the turtle, the other seeing no wrong in eating its flesh. But the compassionate Tris was also a gentle persuader and the woman gave up the endangered turtle, settling for one of her chickens instead.

Back at the barn, Tris showed me how she'd been trained to document and tag the turtle. Once the information was logged, we followed Kai as he carried it down to the sea, each person quiet in their thoughts. Unlike the deformed hatchling I'd placed in the waters off Vanuatu, I felt sure this one would make it. Not only had Tris saved this turtle's life but potentially the lives of future babies too. We watched in silence as it swam away and disappeared beneath the waves. Someday, somewhere, it would surface again and its tag would show how far it had come.

Chapter 24
A Taste of the Sailing Life

We broke early from class one day when Kai spotted *Wildlife* approaching from the north. The catamaran had been undergoing renovations in Neiafu, the capital of the Vava'u chain, in the archipelago. Dave had sailed her back. This year, fulfilling the third of my birthday rules – to do something I have never done before – was going to be epic. How many people get to swim in the wild open ocean with humpback whales and their young calves? It was early June, only another six weeks before they would start arriving from Antarctica.

Dave had been gone for a week. Dior couldn't wait for him to lower the dinghy from the davits, and I was eager to see the sailboat for the first time, so the two of us swam the half kilometre out to sea, where he had anchored the catamaran in eighteen metres of water. We were both so excited we didn't stop to enjoy the fish and coral on the house reef beneath us. The underwater topography soon fell away and we felt the cold of the deeper blue water. After another fifty metres we were climbing aboard one of the most spacious, bright and airy sailboats I'd ever been on. The cabins were roomy, two in each hull, and the salon area provided plenty of space for cooking, relaxing, and school work. Best of all, it had a water maker which could convert salt water into fresh and potable. Add in propane gas that could heat it and we were able to have our first hot showers in three months. Dave showed me around the cockpit and gave me a quick rundown on the navigation system on the helm.

As luck would have it, I soon got a chance to sail on her. The family had to bring the boat back to Vava'u where it had been chartered by a film crew for an episode of *Survivorman* with Les Stroud. Once we left the Ha'apai chain it was thrilling to be out on the royal blue water. It only took a day to sail there so I was already looking forward to making the return passage the following week. In the meantime, Dave and Tris had arranged for me to stay with their friends, Karyn and Boris Von Englebrechten who also lived on a remote island – Fofoa, in the Vava'u chain.

I was incredibly blessed to be accommodated in their Beach House, a building Boris had constructed out of wood and coral rock over a pristine private beach. The finished home was such an incredible achievement and their choice of remote living so unique, they were featured on Kevin McCloud's TV show *Escape to the Wild*. Their three sons, Ben, Felix and Luca had also spent most of their young lives living off grid in the middle of the South Pacific. My volunteer job this week was to help tutor Felix and Luca while Karyn prepped for whale season.

As they were younger than Kai and Dior, their maths problems were less complicated. With a little help from their beach and jungle we learned the 9 times tables. I gave them two minutes to race around collecting anything from nature they could use. For "x" and "=" and all straight lines they used sticks, for "9" and "0" stones, and for anything else a string of seaweed. We had so much fun combining maths and PE in a kinaesthetic way, that the answers stuck. The week flew by. After regrouping with the Sheens at the wrap party for *Survivorman*, we sailed back to Nomuka.

Before long though, I had another, even greater opportunity to sail. The family had ordered their annual supplies from America which were on a cargo ship sailing from San Francisco. Our mission was to collect them when it docked in American Samoa, 350 nautical miles to the north-west.

"Do you get seasick?" Dave had asked me when we were preparing for the trip.

"Never."

"You will be," Kai had chimed in. The glint in his eye told me he couldn't wait to see me lose my lunch.

"If you're ever going to be seasick it will be on a catamaran," Dave had said.

"Why?"

"Because unlike mono-hulled boats that roll from side to side in heavy seas, a cat skitters across the waves. There is no lulling motion. Many times, one hull comes completely out of the water and then smacks back down again."

It was true, I'd never been seasick. I felt queasy once, on the back of a commercial fishing boat when the combination of diesel fumes and rotting guts had made me question my choice of bacon and eggs for breakfast, but I'd never been sick. My confidence waned a little, however, when I had learned Tris wasn't coming with us. She, who'd been a sailor most of her life, and still enjoyed day sails, had recently developed a mal-de-mer and said the trip to American Samoa would be too uncomfortable. She decided to stay home, as did Dior. Still, in my mind, it was such an exciting expedition, my first chance to live on a boat, that nothing could stop me from going.

Leaving Nomuka at sunrise, Dave, Kai and I sailed north to Vava'u. There, we picked up two more crew: Colby, a friend and restaurant owner, and Freddy, a diesel mechanic. But there, we also waited. It took another few days before Captain Dave deemed it a good time to leave. In my nautical ignorance I thought we were waiting because of bad weather. I couldn't figure out why the blue sky and sunshine didn't allow us to be on our way. What I was to learn was that we were waiting for favourable winds. Despite having worked on boats during the many years I taught scuba, it showed me how little I knew about sailing.

Nor had I paid much attention to the route. It looked like open seas for three days, not much to bump into. So why was I feeling nervous at two in the morning, while the rest of the crew slept? Perhaps it had something to do with "standing watch", something I'd never done alone before, even in daylight. Or was it because we were crossing over the Tongan Trench, the second deepest body of water on the planet? Could it be that the wind was howling, waves were breaking over the bow, running along the hard top of the salon and cascading into the cockpit? Whatever it was, it was an adventure.

Because there were five of us, our watches were only two hours long. My job on watch was to keep the boat on course with the aid of the auto-pilot. If it veered off, I was to correct it in one-degree increments. My other primary duty was to keep a sharp lookout for other vessels and to wake Captain Dave if I saw any lights when they were five nautical miles off. He'd been clear about that, five miles off, not one, which would give him less time to react if we were on a collision course. You might as well have told me to keep watch on the galaxies far, far away, because out there in the middle of the black ocean, I couldn't tell the difference between five hundred metres and five nautical miles. So many times, I thought I saw something. Sometimes the light would flicker, other times it would disappear. I didn't know stars, low on the horizon, could play such tricks.

So did Mother Time, because somewhere in that exhilarating, but nervous, two hours I fell down a time-hole and lost twenty-four. It was still four a.m. when Freddy arrived on deck to relieve me, but it was four a.m. yesterday. We had crossed the international dateline.

It was too rough to do much cooking, although, despite three days of pounding waves and nine meals of mostly cold pizza and chicken pasta, much to Kai's disappointment, I wasn't seasick.

We arrived at midday into the harbour of many faces: Pago Pago, American Samoa. On days the winds were still, the tuna cannery on the north bank polluted the air with such a stench, that languishing on the bow was not inviting. When the slope winds blew down the mountain, the anchorage became a skating rink, with boats dragging their ground tackle in the muddy bottom. And on sunny days, the cruise ships emptied tourists onto the winding streets.

None of that mattered. We weren't there to sightsee or relax. We were there to shop. At the warehouse market we each took a cart and one of the pages of lists Tris had prepared. Who knew shopping could be such work. It took five people five hours to purchase a year's supply of dry goods. The entire load required two pick-up trucks and four dinghy rides to get it all back to the anchored boat. On day two, we scoured the smaller shops for items that couldn't be bought in bulk and on the third we collected goods from the San Francisco ship including a book on the Tongan language. Apart from one steak dinner out on the town, and a short drive up the coast, that concluded the trip to American Samoa.

As I stood watch in the middle of the second day on our passage home, I thought about the pretty little sailboats I used to watch through my childhood bedroom window. Now I was on a big one, dancing in those afternoon sparkles. It was the closest I had come to my dream of living at sea. Out in the middle of the ocean, a day and a half from land in any direction, wind filling our sails, sun drying the spray from my face, it was as exhilarating as it got and oh, how I loved it. I was oblivious to the fact that within a week my joy would come crashing down. Although God knows I should have been.

Chapter 25
Flood Tide

A week before my father had died, I had been commenting to a friend on how wonderfully well my life was going. I had a great car which came with my job in my brother's TV production company, shared a lovely apartment in Blackrock with a roommate who was rarely home, and was dating a gentle soul who lived nearby. My life was on track. Within a couple of months of my dad's death, I'd lost it all. Some was coincidental timing, some due to self-sabotage. Regardless, I'd blamed the collapse of the good life on the belief that somehow I didn't deserve it. Then I'd rationalised that the root cause was because I'd voiced my joy aloud and the universe somehow heard me and corrected its mistake. After that, whenever life seemed to go too well, I'd get nervous and dim my light.

Seven days after that splendid sail back from American Samoa, I was standing in front of my tent, listening to the breeze, feeling the occasional dapple of sunlight on my face, and experiencing an unexplained melancholy. We were back on Nomuka, and back to the routine. I had ten minutes before it was time to start school with the children. I was on one of the most beautiful, barely inhabited islands in the South Pacific, living what many, myself included, would consider the dream, but feeling sad. I tried to shake it off. Walking to work, I passed a wandering rooster, Taffy the horse, and Milly, one of the family's rescued dogs. The air was clean and warm.

Compared to other commuters, stuck in noisy, polluted traffic in densely populated cities, I was in paradise. I had no right to feel sad but, by the time I reached the barn, the tears rolled.

"What's wrong?" Tris asked.

It seemed silly to say I didn't know, and whatever it was I didn't feel I could tutor this morning. Tris was one of the bravest women I had ever met, one who had to stare life in the face every day, raise and protect her family in the wild. She didn't get time off to take care of her feelings. And yet, she empathised and headed off to start them on their art project.

Then, as the tears turned from slow streams into raging rivers, I understood what was wrong. I walked back to my tent, picked up my journal, and went to sit down on the large tree root where the edge of the jungle met the start of the beach. Bright sun shone on the vast blue ocean and high tide lapped only a metre away. I began to write.

I wasn't alone, but I was lonely. Worse than lonely, I was isolated. I was living on the outside of a tightly knit family. A unique and incredibly adventurous family, the kind of family I would have aspired to have had myself, but as friendly as they were, their connection with me held no depth, no history. While I saw a few villagers from time to time, I had no real bonds with them either. Most of my friends, the people I could relate with, lived in another hemisphere. I could get an occasional text out, but not receive a response for several days. Phone calls were almost impossible. It was as if I'd stepped back in time to the days of telegrams. Messages could eventually get through but cyber hugs were locked away. I was very much offline and out of alignment.

I thought of my siblings, of the last time we'd stood together in the empty house of my teens. Then, the deluge surged. I cried for my mother. It was seventeen months since she had died and I was caught in a whirlwind of unresolved grief.

At the time of her passing I had been strong, philosophical almost, grateful she'd been spared years of dementia and serene in my thoughts that she was at peace. What I'd forgotten to process was how I felt. I didn't need a list of the various stages of grief, or to question where I thought I was on the scale of symptoms. I'd been down this road before, twenty-five years earlier when my father had left this physical world. I knew the steps. I wasn't in shock or denial. Nor was I angry. I wasn't bargaining with the skies to bring her back. I'd accepted she was gone for good and reconstructed my life without her. I'd processed the phases intellectually. But the only thing I hadn't done, the only thing I still had to do, was to feel. I'd stuffed my emotions down as I often did, my way of coping with the untenable. I'd put a lid on them as if they'd been in a pot of soup and I'd left them to simmer all these months. The contents had burned away. What I was left with was a red-hot pot about to crack. The only thing I could do to remove it from self-destruction was to grab it by the handle and feel the searing heat.

Deep painful sobs, long strangled howls, a downpour of sorrow – I felt it all. I mourned. I lamented. I grieved for my loss. Every time something good or new happened I wanted to call my mam, to tell her I was doing well, to show her I was happy, but I knew I would never again see her smile, never give her another hug.

It had been different when my dad died. Although he had passed before the internet's inception, in a time when home videos were rare and live shots of loved ones seldom existed, I could still see or hear him whenever I wanted. All I had to do was play one of his movies. Granted, it wasn't him, just characters he played, but some of them were close to his own personality, especially the role of Christy Brown's father in *My Left Foot*. I loved to watch the scene where he has one kid on his lap and he is tickling them to the point of painful giggles. It brings back my own childhood memories of sitting on his knee, being tickled and cuddled and loved. Or when he walked into the pub with Christy on his shoulders, saying, "This is Christy Brown. My son. Genius!" Dad was that proud of all his kids in real life too. If I wanted to cry for him, I'd watch *The Mission* because it connected me to him on such an intimate level. I could see and feel him in every scene because, for most of them, I had been standing just off camera. "Gabriel's Oboe" became his calling sign. Whenever I faced any major event in my life that theme music would come on the radio and I would be comforted by his spiritual presence.

But, apart from my mother's roles in *Angela's Ashes, Malice Aforethought* and *Bloom,* she had predominantly been a stage and TV actress. Many of her wonderful performances were in the wind. Unlike my dad, she lived long enough into the internet age we were able to video chat by Skype, but nothing was left of those conversations; nothing had been recorded. There was nothing to play back but an ethereal slideshow in my memory bank. Her profile in the kitchen window when I'd arrive home from school. Her single wave when she'd see me come through the sliding doors at the airport. And the sounds – the sounds she made when she answered the telephone, her cheers from the side-line when I scored a goal in hockey, and her unique way of sneezing and saying *Dia linn* (God be with us) right after.

She was gone, recently gone. I missed her, missed her, missed her. I had no one left in this world who would love me unconditionally. My earth mother was no more. Her absence felt like acid burning the inside of my stomach. Nor did I feel, at this time, any connection with her spirit.

My tears dried up and my lungs stuttered for air. As I grabbed each breath I tried to slow them down, to calm myself, to hug myself from the inside out. I knew that, ultimately, I'd be OK. I was no different from anyone else who'd lost their mother. It's a process, a heart-breaking journey we all go through.

A butterfly landed on the tree root beside me. I watched it pause, then felt it flutter. With a burst of energy, it lifted off and flew away. I followed its flight out over the sea and couldn't believe my eyes. Had I been sitting there for six hours? As my heartache had slowly ebbed, so too had the tide. The foaming waves had subsided, leaving rocks and coral heads exposed. The ocean had drained, the seabed was bare, as was I. But, as long and as torturous as this experience had been, I knew the tide had turned. Cleansing waves broke higher on the sand and I was filled with a new hope, a new understanding, and a new connection with my own soul. The process of grief was complete.

Sheepishly, I showed up for dinner. Poor Tris had had to teach class all day long. The kids were polite, like nothing had even happened. Conversation was ordinary and life moved on.

Chapter 26
Where Giants Roam Free

Weeks passed, school continued. On Saturdays and Sundays, we would go for long swims, snorkel the house reef, or hike around the island. Despite the family's friendliness, the sense of isolation never left me. It hung on my shoulders like an invisible fog. Nothing roused my curiosity. Not even the sighting of a juvenile turtle or baby octopus could thrill me. My personality had gone on a hike. It was early July and I realised I was just hanging on. The second term of school was coming to a close and it was only another couple of weeks until the charter season began. I was waiting for August, for what I'd hoped would be the most spectacular birthday ever: swimming with humpback whales.

In the early hours of 6 July I awoke to the sound of a crash. All my toiletries had fallen off the wooden plank that served as a shelf. I was about to climb out of bed to shoo away whatever animal must have found its way into my tent, when the bed itself shook. Violently. My whole body shuddered from side to side. It lasted less than six seconds but felt like sixty. We were in the throes of a 6.2 earthquake. My first thoughts were of the children. Dave and Tris had left the day before in search of internet, and I was the only adult this side of the island. When the quake subsided, I ran down to the beach and watched the water to see what it would do. Would it suddenly recede? Did we need to move inland to higher ground, all eight and a half metres of elevation? Because of the Indian Ocean earthquake and tsunami in 2004, like many locals and travellers, I had learned to look for the signs of an incoming tidal wave. The resilient Dior had had the same thought. She was further down the beach, also checking. However, it seemed our luck was in, because so too was a normal tide. The quake was over. We went back to bed and tried to sleep as soundly as Kai had done through it all.

The following week, as I took the beach route from my tent towards the barn, I spotted a mushroom-like spray on the horizon. Finally, something to lift my spirits. The first whales were arriving. Over breakfast, I chatted excitedly with the kids and fantasised about my upcoming birthday. However, before the day was out I had to rein it in. Dave and Tris returned. Reservations for their charter business had been pouring in online. The season was booked out. While there might have been a slight gap in the schedule the week after my birthday, there was no guarantee I would get a swim with the whales.

The family were planning to live aboard the catamaran and base it further up the chain, next to an island with an airport. There, they would pick up their guests, ferry them to the boat, and sail off to find the whales. School term would be wrapped up as both children were needed to work as crew. Kai would have deckhand duties, while Dior would help her mom in the galley. The four cabins would be filled with guests and crew. There would be no need or room for me. Instead, Dave and Tris kindly offered me the chance to stay and care-take the barn and animals. I'd already spent four months on the remote island, without cell service, without internet, without connection to friends or family. Remote I could handle; isolated I could not. Certainly not the way I was already feeling. It was time to say a sad farewell to the Sheens and the island of Nomuka.

But there were still three weeks left before my birthday, and the whales would still be calving. I'd waited so long I didn't want to leave without seeing them. Dave and Tris came up with a solution and connected me with their friend Matt on Lifuka island whom I'd met previously when we stopped in at the Ha'apai Beach Resort he ran, en route to Vava'u. Matt's wife was leaving on vacation and he needed help in the kitchen. Could I work as a short-order breakfast cook? Of course I could. Hadn't I cooked eggs and bacon plenty of times in my life? How hard could it be?

Three weeks later, having flipped eggs in the mornings and sold beer in the evenings, I joined another birthday girl, her husband, and Tanya, the whale guide, on Matt's boat. It was a cloudy, rainy day and I was grateful for a wetsuit. Matt crisscrossed the waves for several miles in search of whales, but the surface chop made it more difficult to see their tell-tale spouts.

After a disappointing hour, we were heading back to shore when I thought I saw a puff to our right. Could my affinity with dolphins help find a whale? We strained to see it again. Nothing. Perhaps I had imagined it.

"There!" Matt and I exclaimed together. A small spout of water that was quickly blown over by the wind.

We donned our snorkel gear while Matt drove us a little closer.

"Stay behind Tanya," Matt instructed us as we slipped into the water. "The whales will come to you, if they want."

The water was gloomy; no sunlight shafts pierced the blue. Tanya pointed in front of her and the others nodded; they could see something. I couldn't. Despite my experience, in my enthusiasm to get in the water I had forgotten to defog my mask. I took it off to rinse it while the others watched below. I was putting it back on when the dark head of a whale appeared on the surface in front of me. Then followed the white-ribbed underbelly as she rose in majesty. Her body seemed to twist backwards and her head disappeared from my view. Then the splash. I wasn't scared but I was spellbound. As I searched for it underwater, I realised it was further away than I thought. The others hadn't seen the breach. Then, as if in slow motion, a shape appeared out of the shadows, swimming towards us. It didn't look that big – and then I understood I was looking at the newly born calf. The mama whale was ginormous, at least thirteen metres long. We hung in the water as mother and calf swam past us. Breath-taking. Humbling. Splendid in their grandeur. They were on their way to somewhere else, perhaps another birthday party down the reef.

The encounter was short, but nothing could take away from the joy of seeing these majestic giants swimming freely in their ocean world. The experience didn't come about in the way I had expected but it reminded me that we sometimes overthink our *raison d'être*. Our life's purpose is not carved in cement. It can be as fluid as the ocean: one minute it's as simple as cooking a family meal; the next, as challenging as climbing a mountain. So long as we are *present* in each of our magical moments we can live a meaningful life.

Note: It is with a heavy heart I recall these stories from my experience with the Sheens on Nomuka. Two years later, Kai was tragically killed in a traffic accident during a visit home to Australia. And if that wasn't enough heartache for one family, in 2022 the Hunga-Tonga Hunga-Ha'apai underwater volcano violently erupted causing a tsunami to wash away everything they had ever built on the shores of Nomuka. Thankfully, they were overseas at the time, but every project Kai had helped construct, every tree he had ever climbed, was gone. In 2023 Dave, Tris and Dior returned to Tonga and once again brought visitors to see the majestic humpback whales. They hope to build the Kai Discovery Centre on Nomuka which would educate locals and visitors on animal welfare and the marine ecosystems he so loved. In his short seventeen years on earth Kai was an inspiration to the many lives he touched, including mine. A portion of the royalties from this book will be donated to the foundation in his honour. May Kai's spirit continue to shine and may Dave, Tris, and Dior find solace in the work they do to protect our oceans.

Chapter 27
Gateway to Bora Bora

My time in Tonga was done, but what about the South Pacific? Between the trips to Fiji, Vanuatu and now New Zealand and Tonga, I had been in these southern latitudes three times in the last five years. Could I head north and save French Polynesia for later? Again? While I believe in bucket lists, I also believe in ticking things off them. Bora Bora had stayed on – no, at the top of that list for the last twenty years. Why? For one thing, no matter where I'd been it was always located several days' travel away. Secondly, the over-water bungalows swallow cash, cheques, credit cards, and generally have a voracious appetite for any type of wallet or purse.

It is also the Capital of Honeymoon: a paradise for lovers young and old. Travelling solo can be exhilarating but lonely at times. Nothing accentuates my loneliness more than hanging out on a beach surrounded by couples holding hands. So I had kept putting it off, waiting for some fantasy lover to accompany me on a fantasy trip on some fantasy date in the future. Understandable, but silly. How often would I still be able to make these long-haul flights? Bora Bora was right next door – well, three plane rides away via Auckland and Tahiti.

Shouldn't I just throw out my preconceived notions of how I thought my trip there should be? Wasn't I attracted to the incredible topography, the alluring waters, and stunning scenery?

Surely I could forgo the sex and just enjoy the romance of it all?

"Look mam, I'm here!"

I stood at the airport gate snapping one selfie after another. Perhaps there was a time when we all took photos of the information board announcing our flight and intended destination. Now that we travel so much, we are somewhat jaded in that regard, more concerned about what kind of person will sit next to us and if there will be enough room left in the overhead bin by the time our boarding section is called.

But the childlike wonder came back. Photographs captured my beaming face and the illuminated sign: *Gateway to Bora Bora, French Polynesia.* I bounced with joy, much like a runaway poodle who might accidentally find his way onto a trampoline in a next-door neighbour's garden. I could post my pictures online and my mam would see them in Heaven.

Although I had my Golden Ticket, the plane was open seating. Over the years, I had studied aerial photos of Bora Bora in magazines and online blogs. I'd celebrated many a date night with Google Earth. I knew exactly where the airport was, and suspected the pilot would fly up the eastern side on approach.

I was first on board. The flight attendant smiled and I focused. What I sought was a window seat on the left, in front of the wing. I hoped to give my camera a chance to take the shot of its life – a topside view of aqua blue with thatched bungalows suspended on top. And I got it – the seat that is. People were boarding all around me, but I didn't care. I had the window I wanted and my feet were stowed under the seat in front of me. I buckled up. We careened down the runway and burst into the air, leaving Papeete, Tahiti's capital, behind.

I hadn't found a volunteer project that would house and feed me, nor had I booked a luxury hotel, but fifty minutes from now, I'd be meeting Madame Gloria. In the meantime, all I had to do was sit back and enjoy the spectacular vista. Peering below, I laughed out loud. Yes, I had the desired seat, but I would be taking the award-winning photograph with only my memory because the Plexiglas was all scratched.

We touched down on Motu Mute, one of the many islets that ring the lagoon, and walked across the tarmac to the tiny open-air lounge. Ground staff trailed behind us pushing a trolley full of bags. I picked mine up and followed the directions to the awaiting boats. To most, these were the shuttles to get them to their chosen resorts, where their vacations would finally begin. To me, this trip was like enjoying a free excursion halfway around the lagoon. The main town, Vaitape, lay on the far side of the island. To get there, our ferry circled the mountainous volcano whose twin peaks of Mount Otemanu and Mount Pahia form the iconic backdrop that is Bora Bora. I couldn't stop smiling. The only thing I missed was enough words to describe the intoxicating colours of the azure water.

Madame Gloria, who greeted me, spoke such eloquent French I could understand almost every word. She ran Pension Noni, a guest house in Vaitape where each ensuite room included a mini-kitchen. Mine was clean and cool, and although it wasn't fancy, neither was the rate. Gloria was going to show me how to do Bora Bora on a budget.

Breakfast was included and she began each morning by feeding me fresh fruit and crusty baguettes. After the genteel small talk, she would offer her suggestions of things to do. Top of her recommendations was to circumnavigate the island twice, once by road, then by water. Despite my yearning to explore that first morning, I walked the ten minutes into town, bypassing the tourists dining à la carte, and stopped like a traveller at a local market. Shipped-in goods came with a mortgage so I stocked my fridge with indigenous fruits, and planned to eat my main meal each day from the rolling food trucks. Once my food and lodging were arranged, I set off on my first adventure.

The main wharf was alive with vendors selling day-trips and tours of every sort. While they were all highly appealing, I had made a deal with my budget and allowed myself only one. So choosing was easy. Clearly, it had to be the full day snorkelling adventure among stingrays and sharks, reef fish and corals. I've swum in many a colourful sea, including the Red one, but nothing, nothing, nothing in my experience could compare to the turquoise water of the Bora Bora lagoon. The pool-like hues blinded me with delight. It was as if everything was bigger, brighter, and more vibrant. Life underwater was like watching TV in HD. I wasn't on a private excursion, so I had to share the water with some squealing splashers, but neither they, nor the cruising black-tip reef sharks, could take a bite out of my joy. I didn't even care I was the only single person. Instead, I volunteered my services and took photo after photo of newlyweds who passed me their cameras. I took my time to compose the shots. It was their honeymoon after all, and they were in Bora Bora, for goodness sake. They'd probably spent a small fortune hiring an expensive wedding photographer to capture their enchanting day. They were on the trip of a lifetime. I could hardly let them go home with only a lopsided selfie depicting the groom, missing half his head, while the bride's distorted left arm and enormous chin looked like they belonged to a wrestler on a pre-fight weigh-in.

There, however, my charity ended. While we were on the way back to the harbour, I saw the deckhand signal the captain from the bow. The boat slowed. The captain announced we were making an unscheduled stop. I didn't wait to ask why, but scrambled straight back into my mask and fins. Obviously the deckhand had spotted something in the water. I was first in.

Twelve metres below me, in the deeper royal blue water, three giant manta rays skated over the sand. I floated on the surface watching their progress. While I had ringside seats to their acrobatics, they were still too deep for me to bother with my camera. This would be another memory shot, not one taken in pixels. The rays reached a large coral head, and glided up over it. Their dark backs blended in. I thought the magic was over until one of them turned and started swimming towards me and the surface. A slight movement to my right told me another discreet snorkeller was in the water. It was the deckhand. We both had a head-on view as this five-metre-wide ray approached, his two cephalic lobes guiding plankton into his open mouth. Getting between a mammal and his food has never been smart so I thought to move away, but the deckhand touched my arm and signalled for me to stay. Then, like a plane starting to bank, the ray flipped on one wing, treating us to a complete view of his starkly white underbelly. I clicked and

I clicked, capturing this elegant beauty. Such surprising grace for a creature so big. By the time the other tourists joined us, the rays were gone.

Back at Pension Noni, Maman Gloria chuckled as I flapped my arms and skipped around the patio trying to describe what I had seen. Digging through my mental files of language was pointless. I was quite sure my French vocabulary of undomesticated animals didn't stretch much past rabbit, fox or duck. It wasn't until I added a gaping mouth to the mime, and made devil horns with my fingers, that Gloria clapped her hands in glee.

"*Ah, oui, vous souhaitez dire manta géant.*"

Manta géant? I should have tried in English. Maybe she would have understood had I said *the lesser-spotted, extra-large, fish-that-flies underwater.*

The next day, hoping for exercise as well as exploration, I chose the cheaper option and rented a bicycle instead of a jeep. Despite warnings about steep inclines, stray dogs and potholes, I was determined to experience Bora Bora life off the tourist trail. Pedalling the thirty kilometres around the coastal road takes most tourists two to three hours. I slowed it down to six. Around almost every turn, there was something to savour – the cast of light on the wave-less shore, the steamy heat coming down from the mountain and the inexplicable pleasure in focusing on the now. On the northern shore, the wind blew hard in my face, but pushed me along when I'd turn the next corner. When the road inclined, I got off and walked. When the stray dogs chased, I pedalled faster. At the bottom of gardens, I chatted with kids and sampled coconut oil they offered for sale. Perfumed flowers scented the air. I picked up a Tiare blossom and stuck it behind my ear. My right ear. To all who believed in tradition, it signalled I was a single woman available for love.

I had only one thing left to do and on my last day I made the call.

"*Bonjour*, Intercontinental Bora Bora and Thalasso Spa, how may I help you?" the receptionist recited when she answered the phone.

"*Bonjour, Madame,*" I replied, glad I wasn't paying for a long-distance call. With a greeting that length my budget would have ticked away with every second before I got to ask the question:

"Could I come for lunch?"

"Yes, Madame, for two?"

"For one, thank you."

"Madame would like a table for two at one, *n'est-ce pas*?"

There it was – the *couple* expectation. If I had wanted to mess with her I could have said a table for one at two.

"Just one, at noon, please."

"*Ah, oui, Madame*, I completely understand."

Did she? Perhaps it was merely the result of direct translation. Or did she just commiserate with me for dining solo in a restaurant where none of the tables were laid for uneven numbers?

"Normally, our restaurants are reserved for our resident guests, but we can offer you a two-course lunch for eighty dollars, would that be acceptable, Madame?"

"It would," I replied.

Eighty dollars for a two-course lunch? Was I out of my mind, you might ask? But wait, there's more! Thanks to a tip from Gloria I knew it also included a Day Pass allowing full access to the resort.

Enjoying another free trip across the lagoon, I took the early morning boat they sent for me. When we reached their immaculately maintained dock, I was greeted with the same amount of courtesy and respect as any of the movie stars who'd recently stayed. A bellman whisked me away to reception on one of their monogrammed golf carts. The front desk clerk apologised that the swimming pool was not available to me as it was reserved exclusively for resident guests. I looked to see if her tongue was stuck in the middle of her cheek. Sure, the medium-sized infinity pool looked inviting, but, one metre beyond it was the largest and prettiest swimming pool known to man: The Bora Bora lagoon.

I thanked her, traded my pass for a locker, fresh towels, and a kayak. I may not have been staying in one, but I was able to slalom my way through all the bungalows poised above the water. I met a couple from Brazil who were spending their first day of married life negotiating a two-person kayak. I hoped they would find the challenge equally as funny in ten years' time.

Back ashore, lunch tables covered in white linens had miraculously appeared on the beach. I chose one close to the water's edge where no one would block my view. Dressed in the signature uniform of an upscale restaurant, the waiter brought me a menu. The only nod to the tropics was that he was barefoot in the sand. He welcomed me, uncurled my napkin, and asked me what I would like to drink. He was about to leave when I noticed the menu was à la carte. I shook my head, explaining that I was not a hotel guest but on a visitor's day pass.

"*Oui, Madame*, you may choose an appetiser and main course, or, if you prefer, a main course and dessert."

"From this?" I fully expected a *prix fixe*, a limited menu, the meal you would expect at a banquet: function chicken with crème brûlée for dessert or a melon wedge starter followed by a casserole of beef. Instead, I had Chef's full range to choose from. Like a child let loose in a Lego store, I ran through all my options. For a starter I chose a Jumbo Shrimp Caesar Salad at the cough-worthy price of sixteen dollars and a Filet Mignon for thirty-two. Added to what would have been a thirty-dollar water-taxi ride, a twenty-dollar kayak rental, and a billion-dollar view, I would say I had cracked the code of Bora Bora on a budget. Surpassing all that was understanding I'd wasted energy worrying about feeling awkward in a hotel for honeymooners. I'd been single so long I had forgotten the obvious. All the honeymooners were back in their bungalows – honeymooning. I had the place to myself.

As much as I could have continued to sit there for the rest of the afternoon, gazing at the beach, the water, and the mountain, I had another mission. I checked the time and made my way back to reception, guessing they would be in the middle of turning the house. Departing guests would have checked out and rooms would have been cleaned by now. Final inspections should be underway and the incoming guests would not yet have arrived. I knew it was the sweet spot in which to ask to see a room.

When I told the front office manager I used to be a general manager and human resources director for a hotel group he was pleased to offer me an industry courtesy and escort me by golf cart himself.

As we trundled over the long wooden docks that run halfway out to the middle of the lagoon, I wore two hats. The professional in me discussed the property and guest services with him, while the kid in me grinned from ear to ear. He opened the door to a bungalow on the end and let me enter first. Does pinching yourself work? I was mesmerised. I had seen so many videos guests had posted online, their voices raised in excitement as they gave family and friends a tour of their paradise homes. Yet, this wasn't a video, this was me in real life, touring this iconic room. In the centre of the living room was a glass topped coffee table. He slid the top to one side and showed me how guests could feed the fish in the lagoon below. The master bed faced a window wall perfectly framing the aqua blue water against the forest green mountain. The bathroom and walk-in shower all boasted beach-coloured themes and on the outside deck you could lounge all day reading a book or descend the four or five steps straight into the water. It was stunning and I was brazen, asking the manager if he could take pictures of me while there. He smiled and graciously obliged.

As my plane took off the next morning, I vowed never again to put off a dream. Despite my preconceived notion that I didn't have the money to enjoy it, I had lived for a week on this fairy-tale island for less than the price of a single night in one of the resorts. As for a lover? The pool-like lagoon inside the barrier reef surrounding Bora Bora is open to everyone. It doesn't care where or with whom you sleep.

Chapter 28
The Sarong and the Bunk Bed

Birthday treats and side trips were over. It was time to get back on the
volunteer trail and continue circumnavigating. Still heading in a westerly
direction, I set my sights north of the equator. From the incredible aerial
shots of the Rock Islands, to the photographs of the pristine reefs, Palau
probably ranks high on the bucket list for most scuba divers. It had been on
mine for many years, as had neighbouring Yap, but it's a remote archipelago
in the middle of the western Pacific Ocean. No one ever wanders onto Palau
by accident. Imagine my delight when I found one volunteer project in
Koror, the country's capital. Ellen, who ran one of the most affordable
accommodations on the island, a hostel, needed help with her young sons.

I was chuffed she was happy to accept my help, but getting there took
some planning. Your flight choices are either to arrive in the small hours of
the morning, or plan a long layover in one of the connecting cities of Manila,
Tokyo, Seoul, Hong Kong, Taipei, or Guam. I chose Guam, the largest
island in Micronesia, to see if it was somewhere I might choose to live in the
future. During the seventeen hours I had to look around, I soon learned that,
although it is a pretty island, with much to attract the tourist, any jobs in the
hospitality market would require fluency in Japanese or at least another
Asian language. The other interesting discovery was in Paseo De Susana

Park in Agaña. Torch in one hand, tablet in the other, a miniature replica of the Statue of Liberty can be seen overlooking the bay near Hagåtña.

While ticking boxes on this whirlwind tour, I also took a drive up to Two Lovers Point, a scenic lookout, marking the location of Guam's tale of lost love. According to legend, a young high-ranking maiden, fleeing from an arranged marriage, and her lowly warrior lover seal their fate and union by throwing themselves off the cliffs of Tumon Bay. True Love? Had he been around in ancient times, I could imagine Dr Phil asking "How's that working for you?" Today, like many a bridge in major cities, hundreds of padlocks are clasped to the railings along the site. Modern-day romantics come to profess their eternal love. As the sun kissed the horizon, I watched one man drop to his knee. His soon-to-be fiancée giggled, accepting the combination lock he placed in her hand. They didn't need a key, he said, for she held the code to his heart. Together they entwined their names around the lock and sealed it alongside all the locks from couples who had gone before, oblivious to the fact that many were already rusted. Leaving them to their dusky glow, I turned away, and continued on to my next solo adventure in Palau.

Baba, Ellen's brother, met me at the airport in Airai, and drove me across the Babeldaob Bridge to Miss Pinetree's Hostel off the main street in Koror. Ellen and her family lived a couple of miles away, he explained, but he lived on site. This would be my new home for the next couple of weeks at least. Either hostels have improved since I last stayed in them, touring Italy with my mother back in 1979, or Ellen ran one of the most upscale ones I have ever seen. It was a big old house on a hill, with a large balcony overlooking tree-tops and the water to the west. The kitchen and communal living room could have made it onto the pages of an estate agent's brochure. Large bright countertops, with easy access to the sink, fridge and cooker, allowed plenty of room for visitors to prepare a gourmet meal. As well as the usual communal rooms with bunk beds, there was also a double room, and a family room, for those travellers who wanted to pay a few dollars more for seclusion.

It's always hard to know exactly what is needed in your arsenal for a year's backpacking trip, but even if you never set foot on a beach, a sarong is a multi-purpose must. Tuck one edge of it under the mattress on the bunk above you and you have yourself a privacy screen. Let's face it, when you throw the dice and decide to sleep with five people in the same night you run the risk of encountering one or all of the following night-time oddballs determined to keep you from a good night's slumber.

First there is *The Rummager*. He's the kind of guy who thinks packing is for nerds, that it is way cooler to remove whole drawers full of clothes and turn them upside down into an open suitcase, all the while the taxi driver waiting to take him to the airport, is outside honking the horn. When he gets to his destination, everything works in reverse. He turns the suitcase inside out and spends the night rummaging through all his belongings, looking for shaving cream that may or may not be there.

Then there is *The Fashionista*, the amateur packer, with so many bags, and too many choices. The difficulty of choosing which flip-flops to wear with which outfit gives her the perfect excuse for a midnight fashion show. The runway, of course, passes right by my bed en route to the bathroom mirror.

Let's not forget *The Rustler*, who suffers from ombrophobia. Her fear of rain is such that she puts everything in plastic bags inside her waterproof duffle bag. She's a tactile sort of girl because even though she knows where everything is, she is not content to lift out one synthetic bag quietly to get her stuff. No, she prefers to touch, caress, crunch, crinkle and rustle each bag, reassuring herself that impermeability cannot be affected by the unlikely event of a sudden drop in cabin pressure.

My favourite is probably *The Zipper* – this is the professional packer with a poor memory. He believes in allocated packing. Each item has its own special compartment in a suitcase with twenty-two zips. It is a brilliant system, provided he can remember in which section he put his sleeping pills. At two a.m. all that can be heard is the sound of every zip being unzipped, re-zipped and unzipped again. Like the different tones of beeping you hear when someone is punching numbers on a phone, each compartment's zip has its own unique swish, so much so that I want to yell out in the dark, "You've already looked in that one".

The Hacker is usually the one sprawled on top of the sheets, oblivious to those around him, and exercising his culturally accepted right to hack any phlegm or other obstruction lodged in his throat.

And finally, there is the absolute evil one – *the Snorer*. There is always one in every room. As I look around trying to identify who it is, I can't. Oh God. If I can't hear them now, that means it must be me!

Chapter 29
Dishes and Issues

I heard Ellen the next morning before I saw her. She was chasing her three-year-old around the main dining room, trying to get him settled so she could get back to the computer.

"Come on Kedeb, come eat your breakfast."

"No."

"Mommy has to work."

"Good morning," I said, coming down the stairs.

"Oh, hi. You made it. Welcome to Miss Pinetrees," she said. "Did you sleep well?"

"Yes, thank you." What else could I say?

"Who's this?" I asked, bending down, trying to see if I could distract the child from his run-around. He stopped and looked at me from under his long eyelashes.

"Tell the nice lady your name, honey."

"Hi."

"Well, it's nice to meet you, Hi," I said.

He giggled.

"You want breakfast?" I said, as I resorted to the universal feeding technique for three-year-olds. "Here comes the flying spoon." He opened his mouth, closed it, and giggled as the milk came bubbling out his nose.

"Thanks," said Ellen. "If you would keep an eye on him for an hour or so until I get through all the reservations requests."

"Of course. I'm looking forward to helping. Anything else I can do?"

"Well, if you could help Baba keep the place clean and tidy. He had another late-night pick-up after yours so I don't think you will see him for a while."

"No worries."

Life fell into a routine. In the mornings I would undertake the onerous duty of helping Kedeb watch cartoons while Ellen worked. Who says children nowadays have short attention spans? For the twenty minutes of *Paw Patrol*, nothing could have distracted this sweet child from the TV. However, when it was time to leave to pick up his older brother from school, there wasn't a banshee in Ireland that could compete with his wailing. Until, of course, he was reassured that Ryder and Marshall would still be patrolling on TV tomorrow.

The rest of the time I would clean. Backpackers came and went. Baba would check them in and out, many times driving to and from the airport in the middle of the night. After only a few hours' sleep he would get up, change linens and mop the bathrooms too.

One morning, I had just finished deep-cleaning the fridge when a new guest, probably in his fifties, came downstairs. He must have arrived on the 3.00 a.m. flight because everyone else had already cleaned up and left on their day trips. I said "Hello"; he didn't. I indicated where the pots and pans were; he nodded. I showed him how to turn on the stove; he sniffed. Perhaps he didn't speak English. Even so, I bet every traveller would recognise *thank you* in at least five or six languages, so he could have said it in his own. He didn't. In fact, he never spoke at all. Never mind. When he had finished cooking he took his plate to the dining table and sat down to eat. I pulled the garbage bag out of the bin, tied it up, collected a couple more bags of trash from the pedal bins in the bathrooms, and carried the whole lot out the back door to the dumpster. The day was gathering a wet heat. Even the smell was humid.

I guess not talking helps you eat faster. When I came inside, he was gone. I was about to leave myself, when I spotted his dirty dishes in the sink. What the...? Surely everyone understands the rules of communal kitchens, right? You clean up after yourself. Even if he thought I was the hired help, he could at least have said 'hello'. I had no idea how long he was staying; hopefully only a night or two. Baba could explain the rules to him, but in the meantime, it bothered me too much to leave the place untidy.

Why couldn't he have made a boiled egg instead of scrambled? I mumbled, as I tried to clean the congealed goop off the bottom and sides of the pan. I scrubbed and scoured and scoured some more. Anyone would think the pan had won a free trip to a Day Spa, the way I was giving it an exfoliation to remember. The sponge disintegrated and my fingers were getting sore. When I was still muttering, giving a facelift to an already spotless pan, I knew I had more issues to deal with than a few dirty dishes. Why was I so annoyed? *I'll tell you why,* I answered myself. *I'm annoyed because he's arrogant. Even if he mistook me for a paid employee, there was still no need to be rude. A nod, a smile, a gesture would have made all the difference.* My ego wanted to say, "Hey, do you realise I am a hotel manager? I've directed a staff of over a hundred people? I've managed entire teams of housekeepers? This is not my job. I am not doing this for wages. I am volunteering my time. I am taking a year out to give back." I was annoyed because I felt I had been judged. He saw me as just a cleaner. He had no clue as to my background, my skill set, my value, my worth. Judgemental bastard. He thought I was a nobody. I was hurt.

"I am more than what you see," I said to the frying pan.

There; both the dishes and my rant were done. I found my sunglasses and took myself on a walk along the water. That would calm me down. I thought about members of my staff in the UK, and about how they must have felt. One girl was a trained psychologist, but couldn't find work in her native Spain, so she took a summer job cleaning hotel rooms. Another girl, who cleaned the restaurants, had been a practising attorney in Greece, before the economy collapsed. How had she felt? Did she too feel judged?

I walked and walked, until slowly, my anger dissipated. I picked up a pebble and threw it towards the sea. My exasperated energy carried it through the air until it dropped, like the proverbial penny. Whoa! The circular ripples expanded towards me, bringing with them a humble discovery.

I was a judger too.

What had I said? What had I wanted the man in the hostel to know? That I was a manager, not just a cleaner? *Just.* In that four-lettered word – *just* – I, too, had judged. I judged every cleaner who ever was. I didn't judge the work. I judged the worker. Cleaning is vital to our survival: hospitals, restaurants, bathrooms – we appreciate the effect, without it we would live with infection and disease. But what of the people who clean? My attitude had come from a belief that cleaning is a job from which only the smart graduate. As a society, we applaud the guy who puts himself through college by cleaning offices late at night. We admire the girl who starts out pushing a broom and ends up owning the company. We perceive "cleaning for money" as either a dead-end job, or a bridge to a better life. But what do we say to the people whose life-long careers have been to sweep the roads we drive, change sheets on the beds we sleep in, or sanitise the factory that makes our favourite ice-cream? They are not *just* cleaners; they are an integral part of the human team that makes the world go around. I begged forgiveness from them all.

Chapter 30
Service

It came in a dream that night. The flip switch. The new discovery – service. No matter what job we do, whether or not we get paid, we are all in the business of service. Service surpasses hierarchy. Service is a circle. I serve, you serve, we all serve at the pleasure of our fellow human beings. In service we reveal our purpose and our purpose uncovers who we really are.

I woke up with a refreshed energy. I embraced the day by asking a better question. Instead of asking, *Why do I have to sweep the floor?* I asked, *Who am I serving by sweeping the floor?* The answer was easy: I was serving the guests with a clean environment, a pleasant place in which to relax. Instead of asking *Why am I wasting my time watching animated dogs trying to find a missing elephant when I didn't even enjoy cartoons as a kid?*, I asked, *How am I helping?* The answer was twofold: In watching TV with Kedeb, I was keeping him company and serving Ellen with the gift of quiet time to work.

This new game was addictive. Everything I did, I asked myself whom or how I was serving. Every task, which yesterday would have seemed menial, today had a productive purpose. I was so excited with my new understanding that, had he shown up, I would have even cleaned *he-who-didn't-speak*'s dishes. My gift of service to him would have been an extra few minutes in which he could enjoy his vacation day.

When it came time for my own day off, I served myself. How could I live on Palau and not visit the UNESCO World Heritage Site of the Rock Islands? I'd seen them on countless diving calendars over the years. Green forested islands rising 180 metres from the ocean, in colour contrast with the azure waters below. I used to think they were volcanic, rather than the result of coral reefs that had formed on underwater ridges thousands of years ago, then emerged as islands once the water receded at the end of the last Ice Age. Today, their mushroom shapes make me wonder how long it will be before the erosive wave action completes its assignment and they fall back into the sea.

Palau is learning from the destruction of coral reefs across the oceans and access to this pristine area is by permit only. Permits are easy to obtain, but tough on the wallet. It's a debate to be heard in many an after-dive café: economics versus environment. How does a country both protect and profit from its natural resources? Palau seems to have chosen a balancing act between attracting the tourist dollar but then charging visitors hefty fees so that they don't come in droves.

I picked up my ten-day permit from the rangers' station, but I didn't board one of the sightseeing boats going to Eil Malk (Jellyfish Lake) one of the thirty-six meromictic lakes in the world where layers of water do not intermix. Could I snorkel through thousands of jellyfish on their daily migration from east to west across the lake, in pursuit of the travelling sun? Of course I could. Was I afraid of getting stung? No, since these particular jellyfish are considered harmless, their sting being undiscernible to humans. Did I want to add my sun-screened body along with dozens of other swimmers into their already packed environment? No, I didn't.

Instead I chose to minimise my impact by opting for a tour by kayak, taking a private guided paddle along the resplendent limestone island walls. As we passed by one particular island the ebbing tide revealed a sliver of a gap on the underside of one of the walls. As minutes passed and the tide continued to drop, it revealed a marine tunnel. I gave a couple of energised strokes, lay back flat in the open kayak, holding the paddle alongside, and enjoyed the momentum that carried me under the damp limestone ceiling. I closed my eyes and held my breath until the sun beat down on me again.

The tunnel had opened up into an interior lake, like something found in a Leonardo di Caprio movie set in Thailand. Sunbeams pierced the greenish water, illuminating dozens of jellyfish pulsing around my boat. For a dazzling moment I was alone in a primeval wonderland. Did these ones sting? Drifting in behind me, my guide assured me they were the same variety as on Eil Malk, but I noticed he kept his hands out of the water. We glided with our gelatinous friends towards the evening side of the hidden lake. Not even the broadleaf forest made a sound. I could have meditated my way to sleep. However, it was close to the bottom of low tide, so unless I wanted an underwater swim through the marine tunnel, it was time to retreat. We paddled slowly back, leaving the golden jellies to their nocturnal sink in search of the nitrogen rich waters below.

When we got back to town, I went in search of an Irishman I'd never met. He'd been a sailor. One day, he got off his boat, gave it to a friend I'd met in Tonga, and went to Palau – just like that. Twenty years later, he was supposedly still here, raising four children with his Palauan wife, and managing one of the main diving and tour operators in the country. I'd been asked to say hello. All the dive and snorkel boats must have recently returned, because when I arrived on site, the outdoor area next to the shop was thronging with tourists in various states of debriefing. Some were walking around in shorty wetsuits, dunking masks and snorkels into the wash bins. Others were gathered round a dive guide, getting their log books stamped. With gear already packed away, the seasoned divers, I was amused to note, were already at the bar chugging down a Budweiser or the local Red Rooster. I heard an Irish accent. Judging by the number of staff members paying close attention to his instructions, I reckoned he was the affable big shot.

"Hi, you must be Maurice," I said.

"Must I?" he asked with a twinkle.

Yep, he was the Irishman I was looking for. "Duncan says thanks for the boat; he's still sailing her."

He laughed and shook my hand. "So, what brings you to Palau?" he asked.

United only in *bróg*, we chatted like long-lost friends. Before ten minutes was up, I learned he was hiring. To meet the increasing tourist market, the dive company had grown exponentially. Today it offered diving, fishing, snorkelling, kayaking, retail therapy and a bar and restaurant in which to get over it. Now, with so many departments, they needed an administrative coordinator to tie it all together. With my background in human resources and scuba instruction, I was in the right place, at the right time, with the right skills. Could I, too, live in Koror? Let's see – it was an island surrounded by aqua blue water and coral reefs. Check. It had a warm and sunny climate with friendly people. Check, Check. It was a country other people came to on vacation. It ticked all the boxes, so although it would mean cutting my year of travel short, it seemed crazy not to submit my CV.

My job application progressed to a second interview. They liked what I had to offer. All that was needed was to register the newly created job with the Department of Labour and ensure there was no Palauan national equipped to take on the role. The wait would be thirty days.

If I got the job, working in Palau would be easy; living there, I learned, would not. Accommodation was unbelievably tight. That's the thing about islands; there is no room for urban sprawl. Everywhere I went – restaurants, bars, the post office – every person I met – waitresses, tour guides, locals – I asked if they knew anyone with something to rent. They didn't.

I walked the streets every day. That, in itself, was a challenge. The vast majority of cars I encountered on the roads of Koror were purchased for three or four hundred dollars on the internet. Even allowing for shipping costs, it still worked out cheaper for locals to import used cars from Japan. Where it gets interesting is that Palauans drive on the right, while the Japanese drive on the left. Since the steering wheel is on the opposite side, drivers of these imported cars tend to overcorrect so as not to encroach on the centre line of these narrow roads and wander into oncoming traffic. As a result, they swish deathly close to the kerb, leaving no room for pedestrians or cyclists to make a mistake. So looking for somewhere to live was hot and treacherous work. An ice-cream was mandatory.

I stopped at a gas station that displayed an oversized cone outside. Inside, a collection of aging men sat at the randomly spread-out plastic tables and chairs. Some were playing cards, others reading newspapers, but despite speaking in Palauan, I was fairly certain they were all involved in a group discussion. I'd paid the attendant and was about to leave when the conversation ceased and I noticed several were looking in my direction. I nodded hello. One man pushed a chair out with his foot, offering me a seat. The others chuckled. I debated, but they looked harmless enough so I sat down. Besides, the sun outside would guarantee that the ice-cream would drip over my fingers before I got three steps up the street.

What a laugh they turned out to be. One was a retired army major, another a retired cop, and a couple of others had been in undisclosed government jobs. I had stumbled into the unofficial afternoon meeting of the good old boys of Palau. They were discussing the location for the 2018 Micronesian Games. I asked my new buddies if they knew of any vacant accommodation. Unfortunately, not. But they knew why I was having a hard time finding any.

"It's the Chinese," one guy piped up. "They've bought up commercial properties and now they are bringing over their own staff to service them."

"They take ten-year leases on the rental properties, paying twice the money asked. All cash, all upfront," said the guy by the window.

"There is no way we can compete," said another.

It all made sense, and I knew it wasn't only me. Ellen's own mother was looking for somewhere to live. The house she rented, and shared with three others, was owned by a Chinese landlord. The lease was up and she was out.

"There's a lady on the Chamber of Commerce you might try," the retired cop remembered.

"Really?"

"Yes," he said, pulling out his phone. "She owns apartments on the other side of town."

He dialled the number and connected me with her. I was in luck; she had one becoming available in a month. I thought it was a sign. It was. The sign said I would need at least three month's salary to pay for one month's living.

"Too bad," the cop said, as I handed back his phone. The others muttered in agreement, but seemed unsurprised. My ice-cream was long since licked, so I gave them a cheery wave and left them to discuss the plight of the tourist invasion from China.

My volunteer gig at the hostel was over. Ellen was sweet and said she would have let me stay if she could, but the hostel was sold out. I had to give up my bunk. I explained to Maurice that I couldn't afford to rent an expensive hotel room for the remaining twenty-eight days on the off-chance that no other Palauan could do the job and they could find me reasonable accommodation. Neither of us held out much hope.

The distraction of the possible job meant I didn't have any new volunteer work lined up, but I still had a couple of months left on the invisible timeline I had given myself to complete this trip and settle down. I needed somewhere cheap to live and if I wanted a successful re-entry into the workforce, I should probably get in shape. So, after a twelve-hour layover in Seoul, and a complimentary day trip to local temples organised by Korea's Incheon airport, I flew to Phuket, rented a cute little studio for a nominal sum, and enrolled in a month-long Thai boot camp.

Detox week was tolerable only because it was accompanied by daily massages. Early morning boxing sessions kick-started my day. After breakfast, the range of classes was extensive. Zumba dancing was preferable to yoga because I don't eat enough pretzels to be able to bend like one. I learned TRX was a suspension workout system and not an extinct dinosaur. Weightlifting was still sweaty work and Pilates was deceptively hard.

The food was specially prepared with health and fitness in mind. It was a fun time to be solo because almost everyone else was. It had been the correct decision to come because, although I was fit and healthy after the thirty days, no job offer came from Palau. I turned to the computer to design my next adventure.

Chapter 31
A Fork in the Road

"You're right there," the message read. "You've got to go to Luang Prabang, it's an ancient city of Temples."

I was supposed to be looking for new volunteer projects but got side-tracked with emails.

When we'd been clearing out my mother's house last year, I'd come across a box of photo albums in my old bedroom. It had been cathartic to journey through the pictures stuck to the cardboard pages covered in cellophane. The albums from childhood were losing their glue and many snaps were falling out. I gathered them into an envelope. For all my attempts at living a minimalist life, here were treasures I'd been unable to relinquish. Among them were albums of me and the boyfriend with whom I had left for America all those years ago. There were photos of both our families taken at the last supper we'd all shared the night before we boarded the plane with the mandatory blood test reports in our pockets and our chest x-rays under our arms. Such were the requirements of the Green Card lottery back then, to prove we weren't bringing AIDS or TB into the USA.

At the bottom of the box there was one more album with a cover I didn't recognise. Inside were more black-and-white family photographs, but of my boyfriend's, not of mine. I vaguely remembered packing to leave on our "world tour" and my mother kindly offering to store what we couldn't bring.

I hadn't seen or spoken to him since I'd left the Florida Keys and did not know where he was. But I couldn't dispose of his memories. I had to track him down. Old phone numbers, his family's help, and the internet made reconnecting easy. Since then, we'd sporadically stayed in touch. And now, here he was, at the end of an email telling me I had to go to an ancient city of temples.

For once, I felt geographically challenged. I had no idea where Luang Prabang was, never mind how to pronounce it. All I knew was I had to go there. I had nurtured my body in Thailand, now it was time to nourish my spirit. In loose terms you probably could say I was *right there* if you consider it was in Laos, which happens to share a border with Thailand. But given that it was over a twenty-five-hour trip by road, I could be forgiven for thinking travelling four hours by air would get me *right there* a whole lot sooner.

It was indeed an ancient city, another World Heritage Site. I was ticking boxes on a UNESCO list I didn't know I had. So many gilded temples, so much exquisite fabric, a town abundant in history, where the Mekong river meanders through. It was like nowhere else I had ever been. The biggest surprise of all was the range of cuisine and inventive chefs. Nights can be lonely when travelling alone. Frequently takeout and a good book will eliminate the embarrassment of nodding at hostesses, who seem to raise their voices when asking, "Table for one?"

But on this first night, in this special place, rather than feed from the street vendors dotted throughout the night market, I rewarded myself with a white linen meal in an indoor restaurant with an outdoor patio. The twinkle lights that were laced from tree to tree illuminated the romance I felt from a glass of full bodied red. The patterned butter, the classy salt shaker and the attentive *maître d'* all made me feel I was deserving. I might not have been in Sheba, but I was the self-appointed Queen for the night. The mood followed me home.

A hundred years before I was born, a French man named Henri Mouhot died. I'd laid my bicycle down and was looking at his grave. Such a quiet, unassuming spot in the Laotian woods for the man who discovered the lost city of Cambodia's Angkor Wat. The three other cyclists with me thought the same. We were on a multi-day mountain-bike and trekking expedition out of Luang Prabang. Ambitious maybe, but after the month of training in Thailand, I was still keeping up with the college gap-year travellers – a couple and a single male.

Cycling was easy on the knees. But once we left the bikes at base camp and crossed the Nam Khan river, the trek into the mountain began in earnest. Our guide was lean and nimble with a weathered face that made it impossible to tell his age. We crossed by terraced slopes and rice paddy fields. The trail climbed further into the mountains but, after a couple of hours of us playing follow the leader, thankfully, it levelled out.

We were walking along the side of a meadow when it came alive. Countless children sprinted on to the soccer field beside their school. We had arrived at the Khmu village, our homestay for the night. No need for a verbal language to communicate. Kids, ranging in age from three to ten, grasped us by the hands and dragged us onto the pitch. In the shadow of the towering mountain, we played football in the land of Laos. Luckily, I was put on goal. After the bike and hike, running was out of the question. Better yet, my team was winning, so most of the players were up the other end of the field, which gave me time to photograph the match. Twenty or so little people ran rings around the three tall westerners, hollering each time they scored. When it was over, the children gathered round me staring at my camera. They offered up their vulnerable faces and never blinked as I took one amazing close-up after another. None of them spoiled the photo by raising their fingers in the victory sign salute, something children in the less remote regions of developing countries I have visited, seem to think is the coolest thing to do.

The village was a collection of mud huts, with mud floors. Dinner was a modest rice dish with hot chili peppers that had been dried in the sun. I would have liked to socialise but the number of people smoking sent me into solitude. Built into the sleeping huts were wooden box-like shelves on which we were to sleep. Mosquito nets and a bamboo partition separated me from my two neighbours. Thankfully, neither of them were *rustlers*, *hackers* or *zippers* and sleep came sooner than I expected, despite the oppressive heat.

Day two was to be our longest day of hiking. After Keo, our leader, had collected our lunches from the women of the village, we waved goodbye to our little soccer friends and set off towards the ridge. It was a few minutes after eight, but the sun was already sucking sweat through the pores on my forehead. I'd learned my lesson on the turtle beaches of Vanuatu and was thankful for the face towel hanging from my belt. They said it would be challenging, and challenging it was. The higher we climbed, the more dense the foliage.

We came to a fork in the trail and took the left-hand path. It was muddier than before, perhaps from an underwater stream, because rain was not in season. Despite the squelch, I was able to gain purchase by stepping off the half-buried rocks. However, I must have been losing ground with every step, because, after twenty minutes I could no longer see the others. Their chatter thinned out too, as the verdant trees closed in. Eventually, I could hear it no more. I stopped for a minute. All was quiet, except for the cacophony of jungle life. Leaves rustled in a nearby tree. What was that? Was it a monkey or a flying squirrel? Was that why I was left behind, so I could witness wildlife the others would miss?

No. I heard a crack and then rhythmic scraping sounds. These were man-made. From above, I heard Keo call out. He pranced down the hill like a warrior, carrying a spear. The spear was for me. When he turned it upside down and stuck it in the earth it became a freshly whittled walking stick. As much as I hated to admit it, it helped. The leverage it gave me increased my speed over ground, although I was still ordained to be bringing up the rear. Keo walked with me a while, encouraging me up the hill. Either he had super hearing or I couldn't discern anything over the sound of my thumping heart, because he dashed off, saying the others had come to another fork in the trail.

One of the worst things about being last in line on a hiking trail is being last in line. I imagined everyone standing around at the fork, swigging on water and refreshing their faces. I pushed hard to reach them before they moved on. By the time I did, their breath had evened out, but mine was still auditioning for the opening titles of a psychological thriller.

"How are you?" Keo asked.

"Good," I said, in auto-response, trying to school my brain into believing it.

"We've still a long way to go," he said. We were three hours in, but at least ninety minutes behind.

"Once we get to the ridge, I'll speed up," I said.

He doubted it. On the far side of the ridge, loose scree would be our reward making the downward trail more perilous. A twisted ankle was not uncommon.

"I can do it."

"We could turn back and go a shorter route, so we will make it to our homestay before dark," he suggested.

A silence descended upon us all.

"That's OK," said one of the college kids, but I could hear the disappointment in his voice.

"No, that's not fair to you guys. It's not your fault we are going slow, it's mine."

I was doubting that this particular trek was within my capabilities. If I stubbornly persevered to please the others, would I be putting the whole group in jeopardy, not just me and my wonky knee?

"Are there any other options?" I asked Keo.

"When we have larger groups we have two guides and we could split up."

A second guide? That would have been the obvious solution, but here we were, a day and a half out of Luang Prabang and three hours from absolutely anywhere. Keo took out his phone which, surprisingly, displayed two bars. He dialled. Somewhere in these Laotian mountains somebody answered the call. Keo talked animatedly while throwing several glances in my direction. He paused and asked me a question. I nodded my approval, sealing our fate.

The rest of the group picked up their bags and hiked on up the mountain. I sat down and waited. Someone from the village would come for me. For a "small fee". That was all I knew. I was alone in the mountains, with a bottle of water and cooked rice wrapped in a banana leaf. What if the monkeys could smell it? Should I eat it now for safety? I wasn't hungry but

I ate it anyway. Then I had nothing to do. I sat there, believing, trusting, hoping someone would come.

I was frustrated. After almost a year spent travelling, and a month working out in Thailand, I was in the best shape I'd been in for several years, but it hadn't been enough. My body wasn't twenty any more, even if my mind had thought it was. It was a humbling experience to have to accept my physical limitations for the good of this particular group. I still believed I could do anything I set my mind to. Could I have made the full trek? Possibly. Certainly not in the same timeframe as a twenty-year old athlete. I continued to sit. The sun was making its daily trek across the sky, but still I waited.

It had been twenty-eight years since the last time I had been left in an unknown environment and told to wait. I had done it without question. Back then, I'd trusted, but it had been a mistake.

Chapter 32
Trusting Your Guide

As I waited on the mountain I remembered that accidental "solo" scuba dive I'd made in my twenties. Sitting on that boulder twelve metres below the ocean's surface, I'd done what I was told. I'd stayed put. I'd started out with the utmost confidence that someone would come for me. So, I'd waited. Even when that trust had waned to doubt I still hadn't moved. It was only when I'd remembered that my air, the thing keeping me alive, was in limited supply, that I'd questioned that blind obedience. I shouldn't have waited on the bottom, faithful to instruction.

What if the same was true now? What if no one was coming? I was twenty-eight years older, but was I any wiser? Maybe I should get going? But I had neither map nor compass. Nor had I paid any attention to our route. Instead of utilising the skills I'd learned as a girl scout, I'd allowed myself to be a tourist, lulled along in the security of *follow the leader*. At least on the scuba dive there had been only one way to the surface. Here on the mountain, every leaf looked like the next. Would I wander in circles for hours? What if the trees closed in completely and I couldn't read the sun? What if it fell behind the mountain before I could find my way out. I couldn't bear the thought of sitting here in the dark.

Just as I was considering heading back down the mountain, I was startled by a small Laotian man who mysteriously appeared in front of me.

He nodded, turned his back to me and started walking away. Was this my guide? I thought I'd seen him last night in the village, but I couldn't be sure. It had taken me three hours to get this far, but had he run the distance in ninety minutes? He wasn't even out of breath. He kept on walking down the slope. *Well, if it is him,* I thought, *I'd better start following. If it's not? Well, he must be going somewhere and somewhere is better than nowhere, which is exactly where I am right now.*

We walked in silence for about an hour. Although we were going downhill, I was glad of the stick Keo had made for me. When the scenery opened up to reveal panoramic views across the mountain range, my guide was two minutes ahead of me, but when the trees closed in again, he was only five metres in front. I didn't call out when I needed a rest, I just stopped. Within seconds, so did he. I was in the presence of a real live tracker. He could slow or speed his pace just by listening to how I moved.

By the time the shadows grew long, we'd left the foothills and emerged from the forest at the side of a river. A long-tail boat waited on the near bank, a young man at the stern. My guide said something to him, pointed at me and then at the boat. I guessed that meant *Get in.* It was probably six or seven metres long, painted yellow with black stripes, and had about as much freeboard as my ankle socks peeping over the top of my boots. My guide stood on the bank waiting for his fee. When I paid him, he bowed and took off in an effortless trot. Within a minute he had disappeared back into the jungle from whence he had first miraculously appeared.

In one swift move, the ferry man pushed us off and hopped aboard. I was glad I had sat mid-ships to balance the initial rocking. He pulled the engine to life and dipped the long poled propeller of the mud motor into the caramel-coloured water. And we were off, at a galloping put-put. Had the mechanical power failed us, we probably could have drifted faster with the current.

The scene was exotic, far from the normal ocean views of my travels. Golden reeds grew along the banks. Fields of crops sloped up to caress the base of mountains and the highlands daubed the sky with splashes of purple, blue and green. Five hundred metres downriver, three elephants vacuumed water up their trunks and squirted it on their backs, the end of their working day.

It was an interesting choice I'd had to make up there on the mountain – either to cut the trip short for everyone or to persevere over the ridge. One disappointed the group, the other put it in danger. Neither was optimal, and both were selfish. Worse, both forced me to accept the physical limitations of aging, something that would take time to process. The win-win only came when I stood back and checked the big picture, discovering there had been an option three. Now I was being rewarded with a private voyage, watching the evening rituals of the natural world, a consolation greater than the original prize.

We all have strengths. We all have weaknesses. Any inadequacy I'd felt in my lack of ability to climb the mountain floated away on the third morning of this triathlon-type trek. Reunited with the others, I now led the way, kayaking down the Nahn Khan river back to Luang Prabang. Their shoulders felt heavy; mine were light. This was my comfort zone, but outside theirs. I paddled ahead to enjoy the un-rippled view, but waited for them around each bend. Closer to town the rural route became dotted with houses and then the tips of temples came in to view. The three-day challenge was over. Content in contemplation, I drifted towards the dock. Just like the lesson I'd learned climbing the pole in Fiji, it was OK to be less than perfect. I didn't have to stand on top of the mountain in order to see its peak.

Chapter 33
Hanoi Roulette

One thing travelling has taught me is, when someone offers a recommendation for a place, a restaurant or a movie, much and all as I might love and respect them, it's best to first consider their tastes. A friend I'd met at kick-boxing boot camp in Thailand was excited to learn that my final volunteer project for my sabbatical year of travel would be in Vietnam.

"Oh, you're going to love it, and when you pass through Hanoi you *have* to stay in the Old Quarter," she said. A well-travelled, global-savvy woman, she enjoyed exploration and experiencing new cultures. So, I took her at her word; I would love Vietnam. I didn't.

What I hadn't computed was she was twenty-five years younger than me, and the incessant car-honking and scooter-beeping, which she considered *atmosphere*, for me created the aural nightmare from hell. There was also the fear factor of putting my life in someone else's hands. I'd arranged a car to pick me up at the airport and take me to a budget hotel in the Old Quarter. It was already dark; rush hour was waning from gridlock. Like everyone else, my driver weaved, sped up and slammed on with such rapidity, I counted at least four near misses on our ride to downtown, two of them potentially fatal. But he seemed to think if he continuously beeped the horn he would create an invisible shield around our car making it invincible to accidents. Either that or Vietnam had introduced driving by echolocation.

The Old Quarter reminded me of the narrow side streets in Paris except that the buildings, tall enough to limit sunshine on the streets, were Asian in style. Relieved to have arrived, I opened the car door and the burst of city noise assaulted my senses. The car horns of the highways had been replaced by the high-pitched screech of scooters' hooters. I hauled my pack out of the car, desperate to get indoors and retreat from the racket.

Inside the long, ornately decorated corridor with a cement floor, the smell of sweat and woks greeted me. On a table, pushed up against the wall, stacks of brochures detailed various sightseeing tours and events around the city. A black diary, with pages curled at the corners, was open on today's date. Several names were written in pencil and several had been erased. I spotted mine, or what could pass for a rough imitation of the spelling of my name. This was obviously reception. A middle-aged stout lady appeared from a door behind a wooden staircase. She nodded, uttering a greeting that sounded like the Italian *ciao*, and asked who I was. In exchange for handing her my passport, she gave me a key for a room on the third floor. Despite the smells of sizzling noodles, dinner was not an option, but she said there was a shop across the road.

Indeed there was. Oddly, there was no door *per se*; the entire front of it was open to the street. Stepping up onto the white-tiled floor, I felt I had walked into someone's front parlour. A woman sat on a white plastic chair by the entrance, reading a book. She didn't look up. The rear of the shop opened into a sitting room. A man, presumably her husband, was stretched out on a red velvet sofa. Eyes closed, with hands crossed over his chest, he was either dead or sleeping off his dinner.

On one wall, wooden shelves, painted in white, displayed newspapers, souvenirs, ornaments and various snacks I couldn't quite identify. I did see packets of dried noodles but nothing that looked like a quick and easy meal. I was turning to go when I spied some fresh fruit on a tray on the corner shelf, next to a vase of fresh flowers. Great. Something healthy that wouldn't need cutlery. I picked up two large shiny red apples, dug out some notes to pay, and brought them over to the woman sitting in the chair.

Three things happened at once. She looked up, dropped her book, and started shrieking like a parrot on hormone replacement therapy. Even if I had a couple of words of the vernacular, I still don't think I would have understood; I was fairly sure no *actual* words were coming out of her mouth. Next, she started hollering in the direction of her husband, flapping her arms fast enough to replace the engines of the Boeing I had just flown in on. In a flash, the sharp nails at the end of her bejewelled fingers almost pierced my stomach as she snatched the apples out of my arms and returned them to the tray.

Only then did I notice that next to it was a framed black-and-white photograph of an older couple, a lit votive candle and a statue of a Golden Buddha. I didn't need a translator to finally understand that the apples were not for sale, nor were the fresh cut flowers. Somehow, within two hours of landing in Hanoi, I'd desecrated a home altar dedicated to ancestor worship. I tried to apologise but she started shooing me off the premises as though I was the devil himself. I walked across the street, avoiding wayward scooters, and doing my best to ask forgiveness from the Gods. I waited for a response from on High. The only thing I heard was a loud rumbling. Instead of three "Hail Marys" and one "Our Father", my penance, that night, was going to bed on an empty stomach.

To regain my sanity, the next morning I looked for water – any body of water that would calm my senses. According to the tourist map I'd picked up from the makeshift reception desk, if I walked to the end of the street and crossed over a couple of blocks I would arrive at Hồ Hoàn Kiếm Lake, the name of which came from a mid-fifteenth-century legend. Supposedly, a magical sword was sent from the Heavens to the Emperor to help combat the Chinese in Vietnam. When the war was over a giant golden turtle emerged from the lake and took the sword back, giving the lake its name, which, in English, roughly translates to "Lake of the Restored Sword". If I walked by its banks, I might glimpse the turtle and ask him for heavenly forgiveness for my cultural faux pas from the night before. Alas, redemption would not come easily.

Despite the wads of tissue paper in my ears, I still felt assaulted by the incessant noise ricocheting off the buildings in the narrow streets. Dodging sauntering tourists and vendors on bicycles, I walked as confidently as any world traveller might. I didn't stop until I had turned the last corner, but then I froze in the humid heat. I'd arrived at the end of one of the five major arteries that empties out onto Piaggio Vespa Hoàn Kiêm – a "square" with six unequal sides and a circular fountain offset from the centre. On the other side of it I could see the calm green waters of a lake. It reminded me of St Stephen's Green in Dublin, (without the pagoda buildings) – a refuge of nature in the centre of a major city.

Maybe you've seen the YouTube video entitled "The most insane traffic ever in Hanoi, Vietnam"? I hadn't. But I was looking at the live version of it right now. Cars, buses, rickshaws, bicycles, scooters and pedestrians crossed through this square without the protection of traffic lights, stop signs or rules of engagement. Luckily, everyone had the Audio-Shield of indestructibility – the horn. Everyone, that is, except the poor folk on foot. *Wait now, I'm one of those poor folk.* The mission was intimidating. The last time I'd attempted such a crossing was at France's L'Arc de Triomphe. Back then, I was a daring nineteen-year-old, too lazy to use the underground walkway. Here, there were no subterranean options. The only choice was to either turn around and go back to the hotel or take a death-defying walk across five intersecting lanes of non-regulated traffic.

Fools rush in. I thought I might wait a while and watch the locals. Let's just say the Vietnamese would win Olympic Gold in jay-walking. I was still standing there ten minutes later, watching their gallant efforts. They seemed purposeful, unbothered by the task. They stepped off the path, focused on a point directly across the square and started walking in a slow but persistent manner. Scooters and cars zoomed past them with such orchestrated precision you would think someone had access to the puppet strings above.

After ten minutes studying them, I decided I had to make a move before I got arrested for loitering. I stepped down off the kerb but the immediate cacophony of horns and the threat of instant death coming at me from so many angles had me jumping right back onto the security of the footpath again. It was impossible to know where to look. How could I tell which beeps were meant for me? If I moved out of one scooter's way, I would be in the collision path of three more. If I tried to avoid the car, I would surely be in the way of the bus.

Above the din, I heard the faintest chuckle. An old man to my left nodded at me. Then off he went, walking right into the mêlée of traffic, as if he was out for a Sunday stroll. Forget Egypt: *when in Hanoi, walk like a Hanoian*. Here was my shield. I moved in behind him, much like the cheeky car that hugs the rear bumper of an ambulance parting traffic. As I walked, I focused on the back of his wrinkly neck. Maybe I could call him Moses. If I shadowed him, he would lead me to the other side, preferably the path by the lake rather than the actual *other side*. Moses never looked back. When he stepped up on the pavement he turned left and continued down the path. I stopped at one of the park benches bordering the lake, took a swig of water and congratulated myself on the mammoth achievement of crossing a street. Next, I'd be tying my own shoelaces.

Chapter 34
The Long Night

I'd been comforting myself that my stay in the capital city was going to be a short one. The reason for my trip to Vietnam was to volunteer as an English teacher of middle-income adults at a school in the countryside, close to the sea. There, I would enjoy the idyllic scenery, so notably depicted on postcards and videos of this Asian country. On my days off I intended to visit places like Cat Ba island and photograph the caves and waterfalls. Or wander ancient jungle trails and meditate in the grounds of pagodas. I might even swim in Ha Long Bay. What mattered was that I would bask in the serenity of the East, far away from the noise of city life.

While my morning excursion to the lake in Hanoi had soothed my nerves, the jangling sixty-three-mile train ride to Hai Phong the following day put them right back on edge again. As we were leaving the capital, we stopped several times to rearrange the engine cars. Each time we were shunted forward or back, the vertebrae in my neck took up pole-dancing and the wooden bench seat in third-class offered little in the way of coccyx comfort.

Leaving the city behind, the landscape gave way to green fields and dusty roads, but I still didn't see any sign of mountains or breath-taking views through the rather scratched windows. My Kindle was pushing itself out of my bag, tendering stories of the Orient, but I chided myself for even thinking of taking my eye off the passing sights despite their less than spectacular offerings. Why read about it now when I was already here? After two hours, the fields were once again replaced by housing and commercial buildings. I thought we must have been going through another city. We were, but we were also stopping. This was Hai Phong. Double chiding. My boycotting of travel books had backfired. Had I read any of them at all, I would have known I was not destined for a country village, as I'd hoped, but the third-largest city in Vietnam.

Jiggling my bones back into place, I stepped down off the train and got swept towards the exit by the crowds leaving the station. The square outside was filled with cars, scooters and once again, the incredible buzz of commotion. I scanned the faces of those standing in the shade to see who was looking for a female teacher from the West. Not a glimmer of recognition from anyone, yet they were eager to help.

"Taxi? Taxi?"

Everyone wanted to relieve me of my tourist dollars.

"No, thank you, someone is coming for me," I told them in my best sign language.

One entrepreneurial taxi driver, about twenty-five years old, circled back to me three times. Each time he yelled *Taxi*, I shook my head.

The crowd was thinning out, cars pulled out of the square, people walked away. I watched one family of three adults and a small child climb on top of a motorcycle made for two and, after a kick start and a couple of revs, off they went to play in traffic. There were only two cars left in the square when Mr Entre-persistent came back a fourth time. By now, he was so convinced I would need a ride, he got out and tried to put my backpack into the boot. I took the piece of paper with the contact information of the school out of my pocket. Instead of an address, all I had was a number. Not exactly useful, since I didn't have a Vietnamese sim card. But the taxi driver did. Waving the paper at him, I gave the universal sign of someone talking on the phone. Thankfully, he took it from me, dialled, talked a moment, flipped his phone shut, handed the paper back to me, said "OK" and then drove off.

An employee from the train station came through the gates, meandered up the sidewalk, turned right, and disappeared from view. Presumably there were no more trains coming through for a while. The square was deserted. In a manner I had grown accustomed to when arriving at a new location, I waited. Fifteen minutes passed. The only person entering the square was a young man on a scooter. Perhaps he had left something behind. He drove over to me, took off his helmet and said, "Hi, sorry I am late, I got delayed at the school."

"Hi," I said, "is someone coming to pick me up?"

"Yes, I am here," he replied.

Seriously? He wanted me, with luggage, to get on the back of his scooter, and somehow hold on while weaving through the beeping traffic?

"I don't think so."

He seemed confused. "You don't want to ride with me?"

"Thank you, but no."

And as much as it irked me, I had to ask him to find me a taxi. A non-communicative older gentleman drove me through the bustling streets of Hai Phong. When he forced his way through a group of about twenty pedestrians and turned off the narrow road down a back alley, my senses went on cautious alert. Around another corner we went, the laneway now only wide enough to accommodate one car. This was definitely a dead end. On the left there was a fairly modern-looking three-storey white building. The car stopped. Well, I was either here, or not going to be here on earth much longer. Weirdly, the driver never said a word, but continued to sit there, holding the steering wheel. I was debating what to do next when Scooter Boy arrived and beckoned me to follow him into the building.

Jason, the guy I'd been dealing with by email came down the cement staircase to greet me. He was charming, but busy. He apologised for not having time to show me around, but I could find my room next to the communal shower on the second floor. I found the bathroom alright. My gut told me the other people sharing the facilities were not female. Next to it, the open door revealed a classroom, not a bedroom. I had a look around the large square room. There were two windows overlooking the alley below and the roof of the building opposite. Various posters and English words were stapled to the corkboards on three of the walls. Attached to the fourth was a green blackboard that had not seen a wet duster for quite some time. I was about to leave when I noticed an air mattress standing on its end. Behind it were two tan-coloured sheets and a pillow. It seemed like I might make it into the *Guinness Book of Records* for the shortest commute known to man – I would be sleeping in the classroom where I was to teach.

Meanwhile, I followed the scent of cooking back down the stairs to the ground floor. Scooter Boy and another local were frying up vegetables. A pot of rice was soaking up the last of the simmering water and a tall red-headed guy was setting mats on the floor.

"Hi, I'm Ronan," he said in a distinct Northern Irish accent.

"Hi," I said. "Are you one of the teachers here?"

"Yes, been here two months already." He said, as he put plates and chopsticks on the mats on the floor.

"How do you like it?"

"It's good, I'll miss it. I'm only here for another ten days, as I'm heading back to college at the end of the month."

Scooter Boy, whose name turned out to be Huu, and his friend, Throng Tri, brought over the food. We all sat cross-legged on the floor while we ate an array of spicy vegetables over rice. Huu was a hoot. He was single, had just turned nineteen, but was absolutely averse to dating.

"Why, do you not want a girlfriend?" I asked.

"Too much trouble."

"How so?"

"I just finished with my mother, so I need time for the freedom from the women."

We laughed – such cynicism from someone so young. He was convinced the earth was covered in women whose only job was to tell him what to do. I wondered how long it would take for his hormones to break free and change his mind.

Jason stopped by for a few minutes but didn't eat, and Ronan got going, since he had a night class to teach. I washed the pots and plates, and, because there was no sign of any dish cloth, left them to air-dry. I was tired, and my sense of humour was on strike. I lay down on the squishy air mattress in the empty classroom and tried to figure out what to do. I could still hear the incessant beeping and wondered if it was coming from outside the window or was just a new form of tinnitus burrowing into my head. Thankful for Wi-Fi, I opened my laptop and re-read the communications that had enticed me to this place. What had I read, or not read? Ironically, it was the toughest volunteer gig to get, the only one, apart from Tonga, that had required application forms and essays. Jason had put me to the test to see if I was a match for their project. He'd decided I was; I was about to decide I wasn't.

Vietnamese voices sounded through the wall. Ronan's class.

"I am a girl."

"I am a boy."

"The girl likes to go to the park."

"The boy likes to fish."

It wasn't the repetition of basic sentences that amused me but hearing grown Vietnamese men chanting English phrases in thick Belfast accents.

I must have dozed off, because sometime later, I found myself looking at the inside of my eyelids. Sweat had curled its way around my neck and the sheet beneath my back was a crumpled mess. I was sticking to the mattress. It was dark, the school was quiet, but the night still reverberated with horns and hooters. I couldn't make them stop. They were drilling Swiss cheese holes in my brain. I could totally understand how people drove themselves mad. Forget three weeks, I didn't want to stay another day! But was it fair to leave?

My spirit and ego battled it out.

You have to stay, you made a commitment, said Ego.

What use will I be if it's driving me crazy? Spirit answered.

Sometimes you just have to shut up and put up.

Easy for you to say.

Not everything is about wind chimes and soft breezes, you know.

But I'm nurtured in nature, cities make me crash, Spirit said.

You grew up in a city!

The suburbs of Dublin hardly compare to this populous place.

You said you wanted to travel, to give back, to help new communities, to discover the world, said Ego.

I do.

So, here you are. Discover.

I've discovered I don't like it here.

Aaaggh!

Ego sulked. Spirit won.

Chapter 35
Stuck in a Moment

Once I had given myself permission to leave, I booked a plane ride for the following day. My craving to bypass Hanoi was such that I had to hire a "limousine" service to take me directly to the airport. This leg of my journey had been an expensive mistake. Jason, who had spent time in the West, was understanding. He had obviously encountered the likes of me before and had two more volunteers lined up which thankfully made me feel a little less guilty for leaving.

The driver who came to collect me looked slightly older than ten, his car a long stretch from anything resembling a limo. Regardless, the air was cold and he supplied a bottle of water from the glove box. I looked out the window, watching fields passing by. Maybe I should have found those idyllic postcard locations and made more of an effort to embrace the culture. Perhaps I could have learned the language or bought earplugs to drown out the beeping. But I had to remind myself this was never meant to be a yearlong vacation with unlimited funds. Bora Bora had been an exception. Vietnam was a tick box on a passport, but I was on my way out. Or so I thought.

Traffic had been running at a comfortable pace along the two-lane highway towards Hanoi. Several cars had overtaken us, but we'd still been making tracks. The sudden slowing of the car and the sound of *Du Ma*, the only Vietnamese curse word I knew, roused me from dozing.

Ahead, in the middle of the road, two traffic police, in their beige uniforms with red and gold trim, had created a road block. Some vehicles were being waved through, others told to pull over.

"What's this?" I asked the driver. He shook his head and muttered something.

I couldn't tell if it was the equivalent of a routine check for tax and insurance, or whether they were looking for someone in particular. After a brief conversation between cop and driver, three of the four cars in front of us were allowed through, but both motorcycles were stopped. As we approached the sturdy-looking officer, he directed us to the side of the road. My driver was told to get out. He answered questions for about a minute, then the officer stuck his head in the window and looked me over – really looked me over. I wasn't sure of the protocol. Should I nod, smile, or look straight ahead? He withdrew and told my driver to come with him. Come where? We were in the middle of the countryside. The two of them crossed the road and disappeared behind the trees. Shortly afterward a different officer came out to replace the one who had stopped us. Ten minutes went by and my driver came back across the road. See? There was nothing to be spooked about. He opened the door, but instead of getting in to drive off he took papers out of the glove box.

"What's happening?" I asked.

He said something and held up his hand with his fingers spread out. It could have meant *Stay, don't move*, or *I'll be back in five minutes*. But it didn't mean he'd be back in five minutes, because he wasn't. The next couple of cars were waved through. A scooter approached and looked like it was going to keep going, but finally slowed to a stop. I have no idea what the officer said to him, but the biker tried to take off, then thought the better of it when the police raised a baton in his direction. I could see he fully intended to use it. I assessed my situation. It had been twenty minutes since my driver disappeared behind the trees, the second time. I still didn't know why we'd been stopped. Cars that had been pulled over after us had been interrogated and then waved through. None of their drivers had disappeared into the field across the road.

A sense of vulnerability tried to finagle its way into my consciousness. I was alone in the back of a car I didn't own, in a country I didn't know. A police officer had taken my driver and I was miles from any public transport. The minutes that ticked away jeered at my chance of catching my plane. What to do? In those moments I had to, once again, school my brain to live in the now. I'm fine, I told myself. I'm just sitting in a car, albeit hot, now that the air conditioning has been off for thirty minutes.

Things are always working out for me – a mantra I'd borrowed from Abraham-Hicks.

You wanted to see the countryside, my ego chimed in. *Look out the window. Don't you just love the green fields and tall trees?*

I coined a new mantra:

There is always only now.

The more I said it the more it became true. There was only *now*; but *now* lasted for another forty-two minutes. I was in a meditative state when the door opened and the driver got in. He put both his hands together in the sign of someone praying and nodded his head. He pointed at his watch, then at the sky and drove us off like a cheetah on the run. Had I looked back through the rear window, I might have seen a large building behind the trees, but I would still never know why we had been stopped for an hour and fifteen minutes.

The plane waited for me. In fairness, it also waited for the other 127 passengers too. Somehow, my young driver had got us to the airport on time without getting arrested for speeding. The aircraft was full of excited vacationers happy to be going to Phuket. I'd decided to return to the old studio apartment I had rented during boot camp. It was clean, cheap, and came with free Wi-Fi and a swimming pool. It was as good a place as any to start lining up a job for the start of the year.

Chapter 36
Coming Home

I've never been a big fan of Friday the thirteenth, but this one, in November 2015, was looking promising. I was in a small internet café in Phuket, in the middle of my second Skype interview with an entrepreneurial English couple. They were looking for an administrator for their motorhome rental business just outside of Paris. Their clientele were mostly visitors from the USA and Australia. The job came with onsite accommodation and an opportunity to grow the company. It appealed. I spoke French, enjoyed countryside living rather than the city, and I had plenty of customer service experience dealing with Americans and Aussies. The couple seemed enthusiastic about what I could bring to their business; their main concern was that they couldn't pay me what they felt I was worth. We gave each other the weekend to think it over.

Nine hours later, a night of terror unfolded in Paris: four mass shootings, four suicide bombings, 130 victims dead. France had suffered its own 9/11. I sent the couple a letter of condolence, hoping French tourism would survive. They thanked me, and relieved me of my debate of whether to move to France by hiring someone else. It was the right call, for them and for me.

Natural disasters, and even man-made tragedies like this, somehow bring out the best in humanity. These are the times when neighbours start caring, leaders step up, and heroes are born. Communities come together and countries help each other. Connection is key to survival. Without it, we fail to thrive. We are reminded how short life is, how any of our heartbeats could be our last. Whatever quality time we have left on this earth, we want to spend it with purpose, with people we love. I needed hugs and I needed family. It was time to find home.

Five days later, I was back at zero degrees longitude, my circumnavigation complete, scouring London's Heathrow Airport looking for her. Somewhere in this huge waiting area past security, my sister, Máire, would be sitting. She would be tired. The flight from Dublin to London took only an hour but she would've had an early start. Either she'd be reading a book or chatting to someone beside her, waiting for her connection gate to be announced. She was bound for Austin, Texas, her third time in as many years. Since she'd discovered the American holiday, she liked to spend Thanksgiving with our brother, Conor. What she didn't know was that, on this leg of her journey, I'd be sitting next to her. The surprise was bursting at my seams.

My flight from Phuket had arrived the evening before. Despite a cosy night slumbering in purple light in the airport's Yotel, I still shivered from the cold. A year spent travelling the tropics had thinned my blood, so I went to the bathroom to heat my hands. When I came out, there she was, sitting by herself, reading. She hadn't noticed me, so I pushed the "record video" button on my camera and said:

"Hi."

She looked up and her mouth fell open. Literally. Open it stayed, strangling any words on their way through her larynx. She peered at me, her brain scrambling to recall our conversation from last night. I'd inquired about her trip, and she'd asked about life in Thailand. Chit-chat mainly – or so she'd thought. The phone call had been to convince her I was still in Asia, just wishing her well for her flight.

"Hi," I said again.

Still, she didn't speak. She stood up and her open mouth tried to form a *how*, a *what*, and a *wow*, all in one go.

On the other side of the Atlantic, my surprise arrival in Austin had the opposite effect.

"Oh my God, oh my God!"

My brother, Conor, seemed to have developed some sort of Tourette's Syndrome.

"Oh my God!"

His joy and random utterings made me smile. We rang Aonghus in Dublin. For the first time since we'd settled our mother's estate, the four of us were reunited on a single call, connected by desire not duty, by love not sorrow, and by a new era in our adult sibling relationships.

In the year I'd been "around the world", I had learned and I had taught, I had laughed and I had cried. I'd stood on Arctic ice and melted on the equator's edge. I'd processed grief and battled loneliness. I'd yearned for a partner to share it all with, but was also proud of my solo endeavours. No matter where I'd been, or what situation I'd faced, I'd always found a way. Variety drove me and exploration filled me, but there was something about spending Thanksgiving and Christmas in the embrace of family that ratified my sense of belonging.

With my sabbatical complete, I began the process of re-entry to the workforce, sending out résumés in America and CVs in Europe. Who was going to hire a middle-aged woman who hadn't worked in a year? No one, it seemed. It had been so long since I'd applied for a job online, I didn't know that human resources directors, who used to be the gatekeepers to CEOs, now had computer programmes scanning *their* mail. I had no choice but to hire someone versed in the algorithms to rewrite the story of my professional life.

By New Year's Day I'd sent out over ninety-five applications and, since I was seeking upper-management opportunities the normal timeframe to be called for interview would be at least three to four weeks. To amuse myself while waiting, I surfed the world again. One volunteer project leapt right off the screen. Surely, I could squeeze in one last trip while I was waiting? It would only take a month.

PART THREE
Around the Heart

Chapter 37
The Snakes and the Axe Murderer

It was the third snake that threw me off. Not one, not two, but three. The first had been about half a metre long with hints of green on the underbelly; the second, something similar with a larger girth; but the third one was smaller, all black and coiled up in strike position. I caught my breath. Not a pleasant scenario for an ophidiophobic like myself.

It was January 2016, and I was back in Florida. I'd just boarded *Freed Spirit*, a twelve-metre monohull sailing vessel bound for the Bahamas. After only a couple of emails and a twenty-minute call, I'd agreed to crew her, as a volunteer, across the Gulf Stream and beyond. Officially, the project only required five hours work per day, five days a week, which, in theory, should leave me time to follow up on interviews, but those who have worked at sea know there is no clock to punch when crewing a live-aboard sailboat. Current, wind and tide are the true keepers of your schedule. You've heard it said *if you love what you do, you'll never <u>work</u> a day in your life*. The call of the water still governed my soul. This was going to be such a chance to fulfil my dream of living at sea, I was prepared to overcome any and all phobias. Maybe.

The time had come to take measure of the man called Captain Gary Krieger. Even though the snakes turned out to be *plastic*, it didn't bode well for me to spend a month cooped up with a reptilian lover. In Tonga, I'd learned a valuable lesson. Many young crew would hitchhike the oceans, hopping from vessel to vessel. Captain Dave had taught me to question the safety items on-board and the experience of its skipper. For those reasons, when the opportunity for this trip had come up, I interviewed Gary, as thoroughly as he interviewed me. Just because he was fourteen years my senior and looked like a salty dog didn't mean he was one. More like a sea puppy who'd retired from a long land-based career and an even longer marriage, and then put himself through sailing school to make living on a boat his new way of life.

He seemed friendly though, a nice smile and a decent handshake, nothing like an axe murderer at all, at all. Why is it that, anytime I decide to go off into the unknown, there is always someone in my circle of influence who wants to remind me that all strangers are axe murderers until proven otherwise? Luckily, this is an area where I have, so far, managed to tap into my intuition and keep myself safe.

While my new host may have had a bizarre fetish for fake snakes, and the boat, notwithstanding, was filled with lines, ropes, tools and tape, I didn't see so much as a hacksaw you would give to a ten-year-old heading for scout camp, never mind an axe. Instead, there were two red and silver children's toy windmills on sticks, the kind I had spun out the sunroof of my father's car on the way home from an Irish picnic. They were definitely not big enough to be considered wind generators, so I was hoping there was another source of power on this long-range cruiser – solar panels, perhaps?

Captain Gary showed me below decks where the three-step companionway yielded to a delightful interior of teak and green upholstery. To the left, the navigational station or nav desk was covered in charts and radios, breakers and switches. The galley, an L-shaped design, was complete with three gas rings and a two-shelf oven. The small counter space hid a chest fridge-freezer and the remaining space was taken up with a twin sink. The salon lay in front – another L-shaped banquette design running down the port side and across the beam with a straight settee opposite it on starboard. Between them lay a fold-up table capable of hosting a range of events, from intimate dinners for two, up to and including, a lively cocktail party for eight.

The stateroom and main head, his en-suite bedroom, lay forward in the bow and to the starboard aft, or stern, a second bathroom and the quarter-berth. Like most berths on boats this size, it consisted of a drawer-like bed formed under the seat in the cockpit above. At the pillow end it would be considered a twin, but it narrowed to the width of a small cot towards the feet. The designers say she can sleep a couple, but I doubt they meant a couple of Vikings.

I put down my duffel and peered through the porthole towards the floating docks of Riviera Beach Marina. What joy to be back in the Sunshine State of Florida.

"There are lots of things to hurt you on a boat," Gary said, startling me. I turned around and bumped my head on the bulkhead just to prove his point. "Would you like to go through the safety procedures now?"

"Sure."

I learned plenty of ways this boat could hurt me. There wasn't a square foot of area free from toe-stubbing opportunities. Head-banging came in a close second. Handling lines without gloves offered all kinds of rope burns. The lid of the fridge could either break my fingers, cut my face or, if I was lucky enough for it to fall on my temple, make quick work of actually killing me. Of course, if that wasn't enough, I could always fall off and drown, although I was advised not to do that.

On the other hand, *I* could also hurt the boat. I could unintentionally set fire to it, if I didn't follow the four-step safety procedure for lighting the gas stove. Better yet, if I let the unlit gas drain down into the bilges (because we all know propane vapours are heavier than air, right?), I could cause a mighty good explosion, which would, in turn, set fire to the boat. There were other minor details. Flushing anything down the marine toilet that hadn't passed through my body first would render it inoperable. Since I was told not to jump off and drown that would mean having to keep my legs crossed until arriving at the next available port. I was happy to see, however, that if I did find myself in the water there were all sorts of safety equipment including life jackets with Position Locating Beacons, a six-person yellow life-raft, and an EPIRB to alert search-and-rescue services.

There was a knock on the hull followed by a New York yell:

"Permission to come aboard, Captain?"

"Hey!" said Gary. "Come on down."

Two couples arrived down the companionway. Gary made the introductions. Big Ed and his wife Pam lived on a catamaran, currently berthed in the next marina.

"Pleased to meet you," I said.

"And we're on the catamaran at the end of your dock," said the other man, Craig.

"How long have you lived aboard?" I asked his wife, Liz.

"A few years now," she said. "We love it."

All of them cruised from port to port, sometimes up the east coast of the U.S., sometimes over to the Bahamas and down to the Caribbean. The women were so impressive. They juggled their duties on deck with their cooking skills below and still seemed to have energy to keep their relationships fresh. They were the Martha Stewarts of the sea, and I became quite convinced that Pam could knit you a dinghy by lunchtime.

"So, Gary, I see you got the snakes," said Ed. "How do you like them?"

"Not my favourite things on the boat," said Gary.

"Just wait," said Ed.

What I didn't know at the time, was that, apart from exchanging pleasantries over cocktails, otherwise known as *captain's hour*, the visit had been prearranged for two reasons. Firstly, as his friends, they wanted to assure me that Gary was a good guy. More importantly, they were looking out for their newbie sailor friend and wanted to confirm I wasn't a modern-day pirate who, a couple of miles out to sea, was going to relieve Gary of his boat. I must have passed the test, because, as they were leaving, they gave me a hug and invited me to join them for dinner on Sunday.

That left Gary and me the rest of the evening to get acquainted. He started by apologising for the confusion. A week after the interview I'd called him back to verify my arrival date. He'd told me he thought I wasn't coming, and had found someone else.

"What?" I'd asked in disbelief.

"I thought you said I didn't have enough experience and had decided not to come."

"What?"

"I hadn't heard from you, so I invited someone else."

"I sent you Christmas greetings. I said I would see you in January."

"Oh dear," he said. "Perhaps you could come in February instead, and join the boat in the Bahamas?"

"No."

Silence.

"I feel terrible," he said. "Let me call the other girl and see if she can switch."

She couldn't. Or, didn't want to. She was, however, willing to share the duties if I came too.

When I found out her name was Tuesday, and she was arriving on Saturday, I'd bought my ticket for Friday. Now that I had seen how skinny the salon settees were, I was glad I would have the luxury of the berth with a door my first night. When I'd originally told my family about sailing away with this axe murderer I'd never met, they were concerned. Once they learned another girl was coming they seemed more relaxed. Why? Halfway across the ocean, would an axe murderer gladly dump one body overboard but not two?

"By the way," Gary said, interrupting my surmising that evening, "there's another person joining us as well."

"Uh-huh?"

"A sailing school buddy. I invited him a long time ago but I never thought he'd come."

"His name isn't Noah by any chance?" I asked. Now we had two men and two women. The ark was filling up.

Tuesday turned out to be a petite Asian who loved to cook, and Brad was a businessman from up north, with only ten days' vacation to spare. Pleasantries were set aside as the preparation work began. Stowing a month's provisions inside a twelve-metre boat, while trying to move around three other people and their *stuff*, became a lesson in contortionism. Cabinets and under-the-bed storage were crammed with everything from toilet rolls to rice. Maximising space meant lots of rearranging. Every corner of every cubbyhole was stuffed, not alphabetically *per se*, but following the logic of the person doing the stuffing. Finally, it was done. However, if Captain Gary knew where he had put his nine-sixteenths wrench before, he had no clue now.

On the fourth morning we left America's shores. Winds had been calculated and wave heights scrutinised. After a final check on the weather forecast, we waved goodbye to the boats berthed on either side of us, and motored east. In ten or eleven hours we would dock in the Bahamas. No point in hoisting sails as the wind was right on our nose. About five miles out to sea we entered the Gulf Stream, the fast-moving current that runs from the Gulf of Mexico up the eastern seaboard of the USA. Had we been travelling north, the four-knot speed would have given us a tremendous push. Traversing it, however, was a different story. It started with a gentle sway, a motion that could soothe a sailor's heart or torment a landlubber's belly. The winds, which had been coming from the east, backed to the north. The seas built. Slowly at first, then, gradually, they rose to two-metre waves on top of an ocean swell. The boat rolled. Deeply. One minute the starboard hull would kiss the water, then reach for the sky the next.

Tuesday was looking green and I was feeling hungry. I went below and clipped myself into the safety harness at the galley. By spreading my feet in a wide stance and bending at the knees, I was able to roll with the ocean's pitch. I could hear nothing from above as I was enclosed below decks, right next to the engine. The floorboards heated my feet and I set about fixing us snacks.

When I returned to the cockpit, Tuesday was throwing up — on the windward side. She was too sick to notice the puke flying back in her hair and into the boat. Brad too, looked a paler shade of grey, but he knew enough about boats to dump his breakfast over the leeward side. Captain Gary was happily manning the helm and he and I both sat down and ate.

The stream was approximately forty miles wide and by mid-afternoon we were coming out the other side. The seas had laid down. Tuesday, who had been stretched out on the settee in the salon for most of the day, had recently emerged from below. Brad was gazing at the horizon, looking for solace for his inner ears.

"What was that?" I asked Gary.

"What?"

"That noise?"

He listened. I was sitting in the cockpit on the port side and I was sure I'd heard the engine flutter. We both listened but now it sounded fine.

"There!" I heard it again.

Gary heard it too. It was more than a flutter; this time it sounded like a sputter. Then, the engine cut out. Silence. After hours of talking above the noise, the quiet was calming, although it seemed we were in a spot of bother. We hadn't seen a boat for hours and the Bahamian coast was still fifteen nautical miles away.

Chapter 38
Turning Point

"What do you think it is?" I asked.

At first, Gary didn't answer. Lifting the lid on the port side seat, he muttered, "It might be the fuel filter."

Out had to come fenders, dock lines, buckets and cables, before he could stick his head below. I had no clue what he was fiddling with, but, about five minutes later, we were putting everything back.

"Let's give it a go," he said.

The engine turned over and thankfully engaged. Three miles later, it died again. For the second time in thirty minutes we emptied the lazarette, and this time, both Gary and a new filter disappeared into the black hole. There followed several grunts, and "Pass me this" and "Pass me that". When he climbed out and closed the lid, he turned the key in the ignition. Just like my first car on a winter's morn in Ireland – an old Fiat that could take me from point A to point B because expecting to detour to any other part of the alphabet would've been considered greedy – we heard nothing but *whirring*.

Gary sat for a while, thinking. As the sun made its descent towards the horizon he got on the VHF radio and contacted the harbour-master in West End, Bahamas.

My old TV director brain went into decisive mode. Within ten seconds I had assessed our options. We had come forty-four miles and were twelve miles from our destination. The winds were unfavourable and we had no engine. We could not make it there before dark. Even if we did, we would need a towboat to bring us around the seawall and into the harbour. From what I was overhearing on the radio call, the nearest tow boat cost eight hundred dollars and was in Freeport, forty miles away. We knew there was a storm approaching from the west the following day, so anchoring outside the harbour would leave us exposed to weather. We'd been beating into the wind all day but if we turned around we could sail downwind back towards Florida. Gary's Boat US membership would cover the cost of towing us the rest of the way into port. Parts, or whatever needed to be fixed, would be readily available and the engineer who was familiar with the boat would be on hand to do the work.

"We've got to go back." I said.

Gary looked at me, his lips pursed. Brad didn't say a word. Tuesday commented on how pretty the sunset was going to be. We were still pointing towards the Bahamas.

Gary started talking to himself.

"We should turn around," I said and explained my reasoning.

"It could be just a filter," he said.

"But you've just replaced the filter."

"Maybe we could get into Freeport?"

"It's forty miles away," I said.

"If the towboat left Freeport now, we could try to sail south and meet them halfway?"

"It will be dark by then."

"That won't matter."

The sun was slipping beneath the horizon and still we sat there, suspended on a bobbing sea. No land in sight.

"At the moment no one knows where we are," I said.

He seemed to consider that. Then, he picked up the radio and broadcast our position to the US Coast Guard. Not that the Coast Guard would do anything; we weren't taking on water and there was no risk to life or limb. Yet. They were, however, able to relay a message to the American towing company who suggested they could pick us up if we could get closer to Florida.

Gary said, "It's probably best if we turn back."

Finally.

He turned the wheel to starboard. The wind caught the hull and pushed us around. When we were facing in the opposite direction he looked at me and said:

"I heard you, I just needed to think through the options."

Had I not been caught up in my own anxiety and frustrated at the length of time it took him to make a decision, I would have seen his disappointment. Here was a man with a dream two years in the making. A man who had looked for a new passion in life and had enrolled in sailing school. He'd spent a year shopping for this boat, and another six months updating all its rigging and electronics. He had sold most of his stuff, put the rest in storage, driven cross-country from California, and moved on-board. This boat was now his home. He was a solo sailor who had needed crew to help him achieve his goals. That was why I was here. His efforts had almost paid off. In the end, only twelve miles and a working engine had stood in the way of his dream.

Then he stepped up and became captain-like.

"We'll take two-hour shifts, two persons at a time, and we will sail back overnight."

He disappeared out on deck. Silhouetted against the setting sun, he started attaching a pole to the end of the jib, the headsail. Deciding we all needed comfort food, I went below and cooked a pot of mashed potato from scratch. By the time I came up to the cockpit, it was dark. The wind that had been on our nose on the way over, was now on our backs. The main sail had been raised and the boom that held it was tied off on the port side. The jib was held out to starboard with the pole I came to know as whisker. I was looking at the two sails, each a triangle on their own side. We were now sailing downwind, wing on wing. I didn't know it then but it was the first time he'd ever rigged the boat for this point of sail, having previously taught himself the procedure from watching a video on YouTube.

After dinner, Gary and Brad took the first watch. I cleaned up below and crawled into the quarter berth around ten p.m. The slow roll and forward motion lulled me into a half-sleep. When I awoke I didn't know what time it was, but knew it was late. To protect our night vision, red light illuminated the cabin instead of white. Feeling guilty I might have missed my watch, I went up top immediately. Brad was on the helm, monitoring the autopilot and making course corrections as necessary. He looked better, but tired.

"How's it going?" I whispered.

"Good, but slow. Wind's down to three knots."

"Sorry I'm late."

"No worries, Tuesday sat with me for a while, she's gone below again."

"I'll take over now, if you like."

"Sure. Nothing much on the horizon, but we are being pushed north by the current."

"Got it, thanks."

"It's two a.m. Gary said to wake him when you came up."

"OK."

Brad went below. I looked at Gary asleep on the starboard side, his left arm was wrapped around the winch, holding him in place. Having stood overnight watch in Tonga, I was a little more comfortable in knowing what to do. The night was calm, and the only sounds interrupting my thoughts were the waves slapping the hull. The moon was high and full. I let him sleep.

By the time the sun came up the high-rise condos on Florida's east coast appeared on the horizon. Cell reception was restored and Gary made the call. We were less than three miles out when the red inflatable towboat threw us a line and pulled us to shore. We were then manoeuvred into the same slip we had left only twenty-four hours before. If ever one felt like a dog returning with his tail between his legs, this was it.

"Let's go out to breakfast," Gary said.

The four of us squeezed into a booth at a nearby diner. Never had poached eggs and home fries looked so inviting.

"So, what's next?" Brad asked Gary.

"We'll have to see what the problem is, get it fixed, and then wait for another weather window to try again."

It was five days before Brad was due back to work but Tuesday had the rest of the month.

I didn't say much.

"Are you not going to eat those?" Gary asked me, nudging his knife at some blackened potatoes on my plate.

"They're burned."

"They're crispy, the best." It was the most animated I'd seen him all morning.

"Help yourself," I said in mild disgust.

"Mmm-mmm," he said, crunching one down.

Brad went to the restroom and Tuesday announced she was going to run next door to the Asian market. Gary looked across the table at me and said:

"You're not coming back, are you?"

My face is not my friend when it's time to hide my emotions. My brain had run through all the what-ifs. Brad knew a little about sailing, but given his time constraints it would be unlikely he could make a return trip. Tuesday would be of no nautical help whatsoever. If anything happened to Gary, I would be out there swinging by myself. I was scared I didn't know enough.

"Probably not."

He raised an eyebrow, stabbed another burned potato on my plate and waved it at me.

"Are you going to let one bad night of sailing ruin a whole month?"

Chapter 39
Common Ground

It turned out the boat had suffered a heart attack. Much like a clot can travel through the bloodstream and cause a blockage in the heart, the rough conditions crossing the Gulf Stream had stirred up algal sludge from the bottom of the fuel tank. Diesel couldn't make its way to the engine. Gary had had the right idea changing the fuel filter, and it would have probably got us on our way, had he only known, however, there were *two* valves to be opened afterward, not just one. Regardless, the fuel now needed to be "polished", which required another tow to a boat yard where a transfusion could take place.

After a day of rest, Tuesday and Brad went off in search of a doctor who would write a prescription for anti-motion sickness medication and Gary and I took the boat ten miles up the inter-coastal waterway to the yard. It was a crisp sunny morning and I sat out on deck. Since we were under tow, Gary was able to join me. We hardly talked, but it was lovely just to be on the water without any worries. It took a couple of hours for the fuel to be siphoned off, run through a type of sieve, and put back into the tanks. Once done, the boat was set for another Gulf Stream attempt.

Despite the number of cold fronts that run through Florida in January, the weather cooperated and another opportunity to make the crossing arose the following day. Was I going to walk away from sailing for a month? Allow my anxieties to curtail a dream? I was still undecided. I'd left Malaysia early, Vietnam too. Had those decisions been premature? Had I missed out on experiences that might have enhanced my life? Could I have contributed to the projects if I'd chosen to stay? I'd never know.

I made a contingent decision. If Brad wasn't going, neither was I. It was a cop out, I know. But then I got to thinking, if Brad wasn't going, Gary would need me even more. My biggest self-criticism was that I was an enthusiastic starter, but not always a finisher. Unlike parents, who have no choice but to stay the course and see child-rearing through, I didn't have that responsibility and had given myself permission to quit on many occasions. If I didn't like something, I would just walk away, regardless of the consequences to others. Perhaps it was time to change. I was almost at the point of saying *Yes, I'll go*, – which was progress – but then Brad said he could make the trip so I managed to avoid fully owning my decision.

The four of us set off again. Tuesday wore the scopolamine patch and Gary went from being an absolute novice at navigating the Gulf Stream, to one of the few sailors who crossed it three times in the same week. A mile or two before we arrived, a smiling Gary ordered the yellow quarantine flag to be raised. Bahamas at last. Unfortunately for Brad, there was little chance to use his snorkel gear as he had to fly back to work the next day, which left Tuesday and me alone with the axe murderer. Having lived with Gary for two weeks now, I reckoned the threat was minimal. It would take him so damn long to make up his mind which axe to use, I would have plenty of time to escape.

The wind blew for the next few days, keeping us tied to the dock at West End in the Abacos. It gave me the opportunity to follow up on job applications. I interviewed for an on-board management position with an inland waterways cruise company. It would combine my skills in hotel management with my experience on boats. All looked promising until the end of the second interview when they asked for the transcripts of my Bachelor's degree. A pre-employment requirement, they said. I was taken aback. The company deemed a brand-new graduate, twenty-two years old, a preferable hire to someone like me with a Diploma in Hospitality and years of experience in guest service and employee management. My year at the

Sorbonne University in Paris, countless college courses in California, and State Licensing exams in Florida weren't enough. I didn't have the piece of paper that combined it all. My decision to experience the world instead of the inside of a classroom had backfired.

While I did grumble about unfairness, I also accepted things I couldn't change. By their rigid recruitment standards, I was ineligible. Something better would come along. In the meantime, another tool that has helped me bridge the gap between what I have and what I want is to define *happiness* as *wanting something I already have*. Why had I wanted the cruise ship job in the first place? It was to fulfil my basic needs and to live life on the water. I already had a gig on a sailboat cruising the Bahamas. Although I was not earning an income, I had food to eat and somewhere to sleep. What more did I need in the now? I decided to stay put and continue the rest of the month on *Freed Spirit*.

Once the weather improved, we were able to leave West End. The three of us sailed sixty miles across the shallows of the Grand Bahama Bank. An exceptional day. It was like sailing on a bright blue pool, like the lagoon in Bora Bora. The underside of the white clouds reflected the pure blue water. At the uninhabited island known as Great Sale, we stopped for the night.

I awoke early. The wind had died and day was breaking. I slipped out of the berth, careful not to wake the others, and took my camera up top. In the distance, three other boats were also anchored, their images perfectly mirrored in the glass-calm surface. The sun rose behind the trees, casting the horizon in silhouette. Pink and rose hues spattered the passing clouds. Inky black water morphed into blue. All was still. I tiptoed my way to the bow, trying hard not to sway the boat. My Canon camera had its way, capturing the moment with spectacular shots. I breathed it in.

An unexpected movement on-board rippled the water. My solitude was broken. Standing at the stern was Gary, a professional Nikon raised to his left eye. I'd only seen him taking snapshots with his phone previously. When he lowered the camera he stood perfectly still and the water turned, once again, to glass. Motionless, he too, took it all in. I knew he knew I was there, and he knew I knew he was too. We didn't speak. The only sounds to be heard were the birds of dawn and the immortalising clicks of our cameras. Before he went below, he looked my way and nodded. I smiled. Photographers. We had found a common ground.

After breakfast, we got ready to leave. Gary was at the wheel and I was sitting on the bow, my legs dangling into the open anchor well. I signalled I was ready. As soon as he drove the boat forward the chain slackened and I pushed the button beside me which operated the windlass motor to raise the anchor. With a hook in the other hand I pulled sections of chain across the bottom of the well, to prevent it from bunching up as it came through the hawsepipe. When I had fifteen metres of the chain pulled in, the bow dipped, indicating we were directly over the anchor, and my last tug freed it from the sandy bottom. Once I had it up in the cradle, I gave Gary the prearranged hand signal and he turned the vessel south. Back in the cockpit I helped him raise the main sail and then pull out the jib. We were underway, off on another day's adventure sailing on the Bahamian blue.

Over the next few days, Tuesday and I shared the cooking, and Gary and I took care of all things nautical. Along the way, we stopped at various ports recommended by other cruisers. We *had to* have the famous Conch Fritters in Foxtown, watch the sunset at Green Turtle Cay, and dine on anything at all in Nippers, Great Guana, because it overlooked the crashing waves on the Atlantic side.

As we approached the harbour at Treasure Cay, Gary told us we would be tying up to a mooring ball, instead of dropping the anchor. Unbeknownst to me, it was only his second time to do so. I went on deck to grab the pole hook.

"Do you know how to do it?" he shouted up to me.

I gave him the OK signal and began fixing one end of a dock line to a cleat on the bow.

"I'll come up and help you as soon as I can," he said.

With basic hand signals I directed him towards an empty ball. Once it was alongside the port bow, I reached down with the pole, hooked the floating line attached to the ball, laced the loose end of our line through the eye of the loop on the mooring ball, and ran it back to the same cleat on the boat. Then I repeated the exercise on the starboard side so we had two lines through the eye to avoid chaffing. Birdy would have been proud. By the time Gary came up on deck we were safely tied off.

"Where did you learn to do that?" he asked in surprise.

"Scuba instructors do more than dive from dive boats, you know."

While the water we travelled was blue and gorgeous, the three and a half miles of white sandy beach at Treasure Cay gave us our first real taste of Bahamian paradise. A true vacation spot for many. It was there I understood Gary's schedule. He had none. We'd sailed almost every day but when he came to somewhere he liked, he stopped. The harbour became home and the beach, our playground. We stayed a week.

Chapter 40
The Blowout

Tuesday left on a Thursday. A phone call from Detroit brought her back to the frozen north. Now I was the only crew. The axe murderer and I had been getting along quite well by then, so it was somewhat ironic we should have our biggest blowout the next day on a cay called Man of War.

Having spent the night tied to a mooring ball, Gary decided he wanted to bring the boat into the marina to top up with diesel before we left. We could see the fuel dock from where we were. We should have been able to drive up alongside and tie off relatively easily. However, I wasn't feeling it. The tee-shirt I had hand-washed and attached to the lifelines earlier was already dry, and the Bahamian courtesy flag on deck was blowing rigid in what I figured was a fifteen- to eighteen-knot wind.

"Do we really need fuel?" I asked him.

"We're not low, but it is always good to top up when we have the chance," he said.

I looked at that chance differently. Our docking experience was limited, and often accompanied by an issue. I noticed a large catamaran parked on one end of the dock which would limit our options for casting off. I didn't know enough to take a stance but was definitely feeling uneasy.

Nonetheless, we dropped the ball and headed to the dock. I threw the spring line to the dockhand. He caught it, but we were coming in hot. Too fast for me to fend off the pylon without hurting myself, so we bumped. It wasn't perfect, but at least we were in.

By the time we had finished fuelling, the fifteen-knot wind was gusting to twenty. The catamaran was still tied to the dock right in front of our bow. Much like having to drive a car out of a tight parallel parking spot, Gary had to move the boat astern before he could point the bow out away from the dock. He'd asked the dockhand to hold onto the line attached to our mid-ships and help "walk" the boat backwards until the bow was clear of the end of the dock. First the guy released the stern and bow lines. Then he walked us back. But when only a metre or so of the stern was clear of the end corner, he flung the line at me on deck. I caught it and hauled it in as quickly as I could, lest the dangling end get dragged under water and wrapped around the propeller. We were unattached but still moving in reverse. The only thing holding us to the dock was the wind. It pinned our mid-ships on the end corner and pushed our stern into the fairway behind the fuel dock. Gary tried to correct but didn't have enough momentum to counteract the gusts. The further back we went, the more the boat ended up broadside to the wind. It pushed us parallel to a U-shaped basin of slips. Protruding over the edge of the bow pulpit, our two anchors were ready to rip through the Bimini cover on the back of a motor yacht that did not look cheap. I dumped the line in a pile on the deck and ran to the bow to fend us off. The fairway was barely as wide as our boat was long, and our dinghy, which was tied up on the stern davits, caught on the pylon on the slip behind us. There was no room to go forward or back and the wind kept pushing us further up the fairway against boat after boat.

"We're in trouble, here," Gary shouted from the cockpit.

"Ya think?"

I ran back to help him, almost tripped on one of the bloody plastic snakes, but then heard a shout from the dock. The bow had cleared the first motorboat but was on a collision course with the next. Diners at the waterside restaurant were on their feet, hoping to witness the nautical version of a train wreck. I grabbed the mooring pole and managed to fend us off two kayaks hanging from the upper deck of a Fleming trawler. The next one was a sailboat, also with a dinghy up on its davits. Had I reached out I would have caught my hand between our standing rig and their dinghy's propeller blade. We cleared it by three inches, but we were now pinned at the top of the U-shaped set of slips.

Gawkers were yelling from all three surrounding docks. None of the comments was helpful. The only one in control was the wind. One man jumped into his dinghy off our bow with the idea of towing us out. A gust caught our stern and pushed it to port. It would have helped except our bow now turned to starboard and our anchors were about to decapitate the man in his dinghy. I yelled, he ducked. Just in time. The slight move, however, had unpinned us, and the wind brought the boat perpendicular to our original position, head into the wind. We could've drifted backward into an empty slip behind us. Instead, Captain Gary saw his moment and gave it full throttle ahead. Like a scene out of *Fast and Furious*, we skidded left out of the fairway, roared past the fuel dock and zoomed out the channel. So much for minimum wake. I hoped the poor guy in the dinghy liked rollercoaster rides. It was unlikely we'd ever dare show our faces in that harbour again.

We docked in Hope Town, Elbow Cay, an hour later. Gary didn't need a Master's degree in body language to pick up on my mood.

"You look annoyed," he said.

Annoyed? I couldn't speak.

"Everything's fine," he said.

"Fine?" I shouted. "Everything's fine?" I was fuming. "I just saved you about fifty thousand dollars!"

"Yes," he said, "you were great, thank you."

"Thank you? We're lucky I didn't lose an arm."

"I know. I am so glad you're OK," he said.

"It was crazy up there."

"I know."

"I said it wasn't a good idea to go in, in the first place."

"Did you?"

"Yes."

He looked at me.

"I saw the catamaran was there," I said, "the wind was blowing, it was going to be too tricky. I said we shouldn't go in. And what is it with the damn plastic snakes?"

"I thought you just asked if we really needed fuel."

I stormed off – well, as far as you can storm off from another human being on a twelve-metre boat. I plonked myself up on the bow, stared at the water, hoping the lapping against the hull would calm me down. I was annoyed alright – annoyed at him, annoyed at the dock hand, annoyed at the gawkers, annoyed at everyone yelling at us. Annoyed, annoyed, annoyed. It was a wonder I wasn't annoyed at myself. Then I thought – damn him. He was right. Now I *was* annoyed at myself. I had never actually said we shouldn't go in. Instead, I had wrapped it in an Irish way of talking, only asking if we really needed fuel. Why? Because he was the captain and it wasn't my decision. I'd hoped he would've understood the real reason behind my question.

I stewed for a few minutes more until I heard Sister Mary Pierre's voice ringing above the tinnitus in my ears.

"Now, girls," she would say to us in class, "it's important that when you grow up and get married you must never let the sun go down on a row."

What a Dominican nun knew about the trials and tribulations of marriage was beyond our eleven-year-old minds, but the saying was so drummed into our heads, it had become part of my fabric. The sun hadn't set yet; there was still time. I went below. Gary was sitting on the sofa, playing on his phone. He wasn't smiling.

"I'm glad your boat is OK," I said.

"Thanks."

"I'm sorry I yelled at you."

He put his phone down. I knew to be quiet.

"I was doing my best," he said, "but I had no chance against the wind. I was fighting with the helm, the engine controls, desperately trying to manoeuvre us out of that mess."

"I was frightened we were going to cause damage," I said.

"I'm glad you didn't hurt yourself. It's just a boat, I have insurance." He saw the look on my face. "But," he hurried on "I appreciate everything you did up there."

Good move.

"They're supposed to scare away the birds."

"Huh?"

"The snakes. You remember Ed? He told me they'd stop the birds from pooping on the deck."

"Do you think it works?"

"No."

"Oh, for God's sake. Can we get rid of them, then?" I asked.

"OK."

"Thank you."

I managed a grimace of a smile, but he still seemed mildly pissed off. Desperate to get the approval of a dead nun, I asked:

"So, are we good?"

"We're good," he said.

Chapter 41
The Double Fix

I knew we were good, but we weren't great. Not as great as we had been, or could be. While I was cooking dinner, I came to understand an important principle. Sister Mary Pierre's mandate for never letting the sun go down on a row was only half the solution: the *First Fix*.

When there is a row, a hurt or a frustration, both parties may have a different way of processing. In my case I always want to fix it right away. I don't function well in a superficial conversation when I still feel the niggles going on underneath.

Others might use the three-day process. They prefer to walk away – perhaps to their friend's house to play video games, or to the pub to have a drink with the lads, or drive to the gym and bench press twice their weight. In Gary's case, there was nowhere to go except down the rabbit hole of his phone.

The first fix will get you back on speaking terms, maybe even a hug, or in relationships, make-up sex. You may think everything's fine, but, if you still have an emotional charge attached to the issue, it's not. If you still feel you haven't had your full say, spit out everything that is specifically bothering you about the row, then things won't be as fabulous as you'd like them to be. Underlying wounds won't heal and unexcised bacteria will fester. It could be weeks, months or even years, gnawing away in the background, until one day there is another fracas, and, in the middle of an innocuous row about loading the dishwasher, up comes a geyser of accusations culminating in "You never liked my mother, anyway."

The *Second Fix* works when both parties are over the hurt of the event. Space or time has helped thaw any resentment and we are ready to talk things out without any self-righteous filters. We can discuss what triggers us and show the other person how to recognise what we need in the moment, whether that be space or engagement. The row isn't truly over until both the first and second fix are wrapped in a bow completing what I call the *Double Fix*.

The next day, I was doing laundry at the Hope Town Inn and Marina. A guy with a beard walked in. He emptied the middle washing machine, which had just stopped spinning.

"Use this one," he said, "it takes a dollar twenty-five in quarters instead of the five-dollar tokens."

"How come?"

"They're waiting on a part to convert it."

"Thanks."

As he loaded up a dryer, we chatted about sailing. He and his wife had been cruising to the Bahamas for quite a few years.

"Any tips for my captain? I asked. "He would love to cross the Northeast Providence Channel down to the Exumas."

"Yeah, it's easy," he said, "you just have to wait for weather."

"His ambition is to get all the way down the chain to George Town. He is thinking of crossing on Saturday."

"That's what we are planning too, but we're going to 'stage' from Lynyard Cay the night before."

"Oh." I wondered if Gary knew to do that too.

"What's the name of your boat?" he asked.

"*Freed Spirit*. Captain's name is Gary."

"Yeah, I've seen it." He reached in his wallet and handed me his "boat card", as they are known. On it was the name of his sailboat, *Seaquel to...*, a couple's picture of himself and his wife, Paula, and information on how to contact them. This was how sailors, cruising up and down the islands, kept in touch. They might forget your name, but they would remember the name of your boat. Gary had a boat card too, with a picture of him on the front and his boat on the back, but I didn't have one with me.

"Tell your captain I can drop over later and give him a few pointers, if he likes."

"That would be great. Thanks. I'm Niamh, by the way."

"Irish, are ye now?

"Yep."

"Joe, Joe Fay."

Joe was good to his word and arrived later that afternoon. I left the pair of them alone to pore over charts, thinking Gary could use some male time and I could use some space. I needed to think. I'd been on-board a month. Hope Town was only a ferry ride from the international airport at Marsh Harbour. This would probably be my last chance to fly back to the mainland. If I crewed the crossing to the Exumas, I would have to continue down the chain until the next major airport. That could be several weeks away. As far as looking for a job was concerned, the further south we went, the more limited internet access would be. Skype interviews would be next to impossible. If I hurried back to the mainland and found work, I could save lots of money so one day I could retire and sail away to a deserted island.

Yet, here I was, already. Young, still fit and healthy, crewing on a sailboat in some of the most wonderful waters I had ever seen. The Exumas were reputed to be the islands of brochure paradise, many only accessible by private yacht. Sailors had told us we could stop anywhere along the chain and enjoy beautiful beaches. If we came to one someone was on, we were to sail further south until we found one for ourselves. I would be living the life many people dream about. Why would I quit that now?

When I returned to the boat, I noticed the snakes were gone and the boys were wrapping up.

"See you Friday night," Joe said to me as he jumped off and disappeared up the dock.

Gary was excited, beaming like a child. "Joe says we can buddy-sail with him and Paula, across the channel. We're going to meet them at Lynyard Cay and maybe have dinner on their boat Friday night."

Although Gary and I had cleared the air the night before, it had only been the First Fix. Today, we'd taken a step back. I was calm and he was relaxed. We sat and chatted through the events. Just like the first crossing of the Gulf Stream, we understood we could experience the same event but had different ways of processing it. He had been afraid for my safety; I had been afraid for the boat's. I agreed to be more direct in my expression; he agreed we would discuss our options before committing to a decision. We agreed to our differences and put it behind us. And so the Double Fix had been achieved.

"Speaking of decisions," I said, "I've decided to stay."

"Ah," he said. "I didn't realise you were still debating that."

"Well, it's too late now for you to get a new volunteer."

"It might take a while, but I could wait here until one flew in."

"But you'd miss crossing with Joe."

"What about your job hunting?"

"It'll have to wait."

Six a.m. came too early on the morning of our departure from Lynyard Cay, especially after a night of hilarity. Joe had regaled us with stories of trips to his ancestral village in Ireland, and the antics he and his ninety-five thousand cousins got up to, growing up in Boston. We were looking forward to more fun along the way. The sun had not yet claimed the dew on deck, so I was cautiously moving about the rigging. When sails were prepped and the bridle taken off the chain, we weighed anchor and followed *Seaquel to...* out into the blue. It was our first time buddy-sailing, and although we were still a hundred per cent responsible for ourselves, it was comforting to see a set of sails other than ours when we lost sight of land. When I looked behind our stern, I saw another seven boats that seemed to have listened to the same weather forecast. We had ourselves a flotilla. Wind on our beam, sun on our faces, it was the epitome of a glory day at sea. The boat heeled ten degrees, we were making almost seven knots. By sunset, we arrived at Royal Harbour, a sheltered spot to rest the night. Only one more day's sailing to reach the Exumas, but what a day that would turn out to be.

Chapter 42
The Coral Garden

Our departure from Royal Harbour began much the same as the day before. Early. The full moon had not quite gone to bed. Gary was still on his first cup of coffee and I hadn't yet brushed my teeth, but we were already underway.

"We have to get through Current Cut at slack water," Joe had told us.

It was about seven nautical miles away. The tide was due to turn at 7.45. If we were late, the body of water that squeezed through the narrows between Eleuthera and Current Island would come at us at three to four knots. Steering through it would be anything from difficult to downright hairy.

"*Freed Spirit, Freed Spirit, Seaquel to...* on channel sixteen."

"*Seaquel to...*, this is *Freed Spirit.*"

"Switch channel zero eight."

"Switching."

"Hi Gary," Joe said, after we re-joined him on channel eight. "As we approach the cut, I'm going to slow down and take a look. You guys hang back and give me room to go through."

"Roger that."

"As soon as you get past the rocks make a hard turn to starboard."

"Will do, Joe."

"It's a hard right, Gary."

"Roger."

"Let's stand by on eight."

"*Freed Spirit* standing by."

Gary pulled back on the throttle. We hung back like Joe suggested, slightly off to one side. At first, it looked like Joe was disappearing into the mangroves. We couldn't see the opening, such was the narrowness of the cut. When we lined up behind him we got our first view. Joe was already through and making a ninety-degree turn. The water, however, looked anything but slack. Tide tables had been misjudged and the breeze was picking up. We were still under sail, but with the engine also running.

"Here we go," said Gary, as he increased power from idle to 2,700 rpm. We were about three-quarters way through when Joe broke in.

"Turn to starboard, Gary, hard right."

A row of rocks pierced the water on our starboard side.

"We're too close to the rocks," Gary replied.

"Turn now, Gary, turn," Joe insisted. "You're getting set."

The current had indeed got a hold of us and we were being pushed south, past the turn. On the surface it looked like we had a wide body of water in which to turn, but underneath, the channel, with enough depth to carry us, was no more than two or three widths of the boat.

"Point your bow at the rocks, Gary, point at the rocks."

Gary couldn't answer. He needed both hands to fight the wheel. The wind was catching the sails and the current was commanding the rudder. I pointed in the direction Joe wanted us to go.

"I know," said Gary, his knuckles white. The only way to get control was to increase speed. Trusting Joe, and not his visual instincts, Gary pushed the throttle forward. We were heading straight for the rocks. With one hand over my mouth and the other holding tight to the railing, I braced. Just before we hit, he swung the wheel, making a sharp ninety degree turn. The jagged boulders whizzed past, a metre or so from our starboard side. It seemed to happen in slow motion, but was over in a flash. We motored on, out of the narrows and into deeper water.

Joe's voice came over the radio. "Good job, Gary."

It was a couple of moments before Gary got his voice back, and when he did, we both just laughed. I could see the tee-shirts we would proudly wear: *We survived Current Cut!*

With the stress behind us, we relaxed, chatted and listened to John Denver as we sailed along. "Calypso" was the perfect song of the sea. The melody waltzed with the sway of the boat. The waves fell to ripples and the blue water turned azure. It was late morning, the sun was high, and all was good with the world. Until ...

"*Freed Spirit, Freed Spirit, Seaquel to...*"

"Uh-oh," said Gary, giving me half a grin.

"Go ahead *Seaquel to...*"

"We're coming to an area with some coral heads, Gary. Can you see the one off our port stern?"

"Not yet."

"No worries, you'll see it when you get up close. Just follow us."

"Roger."

It was indeed easy to spot. A large dark patch against the azure water. We both took out our cameras.

"*Freed Spirit*, there's another one on our starboard."

Gary acknowledged.

"So pretty, isn't it?" he said to me.

It was indeed. How I wish we could have dropped anchor in the sand and snorkelled around it.

At first we followed Joe's line, but as the coral heads grew more plentiful, and the distance between us too great, it became impossible to trace his path. We were on our own. As beautiful and as fragile as these coral heads were, they had the potential of putting a hole in a fibreglass hull, especially one like ours, moving at six knots.

"There's another one," I said.

"See it." Gary answered, and pushed the autopilot button twice, making a twenty-degree correction to avoid it.

"Another at eleven o'clock," I said.

"Got it."

They were popping up more frequently, and Gary was correcting left and right.

"Would you like me to go on deck and keep an eye out?" I asked him.

"Probably not a bad idea."

"Just so we are agreed, when you see me pointing it will be the course to travel. I won't be pointing at the coral, OK?"

"Got it," said Gary.

When I got up on deck I saw several all at once. I placed myself in front of the mast so as not to block his view. We needed to avoid the one off our bow. We couldn't turn right because there were two more blocking our route. The one off our port was at mid ships so I raised my arm and pointed to port. Nothing happened. We were still heading for the one off our bow. I looked back to check. Gary had made his correction but there was a lag before the boat responded. I waved my arm to port again, the boat started to slowly turn. We just missed the one in front. The next one came up fast. I gave Gary the signal to slow. He threw the boat in reverse for a second, which gave us time to manoeuvre. I pointed to starboard and this time the boat moved almost immediately. He had taken it off auto-pilot and because he was manually steering the lag time was greatly reduced. It showed me the time I would need between coral heads. The next three were all to our port but I reckoned we would clear them by one or two metres. I gave Gary a signal to keep straight. Another one loomed up on starboard and I pointed to port. The radio was eerily quiet. Joe was far ahead of us by now, but he, too, was weaving as much as us. The height of the sun helped point the corals out, but it was also beating down on my face. I had come up without my hat. They were coming steadily faster; I didn't have time to run back.

Choosing a route through them was like playing chess; I had to think three or four moves ahead. If not, we risked finding ourselves completely boxed in. The next one we approached was right on our bow, but I gave Gary the signal to go straight. I could feel him slowing down, but I insisted he kept going. I could tell he was watching them as well as me. I needed him to just watch me. He could see those in the distance but the closer in we got, they disappeared from his view. I took a second to look back at him and mimed:

Watch me, not the water. If this was going to work, he had to trust my route and I had to trust his reactions.

A colossal head loomed in front of us. We were blocked on either side. I needed to get us far enough forward to be able to pivot at the last minute. I knew he could do it; so too could the boat. Hadn't I just seen it happen at Current Cut? When the port coral was behind my shoulders I furiously waved my arm to the left. We hadn't rehearsed this detail of signals, but I hoped he could tell the difference between *turn left* and *turn this bleeping boat left NOW*. He made the turn. They were coming fast now, like black spots on an otherwise white Dalmatian. They didn't look pretty any more, just obstacles of nature we had to navigate. The breeze was picking up and coming from behind. To avoid the boom swinging violently across the boat, risking damage to the rigging, I guided us to port as often as I could. If only we'd dropped our sails before we'd entered this lion's den. I felt the deck vibrate beneath my feet. Gary had turned the engine back on. We would certainly need the help.

"*Freed Spirit, Seaquel to...*"

Click was all Joe got from our radio.

"We haven't seen one for five minutes now, I think we are out the other side." Joe's boat was far in the distance, so we still had at least a mile to go.

For ninety scorching minutes I determined each twist and turn, and for ninety minutes, Gary reacted. Each time I pointed left or right, the boat would move accordingly. Together, we manoeuvred our way through this hazardous beauty. I became the conductor and Gary, first violin. When we were out the other side, I went astern and sat down by his side. We smiled, but didn't speak. After an hour and a half of non-verbal communication, words were hardly necessary. What we knew in that moment was that a bond had been forged. We were more than captain and crew; we had become a team.

The Exumas were as magnificent as everyone said they would be. Island after island, cay after cay, the golden beaches were addictive. Each morning we'd pull anchor and say a sad goodbye to our deserted island, only to moor at an even more beautiful one later that day. Some nights we would dine with Joe and Paula. On others we ate by ourselves, talking the night away. Our voyage through the Coral Garden, as I'd nicknamed the minefield, had brought us close together. Our mutual respect had deepened, our friendship, expanded. The boat seemed to have grown larger, more spacious. As we moved from galley to saloon, or cockpit to deck, I never felt he was in my way, nor did he feel I was in his. Nautically, we danced. Somewhere in those Exuma days, a spark ignited between us, and we kissed the flame. Gently, at first, nothing more than a sweet connection. It was tentative, as if we'd begun to date, although we kept this discovery to ourselves.

Chapter 43
Pigs Might Swim

Pigs may not fly but they sure can swim. Joe and Paula had been showing us the sights, as we cruised south. Big Majors, a hilly island and home to a sounder of swine, was a must-see. We approached the beach by dinghy. Hungry boars and sows swam piggy-style out to greet us. Unlike a dog, catching a carrot by mouth was not in their DNA. If we didn't feed them by hand, their trotters would clamber up the pontoons. Fearful for our flotation, we beached the tender and got out. They swam after us, back to shore. What they craved was water, fresh water, so we gave them some of ours. People arrived. These swimming pigs were famous, bringing fast boats filled with tourists. On nearby Staniel Cay, or as far away as Nassau, you could buy their likeness on a tee-shirt, a mug, an apron or a cap.

We saw them, photographed them, and had our fill, so we planned to leave early the next morning. Watching Joe pull up his anchor rode by hand, I was glad we had a windlass motor to do the job. Ours wasn't made of rope like his, but of three-eighths-inch chain weighing one and half kilos per metre. As soon as his anchor was aboard, Paula turned the boat out to sea. On *Freed Spirit*'s bow, I pushed the button. Instead of the sounds of a motor turning and the clanking of the incoming chain, all I heard was a click. I tried again, click, click. Dead. The motor was dead. Or the breaker was dead. Or the solenoid was dead. Or the gear box was devoid of oil, and therefore, dead. Whatever it was, it meant another night with the piggies. Or maybe seven.

Gary had a new breaker switch flown into Staniel Cay, and within a week we were underway again. Ten miles south, at Little Bay, we caught up with Paula and Joe. Their boat was among several anchored in the cove. Word went out on the VHF to prepare for captain's hour ashore. Thirty sailors, all with stories, mingled on the beach as the sun went down. Some were heading south; others were on their way back north. Most were married couples, living out their retirement dreams. We sipped wine and nibbled on the hors d'oeuvres each boat had brought. Around the campfire, a Canadian with a guitar roused us into song. Logs crackled and voices soared. Old friends hugged and tales were told. The firelight warmed my heart. There was nowhere else I wanted to be and nothing else I wanted to do. It made me happy and, at the same time, sad. These sailors were living the life I wanted, a life I almost had. As the impromptu party broke up, the ubiquitous boat cards were exchanged. Compared to those with photos of smiling couples, Gary's boat card confirmed he was a solo sailor and we were just captain and crew. Despite the hints of a fledgling romance, I understood what was real. It was his boat, his life, and I was on borrowed time.

The following evening, we brought our cushions up on the bow and toasted the sunset.

"What's up?" he asked.

"Just thinking about last night on the beach."

"Wasn't it fun?"

"Yes," I said. "Did you notice almost everyone was a couple?"

He was quiet a moment.

"What do you think is going to happen when this trip is over?" he asked.

"How do you mean?"

"What are your expectations?"

I couldn't see his eyes behind his sunglasses.

"You know I care about you," he said, "but I'm not looking for a relationship."

"I know."

"After a long-term marriage and a few years with a girlfriend, I just want the freedom to sail, to travel, to meet new people, to live the way I want to live."

"I know. I'm happy for you."

"I'm just not in a place to offer you what I think you want."

A fish emerged from the water and flew a metre above the surface. We both watched it as it returned below.

"Don't worry," I said. "I understand this is a summer fling."

He gave a conflicted smile.

"But," I said, "here's what I know for sure: I love living on the water, I love sharing the experience with someone special, this is the life I want. Maybe not now, or in the near future, but I *will* have this life."

"I believe you," he said.

Chapter 44
Anchored

"I've been thinking," Gary announced one morning, after we'd had a dingdong over nothing. He may have said I had too many rules and my personality was rigid. I may have called him an asshole.

"Uh-huh?" I said, wondering what was coming.

He said, "I think we have been brought together for a reason—"

"What, to hold up a mirror to each other?"

It was out of my mouth before I realised I had cut him off. He paused.

"Maybe so," he said.

I felt sure that wasn't what he had intended to say, but I couldn't bring back the moment.

I went up top to hang out some wash cloths on the lifelines. As my self-amused brain is wont to do, I started talking to the cloths.

"Oh, so you want to be next to the yellow one," I said. I had put a blue cloth on the bottom rail but then figured it might get lonely.

"You realise you say that kind of thing out loud?" Gary said.

"Jesus!" I yelped. "Don't sneak up on me like that!"

"There's only two of us on the boat, who did you think it was?"

Adrenaline flooded my blood and tingled down the back of my knees as it always did anytime I got a fright.

"You startle easily."

"So?"

"You're a delightful kook."

"I thought you liked my cooking?"

"Never mind." He laughed. "You and your washcloths ready?" He started the engine.

"Ready, captain." I put the last peg on the newly located blue one, and went up on the bow. I opened the door to my "office" – which others might call the lid of the anchor well – and pushed the button on the windlass. *Click.* I must have forgotten to turn on the newly installed breaker in the cockpit first. I signalled Gary, asking him to do it.

"It's on," he mouthed.

I pushed a second time. *Click.* Not again. Time to go back and tell him that something other than the breaker was also broken on the windlass.

"Now, we're screwed," said Gary.

I'd never heard him swear before.

"No we're not," I said. "Joe's not the only one who eats spinach, you know."

Back in my "office", I put on my gloves and braced my feet against the bulkhead. I had thirty-metres of chain in the water and a twenty-kilo anchor bedded in the sand. I signalled Gary to drive slowly forward and began hauling her in by hand, the way I'd seen Joe do it. It was going well. I put my shoulders, back and arms into a rhythmic movement, just like being on a rowing machine at the gym. With twenty metres of chain on deck, I was almost done. We were above the anchor. Then the wind picked up, pushing the boat back. My arms were stretched; the chain was taut. I needed Gary to increase speed to give me some slack, but I couldn't raise a hand to let him know. I was stuck, just hanging on. I flexed my knees and got a little purchase, but a gust caught the boat and the safest thing I could do was to let go. Perhaps I'd watched too many hospital dramas, but I stuck my hands in the air and shouted "Clear!" The chain whipped over the deck with the clatter of a freight train as it went. All twenty metres went plummeting into the water and I was back where I started.

A hundred yards away, Joe heard and saw it all. *I can do this,* I thought, and signalled Gary to go again. I started to haul, to get in a rhythm. The wind wasn't as strong and the first fifteen metres came in quickly. I had twenty in, then twenty-five. I could feel a new resistance as we pulled taut over the anchor head. I held on. If Gary kept driving slowly forward, then reversed, it would break free from the sand and I could pull her in.

I'm not sure if it was another gust, or if Gary held too long in neutral, but, my arms were stretched to the max, and the chain creaked with strain. I couldn't hold on. I threw my hands in the air and this time shouted more than "Clear!" Twice I had pulled most of her in; twice I had let it all out again. I signalled to go again.

Gary popped his grim-faced head from under the Bimini and shouted:

"I think I see Joe coming to help."

"I can do it."

My mistake was now obvious, even to me. I hadn't locked in my gains. Out of the corner of my eye, I saw Joe lower his dinghy.

"Let's go again," I yelled above the breeze.

"Should we not just wait?"

"We've got this."

I felt we needed to show we could take care of ourselves, that I could do as much as any guy. Gary shrugged, but put the throttle in forward. I started hauling. This time I wrapped the regained chain around the aft bow cleat. I pulled in three more metres and wrapped it around the forward cleat. I then tightened the slack between the two and re-secured the aft. The excess three metres, I now pushed into the well. There! I had three in and no matter what happened it was staying on-board the boat. With the chain tied off, I could use hand signals to keep Gary up to speed. I repeated the exercise on the next three metres, and the next, and the three after that. Joe's dinghy was on its way. I saw the fifteen-metre marker on the chain come aboard. I cleated it off just before the boat rocked. Joe had climbed aboard. I pulled in another five before he reached the bow.

"OK, Niamh, let me help."

I had only ten metres to go. I knew I had it now.

"Come on, you need a break."

Reluctantly, I stood aside and watched him pull in the rest. The anchor rolled up sweetly and we were floating free.

"Thanks, Joe," I said, "appreciate you coming over."

"You had it," he said, and patted me on the back.

He drove back to his boat, pulled up his dinghy, and both boats got underway.

"You're amazing," Gary said, when I came back into the cockpit.

I went below to stew. I was mad I didn't get to prove that I could do it, that I could have finished the job like Joe, or any other able-bodied seaman. But why was that so important to me? What did I feel I needed to prove? I thought about it, tried to figure it out. A hint of understanding emerged. For years, I'd been showing the world my masculine side, believing that the men in my life – my dad, my brothers, my boyfriends, my husband, my employers – would respect me more if I could prove I was as useful as one of the guys. What was that about? I dug deep, trying to answer a fundamental question. Why was I the way I was?

When I was honest with myself I realised it all came back to my body image. I saw myself as an overweight, big-boned Viking woman. I felt I didn't have the framework to show off a fitted skirt, or slim enough calves to look elegant in high heels, or the sort of delicate hands that make jewellery look dainty. I had never turned a man's head with my looks. So there was little point in caring about my appearance. I chose comfort over fashion. I hated shopping for clothes because the mirrors spat back an image I didn't want to see. The more that depressed me, the more I overate, overdrank, overcompensated. If I could never be that petite female, then I'd better be as strong, as capable and as competent as any man.

So I'd supressed all my feminine energy, believing that without the looks the rest of the traits would seem weak. Tomorrow, I would have another chance to show my capabilities, but for now, I needed to embrace my femininity.

Ten minutes later, I came back up to the cockpit wearing a dress and carrying my iPod. Gary smiled, but didn't say a word. I turned the music up high and danced like a *natural woman*.

Chapter 45
Soul Gazing

Over the next few weeks, I lowered and raised the anchor by hand. Some days I managed, some days I asked for help, but never again did the freight train leave the station. As we made our way down the Exuma chain, we found a better way to communicate. We fine-tuned our hand signals and made up new ones. If we needed words, we spoke them; if we didn't, we just laughed.

He showed me how to plot a course, and I taught him what I knew about tides. He started helping wash the dishes, I relieved him more on the helm. Phone service was spotty but when his family called, I would listen to my iPod, to give him privacy in the twelve-metre space. We had no TV, no radio, and rarely had Wi-Fi. After dinner, we would chat for hours and never seemed to get bored. We discussed everything from sailing to scuba diving, from travel to relationships, and from childhood stories to spiritual psychology. I loved hearing his thoughts on life, and he liked listening to what was left of my *bróg*. Nothing was off limits.

One day, I even told him about the tradesman who had molested me as a child. His face fell.

"It's OK," I said. "I got over it a long time ago."

"How?"

"How what?

"How did you get over it?"

"I just did. It happened. It's in the past. I moved on."

"Did you ever tell your parents?"

"Not then. I was afraid I would be in trouble."

"What?"

"Maybe I was partly to blame."

"You were a *child*!"

"Yes, the first few times, but not when he came back to build the second house. I was thirteen, almost fourteen."

"You were still a CHILD!"

I'd never seen Gary so angry. I was almost sorry I'd told him.

"Did you ever talk to anyone about it?"

"Like a shrink?"

"A professional trained to deal with childhood issues."

"In Ireland we didn't run to a therapist every time we broke a nail, you know."

"You didn't *break a nail*."

"Yeah, well, I'd 'forgotten' all about it until I moved to America."

"What reminded you?"

"The subject seemed prevalent on some of the talk shows."

"What did you think then?"

"I wanted to tell my mam, but I was afraid of hurting her feelings. I mean what could she do about it, years later? Nothing. Except maybe feel bad. I didn't want her to feel I was criticising her, that she and dad should have known."

"We're not responsible for other people's feelings, just our own," he said.

"I know. But ..."

"Did you tell her?"

"I wrote her a long letter and asked her to call me as soon as she read it."

"And?"

"She told me she was sorry that happened to me."

"That was it, that's all she said?"

I twirled my glass of wine, remembering that conversation, or lack of it. I'd written the letter to help me sort out what I wanted to say, and sent it to

her so she could absorb it before we talked. Phone-calls home had a flat rate
for the first three minutes only. I didn't want to waste the time like we
usually did – talking about how much the call cost and whether it was
raining.

"Did you get the letter?" I'd asked her.

"Yes, love."

After the longest pause she said:

"I'm so sorry that happened to you."

I don't think either of us knew what to say after that. I'd just wanted her
to know, and now she did. It was probably the first time we didn't use up
the whole three minutes. In all the years I'd been home to visit her since
then, neither of us had ever brought it up again.

"So, that was that," I said to Gary, draining my glass. "Sure, didn't I turn
out OK in the end?"

He wasn't ready for me to lighten the mood.

"When did you learn to disconnect from your emotions?" he asked.

I sighed.

"Not everything can be solved by talking about your feelings, you know,
sometimes you just have to duck."

"Huh?"

"Duck! If I'm threatened physically I'm not going to hang around trying
to negotiate with my attacker, I ..."

I was no longer on the boat, but standing in our kitchen, aged sixteen,
listening to my dad on the phone. Along with about twenty other fifth-year
classmates, I'd been invited to attend a school retreat at the recently
established Glencree Peace and Reconciliation Centre in Wicklow. The
subject was Interpersonal Relations, and if I remember correctly included
elements of justice and violence as well as verbal and non-verbal
communication. I'd been looking forward to it. If nothing else, four or five
days away from the tension in the house would be a relief, but my dad
thought the whole premise was poppycock. Miss Cullen, our civics teacher,
had phoned to explain to my parents how I might benefit from attending.

"If someone comes at my daughter, swinging a punch," my dad had said,
"I don't want her to stand there discussing her feelings and telling her

attacker how he should get in touch with his. I want my daughter to know how to duck!"

Apparently, I'd been "ducking" every emotional crisis since then. Although my dad had signed the permission slip in the end, and I'd spent a few days listening and talking in a "safe environment", learning how my interactions could impact another human, both positively and negatively, I had put it all aside when I got back home. I didn't want to be ridiculed for talking "poppycock" at the dinner table. Instead, I continued to just "get on" with things because no matter what happened to me, there were always people worse off.

What I hadn't realised until these types of conversations with Gary was that I had never questioned my feelings. I recognised them, I knew what they were, but I never really asked myself why I was feeling a certain way, never asked what triggered my various emotions.

"So, how d'you like them apples, Dr. Freud?" I said, when I relayed this revelation to Gary.

"I'm not a psychiatrist," he said, refusing to let me deflect, "but you've said you struggled with your weight your whole life."

"Yeah?"

"Did it ever occur to you that that could be related to your being molested as a child?"

"Not every fat person has been sexually abused," I contested.

"I hear you, but people of normal weight rarely eat for comfort either. How about the times you lost weight? Why did you put it back on?"

"I dunno. I like food, I guess."

His look told me he wasn't taking that for an answer.

"I did every diet imaginable but I never seemed to get to my goal weight."

"Why? What happened when you got close?"

I had to think about that. "People started to compliment me."

"And?"

"And it felt weird. I wasn't used to people looking at my body. I felt kind of … naked. Exposed."

He sort of smiled, and I sort of got it. Wow! I'd never put the pieces together before. What an epiphany. I'd not only used food and alcohol to comfort me when I was lonesome, unhappy, or depressed, but also as a defence mechanism. If I was fat no one would look at me twice. I wouldn't attract unwanted attention. I could supress my shame and hide behind my skin.

The conversation had been tough, but I realised it was a gift. While I thought I had come to terms with being molested as a young child and had made a concerted effort not to allow it to define me, or fall into a state of victimhood, I realised I'd buried my emotions about what had happened and that somewhere in the recesses of my mind I'd been stuck in a story of guilt. All these years my brain had conditioned a belief that I'd been "asking for it", that it was my fault. Gary's anger somehow highlighted how ridiculous that was.

It was time to make a shift. Time to start loving the innocent child within me, forgiving the teenager who'd blamed herself, and absolving the younger adult who'd sublimated who she was so that she could find someone to want to marry her, to give her children of her own to love and protect.

But the task was daunting. How do you forgive yourself? Where do you start? Gary explained the process he had learned to use in his own life.

"I start with looking at my 'story'. We all have our stories," he told me. "Parts of them are true but much of the stories we tell ourselves are false. Ask yourself what part is true, if any. Once you've determined what's false you can forgive yourself for believing it to have been true. Then determine what other truths existed, or do exist, and reinforce those."

Over the weeks that followed, I allowed this process to percolate. I ruminated. I journaled. As I wrote and wrote, answers emerged. It became clear to me that the false part of my story was believing that, as a young teenager, I was responsible. The truth is, I was still a child. Yes, I was looking for attention and craved physical affection. My mother loved me in her own way, but most of the hugs I received as a child came from my father, and he was absent much of the time. The truth is, the tradesman had set the stage when he pushed his tongue into my eight-year-old mouth and forced me to fondle his penis, a violation I had accepted as OK, and one I returned to when hormones flooded my body. The truth is, I was only thirteen, and no matter how mature I thought I was, I was not an adult. The truth is, a normal, well-adjusted older man would have sent me on my way, or told me to find a boyfriend my own age, or even told my parents. The truth is, he was a predator who molested me.

As I dissected my story, cast out the falsehoods and accepted the truth, a sliver of space opened, just wide enough to allow the first feelings of forgiveness in. Gary and I talked about how I could translate those feelings into positive statements that would eventually make their way into my psyche and take up residence as my new reality.

I forgive myself for accepting the falsehoods as true.

I forgive myself for judging myself as responsible; the truth is, I was a child.

I forgive myself for believing that what happened to me didn't require therapeutic help.

Compared to the horrors others have suffered at the hands of abusers, I had believed what happened to me was inconsequential. I wasn't raped, beaten, or murdered. But the truth was, while it may not have ranked high on the scale of one to ten in another person's experience, it was a ten in *my* life and deserved my attention.

As I made these statements, adding new truths as I uncovered them over time, I also forgave myself for ignoring my health by overeating and overdrinking. I made a new promise. I would take on another diet, a final one, a lasting one. I would take care of myself, for me, and for the rest of my life.

Although it would take a couple of years for others to notice the overall effect, these acts of self-forgiveness and self-love reached deep into my subconscious and the first kilo of protective fat I'd been carrying for so many years melted away.

During these evening conversations Gary also showed me how to *soul gaze*, to look directly into each other's eyes and see beyond the superficial, to observe the beauty we all possess and to journey "around the heart", to perceive the loving essence of each individual and to understand, in our depths, that we are all essentially the same. It harmonised our energy and we connected on a level I'd never experienced with another soul. It was deep, it was personal, the discoveries profound.

On one particular evening, we figured we were talked out. We knew almost as much about each other as we were ever going to know.

"What about a game?" he said.

"Like what?"

"Cards? Can you play poker?" he asked.

"Been a while, but yes."

"How about strip poker?"

"Might be a short game." All I had on was a tee-shirt, shorts and underwear.

"How about we each go to our quarters and get dressed as we wish before we start?" he said.

"OK," I said, "but we only get ninety seconds."

"Agreed. I'm setting the timer. Go."

Chuckling, I ran all two steps into the quarter berth and closed the door. First, I took off my tee-shirt and shorts and put on extra sets of underwear, then two tee-shirts, a pair of leggings, and socks.

"Sixty seconds," he yelled.

I couldn't stop giggling. With hardly enough room to turn around I got my sweater and fleece out of my dry box and put them on.

"Are you ready?" he called out.

"Hey, it's not time yet." I couldn't stop laughing as I crammed as many pieces of clothing onto my now overwarm body.

"Ten seconds."

"Coming."

I donned my woolly hat, a jacket and scarf, and for good measure, sunglasses. I was so bulked out I barely fit through the narrow door.

"What took you so long?" he said.

I started laughing so hard I almost wet my pants. Sitting at the table, ready to play strip poker, was Captain Gary. All he was wearing was a baseball cap!

I won the first game, and he took off his hat. Unfortunately, I also won the second. The more I won the more Gary laughed. It was twenty-six degrees outside, and probably thirty-three inside the cabin. Sweat rolled down my temples. Eventually, I got smart and tried to lose.

"By the way," said Gary, when I lost my first hand, "I get to dictate which piece of clothing you remove."

"What? That's not fair."

"Sure it is, take off your bra."

"Which one?" I was wearing two.

As the game progressed I had to struggle out of undergarments while leaving sweaters and leggings in place. Not wanting to provoke a medical emergency, we eventually had to call it quits. Never mind a royal, Gary worried about my hyper-thermic flush. I never played cards with him again.

Chapter 46
Can't Say Goodbye

We came to an enchanting island called Lee Stocking, so beautiful we stayed two nights. In the morning, we climbed the short hill behind the beach to look back down on the peaceful bay, our new and temporary home. The turquoise water was so clear, it looked as if the sailboats were suspended in mid-air. The scene was too inviting to stay standing in the heat. We skipped and jogged back down the hill and swam out to the boat. Sunlight illuminated tiny crabs on the sandy floor, four metres below. When we reached the stern, we slowed and rolled face up. The water was glass calm. I was overwhelmed with the desire to make snow angels on its surface. I could tell Gary was happy, too. He flipped upright, making jumping jacks right in front of the name painted on the boat. That's when I got out. I dried my hands and grabbed my camera. I leaped into the dinghy, pulled the engine to life, and drove a suitable distance.

"Where are you going?" he called out.

"Do that again." I called back.

Without further question, he dropped vertically beneath the water. I swung the dinghy around, parallel to the boat, and lined up my shot. As he exploded through the surface, he flung his arms high and wide, and a beaming smile lit up his face. The image in my lens would be forever captured in my mind. Sun-sparkled water droplets were caught in mid-air, and over his shoulder were the words that depicted his life and boat: *Freed Spirit*. In that crystallised moment, I knew I didn't want to say goodbye, not to him, not to the boat. Right then, I decided I would not fly out when we reached George Town, our most southerly intended port. He would still need help to bring the boat back to the States before Hurricane Season started in June. We had such a rhythm now, I couldn't imagine him starting again with a new volunteer.

"Cheers!"

We toasted that magical day at sunset, sitting on the bow. Orange and red clouds rumpled the fading sky. The air was still, and my heart was grateful. I'd learned so much, experienced so much, more than I could have hoped. Spending this time with Gary had helped me relax, put life in perspective. I was becoming less rigid, less critical, less judgemental, more tolerant, more patient, more easy-going.

I took a sip of my wine, then said: "You make me a better me."

He smiled and touched his heart. "That's beautiful," he said, gazing out to sea. "I've learned so much from you too."

I smiled. We sat in silence awhile, watching the night draw in.

After dinner, he offered to wash the dishes. I was happy to sit and read.

Crash!

I jumped and screeched at the same time. The boat had lurched and the lid of the fridge had slammed down on the counter.

"Man, but you have a hell of a startle reflex," he said, laughing.

"It's not funny."

"It kind of is. So, what do you think that's about?"

"Why does everything have to be about something?"

I went back to reading my book. I tried a couple of paragraphs but, now that he had shown me how to open the door to my feelings, his question had needled me. Why *did* I startle so easily? It seemed to me it was only something that had developed in the last few years. I would jump at the sound of a horn, the unexpected ring of a phone, the sudden appearance of someone behind me or any kind of loud bang at all. Why? Intellectually, I knew jumping at sudden sounds must have something to do with anxiety, but what was I anxious about? Gary had somehow provoked me into wanting to understand myself more and more. So why did I jump at noises?

An image I'd once seen on TV flashed in my mind. A big close-up of a child's face. Off camera there was a loud bang. Instantly, the young girl's eyes blinked. Voices shouted, her face contorted. It was a commercial for a marriage counsellor. Could it be? Could my startle reflex be a product of my childhood, from those days my parents were breaking up? I used to push away my feelings, always trying to stay strong, but, in truth, I was living in a permanent state of anxiety, wondering what the next slamming door would bring. Could that be it? Or was it caused by the shock of waking up one night in the flat I shared with a room-mate and seeing a strange man sitting on my bed, a metal briefcase by his feet. He had apparently wandered out of a nearby mental health facility and somehow found his way up onto the third floor of our building. And if it was, could the simple act of identifying the source stop the involuntary reaction? I'm not sure. I still get shivers wondering about what was in the case.

"I forgot to tell you," Gary said, interrupting my ponderings, "I got an exciting text from my buddy, Lon."

"Oh yeah?"

"Yeah, he and his friend are coming to sail with me, they'll meet the boat in George Town."

"Oh..."

"What?"

"Nothing, that's great. Good for you."

Another reason why old-fashioned paperbacks make great reading – it's hard to hide your face behind a Kindle.

"What's the matter?"

"Nothing, I didn't know you had someone lined up already."

"Well, I'd mentioned it to him ages ago, but only just heard back."

"So how long have I got?"

"For what?"

"Before I need to leave the boat?"

"I think they arrive on the third."

So, that was that. I had fifteen days until this fairy-tale was over. At least it would give me two weeks to book a flight.

We stopped at Emerald Bay the following day, to take on diesel and water. It was our first time docking since the catastrophe in the Abacos. I threw my spring line to the dock hand, then the bow, and Gary threw the stern. It was unrefined but an enormous improvement overall. Joe followed us in, with Paula standing on their bow. They passed the dock and made a 180-degree turn. Joe was coming slowly, head into the wind. By the time his bow lined up with the dock, he was almost at a stop. As calm as you like, Paula leaned over the lifelines and looped her line on the cleat on the dock. Joe stepped off the boat and made the stern line fast.

"So that's how it's done," I said to Paula. Our bows were nose to nose.

"I told Joe when we started cruising I didn't mind going on deck, but there would be no hurrying and certainly no scurrying."

I laughed. They'd made it look so easy.

"Wind, tide and current," said Joe. "That's all you've got to know."

Twenty miles later, we arrived into Elizabeth Harbour, a naturally protected body of water between Great Exuma and a barrier island one mile to the west. I'd never seen quite so many boats. At least five hundred were anchored, wherever they'd found a space. Gary looked for one for us. His skill in manoeuvring the boat in such tight quarters, had grown exponentially. Our hand signals were clear, and with a minimum of fuss we dropped the hook. Once we were sure the anchor was set, he turned off the engine and I completed the log. Then we sat there, dazed. This was it. This was the spot for which we had reserved the champagne. Six hundred and fifty nautical miles sailed from when we'd first left Florida. We'd arrived at the southernmost point Gary had hoped to make, the mecca of yachting for south-eastern cruisers, the prized destination: George Town, Bahamas. The sense of anti-climax was overwhelming and surprising.

Chapter 47
Got It Bad

"What's the matter?" Gary asked when he came back from dropping the trash ashore. He could see I'd been crying. We'd been a day or two in George Town. Our newfound friends and mentors, Joe and Paula, had already turned around and headed north. My time aboard was almost up. I was supposed to be researching flights.

"He found me!"

"Who?"

"Ivan!"

"Who's Ivan?

"The boy from Bolivia."

"You never mentioned him before."

I told Gary the story of Ivan and how the sponsorship charity had refused to give me his personal contact details after he turned eighteen.

"How did he find you?"

"Facebook!"

"Wow. So what's he been doing?"

"You're not going to believe this. After school he went to study in Cuba, lived there for nine years and became a doctor!"

"You're kidding!"

"Now he is back home in Bolivia practising medicine in his home town of Oruro."

"That's an incredible story," said Gary.

"I'm so proud of him," I said, unable to stop the tears.

"And you should be so proud of yourself," Gary said. "Look what an impact you made on his life, on the lives of those he heals."

"I just sent some money and wrote to him."

"No," Gary said, "you opened a door for him and showed him he mattered. You're an amazing woman."

I snuggled under his offered arm and embraced the compliment. I did feel proud – proud I had made the commitment and proud I had seen it through. Something I had started *and* finished. I was also overjoyed to communicate with Ivan again and vowed I would find a way to meet him someday.

I stood up to wash my face. "By the way," I called out from the bathroom, "I got so caught up with Ivan, I haven't found a flight yet."

"Perhaps we could find you a boat?"

"How do you mean?" I said, coming back into the salon.

"There's plenty of them here, I'm sure we could find you one for a week."

"Why a week?"

"Just while my friends are here," he said.

"What? They're only staying a week?" I couldn't hide my surprise.

"Yeah, they leave on the tenth."

"I thought they were coming to sail you back to Florida."

"Why would you think that?"

Had this been a misunderstanding, or had he deliberately misled me? For two people who could gaze at the depths of each other's souls you'd think we could figure out a couple of words in English. Time to get this straight.

"So, what are you saying? You only want me off the boat for a week so you can have a 'guys' trip' with your friends?"

"I guess."

"You'd like me to hang out in George Town and come back on-board after they leave?"

"It's up to you. I thought you were still job hunting, but if you want to make the passage back to Florida, it's OK with me."

I didn't say another word. My brain was too busy rattling.

In the end, he found me somewhere ashore, housesitting for an estate agent. While he and his buddies sailed to Staniel Cay and back, I lived in a house with doors. And toilets you could flush. And running water that was hot, and a TV with movies to watch. An easier life on land, a life I could have back. Yet, every day on Facebook, I scrolled his page hoping to see where he was. I viewed the photos he shared, and the new places he visited without me. I watched the local weather and studied the marine forecasts. I checked the winds and tides to make sure he was safe. I played the same song by Adele, over and over again. And when I found myself counting the days, I knew I had it bad.

In a million years, I would never have picked Gary out of a line-up. He was not at all my type and we were years apart in age. My first boyfriend had been twenty-six years older than me; my next, eighteen. I'd scoffed at those who said it was because my father was absent so much of the time. I'd insisted I was just attracted to older, more mature men. It wasn't until after my father died and I was living with the next boyfriend, who was six months younger than me, I wondered if maybe they'd had a point. Looking back on it now, I also ask myself if the encounter with the paedophile could have been an influence? I don't know.

Regardless, I knew my attraction to Gary had nothing to do with his age. I felt at home with him, somehow more myself. It was my first true experience of what an adult and healthy relationship should feel like. However, he'd come out of a long-term marriage in search of freedom and adventure. He wanted room to breathe, not another relationship. Of that he'd been quite clear. I didn't know what it was we shared, and I knew it had no future. There was something though, some connection, some sort of energy that was unexplained. I knew it would have to end, but hopefully not just yet.

On the seventh day of that long week, I saw him sitting on a picnic bench near the Exuma market, waiting for me. He didn't see my approach.

"Hey, how are you?" I said, tapping him on the shoulder.

"Great!" he said, giving me a peck on the cheek.

"Did your friends have fun?"

"Oh, they loved it."

"I bet."

"How did you get on?" he asked.

I kept it light, recounting the funny stories of my landlocked week. The house had been two miles out of town, and although I'd been told it was easy to hitch-hike, I could never seem to get a lift. On one particularly hot day, I told him, a white station wagon, which had passed me the day before, had stopped, and I'd jumped right in. The driver was around thirty, but he'd explained he was nervous about picking up strangers. So, I'd asked him why he'd stopped today.

"And what did he say?" asked Gary.

"That he'd seen me for the first time yesterday so he didn't stop. He didn't know me then."

Gary laughed. "So on day two you weren't a stranger?"

"Apparently not."

"Maybe, overnight," said Gary, "he figured out you didn't have an axe."

Chuckling at our in-joke, we started walking down the street towards the dinghy dock.

"So, any plans?" Gary said.

"Yes, I thought I might sail back to the United States with you."

"That's nice, but I meant for dinner."

I laughed. Our future was confirmed, at least for the next two months.

Chapter 48
Collision Course

On the windy morning we left George Town, the clock had stopped in fright. Somewhere around half-past early, we were northbound out of the harbour. I had so many mixed emotions. His buddy, Lon, had invited Gary to his wedding. Instead of slowly making our way north, we were trying to make tracks.

"What will you do next?" Gary asked after breakfast.

"Find somewhere to live in the short term, I guess. There's not much point in looking for a job now," I said. "It will only be another two months after we get there until my family reunion in Ireland. A new employer would hardly give me the time off. Do you want to come, by the way?"

"To Ireland?"

"Yes."

"I've never been."

"I know."

He said nothing for a while, then:

"You understand I—"

"Relax," I cut him off. "I'm not looking to have your baby. Ireland is a cool place. If you want to see it, you're invited."

"What will you do in the meantime?" he asked.

"I've an interview for another volunteer project in Turks and Caicos."

"Oh," he said.

"Why?"

"Well, since I am going back to California for the wedding," he said, "I'm going to stay on for a few months to spend time with my kids and grandkids."

"That will be lovely for you."

"The boat will be at the marina. If you want, you could stay on-board while you are waiting to go to Ireland."

"Really?"

"Sure."

"You mean I could work on the boat in the mornings, get the stainless steel polished, varnish the woodwork, and have free time to write in the afternoons?"

"That would be fine by me," he said.

"Thanks." I said. "I might just do that."

The end was coming, I knew, but it wasn't over yet. We still had another four weeks to sail together and I was determined not to ruin it by being sad about something that had not yet happened. I turned up the music and, along with John Denver, we sailed "on a dream on a crystal-clear ocean".

When we got to the north of the Exumas, we checked the charts and took the long way around, avoiding the Coral Garden. After Royal Harbour came the crossing to Lynyard and the Abacos chain. Each passage that had been a milestone on our way south was now just another bit of ocean to sail. We did it all by ourselves, confident in our abilities. Gary had become a seasoned captain and I an experienced mate. Within four weeks we were back at Great Sale, the first island where we had discovered our mutual love of photography. It seemed fitting this would be our last sight of land for days. Instead of crossing to the nearest point on US soil, we took a chance and made Brunswick, Georgia, our destination. It would be a daring three-day non-stop passage in open waters which would take us across the Bahama banks and up the middle of the Gulf Stream. As we set off, we found that the *Spot*, the battery-operated gadget we relied on to broadcast our GPS co-ordinates, wasn't working. Facing three days alone at sea we had to come up with another solution that would let people know where we were.

Gary took a photograph of our plotted course hoping we could email it to friends and family. But the phone had zero bars. The charts showed an island with a cell tower twelve miles to our north. We couldn't see it, but we knew it was there. Big Ed from New York had once told us if you hoist a cell phone up the mast, the elevation would give a greater range. We decided to give it a go. We put the cell phone in my nylon back pack, clipped it to a spare halyard and Gary hoisted it up the mast. We were so enamoured with this solution I went out on deck with him to photograph the triumph. What Ed omitted to mention, assuming we'd already know, however, was we needed to add a downhaul line as well. Now, not only was the cell phone stuck up the mast, so was the halyard clip.

"Maybe when the wind picks up it will blow it down," said Gary.

"Maybe when the wind picks up it will wrap it around the mast even more," said I. "There is only one thing for it."

"I know," he said.

"One of us has to go up there and get it."

He nodded, having figured that out too.

"I supposed it will have to be me," he said.

"Have you ever gone up the mast in a boatswain's chair?" I asked him.

"No, have you?"

"No."

"Have you ever hauled someone up?" I asked.

"I've seen it done."

That inspired no end of confidence.

"The important thing is controlling the descent," he said.

Indeed. An uncontrolled rappel down the mast of a boat underway, with no one at the helm, might be quite the spectacle. Regardless, the obvious choice was for me to go up. If anyone was going to bounce off the deck and into the ocean it would be preferable if it was me. The boat would need a captain.

With trepidation on both our parts, I sat onto the canvas-covered wooden plank some smart-ass designer called a chair. We then clipped it to the main halyard as that sheet ran back to a winch in the cockpit.

Gary unzipped the windscreen at the front of the cockpit so we could keep in contact. He then put the handle into the winch and turned. I rose above the boom.

"How are you doing?" he asked.

"Fine."

"I'm going to stop every few feet to check on you."

"No," I said, "keep going."

I wasn't wickedly scared of heights but I remembered the pole in Fiji, and this one wasn't fixed. The higher up I went the more the mast swayed from side to side. We weren't tied to a dock; we were in the middle of the sea. I wrapped my knees and arms around the mast, with my nose only two inches away. We stopped again.

"How... are... you... doing?"

"Fine," I said.

Gary's stopping every metre had nothing to do with checking on me, but everything to do with catching his breath. I bet, by now, he wished his volunteer mate was a lithe teenage boy and not some woman as voluptuously endowed as me.

"Stop!" I yelled. "Let me down."

Because I was focused on the section in front of my face, I hadn't noticed I'd already passed the first spreaders perpendicular to the mast, and now my knees were caught underneath them. If he kept hoisting something was going to give. I was hoping it wouldn't be my bones. He slackened. I hauled my legs out and we started up again. I was close to the second spreader. The one clever thing we had figured was for me to take the mooring pole up with me. I reached above my head, hooked the halyard and pulled.

"Got it."

Down came the bag. And so did my wobbly legs. Gary came on deck to help unclip me from the chair. He started to fold it up, but stopped.

"What?"

"Glad we didn't see this before," he said, pointing at the label.

I read aloud: "'Maximum weight allowance...' Oops!" It had been designed for that elusive skinny mate after all.

"How about the email, did it send?"

"No."

All for naught; we were on our own.

By the time darkness fell that first night we were across the shallows of the Bahamian banks, and entering the edge of the Gulf Stream. This time we weren't trying to cross it, we wanted to ride it north.

"Do you know what I'm thinking?" I said.

"Never."

This was probably going to be our last coherent conversation as we would see little of each other over the next few days because one of us would be on watch while the other slept.

"We're going to see dolphin tomorrow," I said.

"Is that a prediction?"

In the four months we'd been cruising, we'd seen varieties of fish, eels and even sharks, but we hadn't seen a dolphin.

"Not only are we going to see them," I said confidently, "they're going to ride our bow."

I still had plenty of energy that first night so I took a four-hour watch. I had one ear open for the VHF radio, the other plugged with music. The first few minutes passed slowly, but then it got busy. Cruise ships never look so big as when they cross the path of a twelve-metre sailboat. I moved over.

Towards the end of the second day we were nearing the western edge of the Gulf Stream when a small bird flew into the cockpit. It landed in my hair.

"Get it off me, get it off me!"

Gary started laughing and, worse still, taking photos.

"Seriously, get it off me!" I could feel its talons digging in to my scalp. The more I squealed the more Gary laughed.

"Bet you wished I'd kept the snakes now."

If I'd had one of his damn snakes at that moment, I would have thrown it at him, fangs first.

"GET-IT-OFF-ME."

"You've swum with sharks, jumped out of airplanes, and you are afraid of a one-ounce bird?"

I was. Maybe it was irrational, or maybe I watched Alfred Hitchcock as a child, but birds freak me out. The bird must have sensed it too as it flew out of the cockpit and onto a line hanging down from the boom. The seas were calm, so, camera in hand, I stepped out on deck to take the unique shot but I saw a black shadow near the boat.

"They're here!" I shouted. "They're here!"

"Who's here?"

"Dolphins!"

"Where?"

"I knew they'd come. I knew they'd come."

I ran up to the bow where they rode the wake. There were three of them: a bull, a female, and a calf. Atlantic Spotted Dolphin. For the second day in a row, the helm was left unmanned. Gary followed me up. Between us, we photographed the joy, the thrill, the speed. Switching back and forth beneath the bow, they propelled themselves with such precision. Sometimes they'd swim wide and crisscross each other on the way back in. Other times they would dart out in front, curving their sleek fins to the sky. The male rolled on his back and showed us his spotted belly. At first I thought they were playing, but they were surfing. Like the forgotten bird, they too, were hitching a ride. Using the bow wake to conserve energy, they were probably moving from one feeding ground to another. I preferred to think they were escorting us out of the Gulf Stream, bringing us home. When they peeled off, we were once again alone.

"How did you know they would come?" he asked.

"Somehow, I always know."

The excitement had revived our energy so by the time the second night fell we were out of sync with watches. I'd been down for a couple of hours, but couldn't sleep. I came up at four a.m. Gary wasn't tired either. I took a look at our course line on the chart plotter.

"It would be better if you go down now, so you are up by seven thirty," I said.

"Why?" he asked.

"Because that's when we should be approaching the entrance to Brunswick."

"It's a wide channel," said Gary. "You'll be well able for it."

"Get your ass in bed now, Mister."

"That'd still be Captain to you, matey."

The wind picked up overnight and so did our speed. The motion must have lulled Gary to sleep because I didn't see him the rest of the night. As the sun rose behind the stern, I saw the first of the channel markers on the way into Brunswick. It was only ten past seven. He still had another twenty minutes. I'll give it a go, I thought. I lined her up in the middle, trying to keep equal distance between the red and green channel markers. These were not play toys but steel buoys at least three to four metres tall. Crashing into one of them would not enhance my nautical résumé. I made it. Another fifteen minutes to go. Perhaps I could get through the next set. As I looked down at the electronics and then up at the markers it was obvious the channel narrowed in. I saw a large white charter boat coming at me at twenty knots. Perhaps he was blinded by the rising sun, because he wasn't moving to my port. We were on a collision course. I had no room to my right, waves were breaking on the shallows. He kept on coming. Fast.

"GARY!" I yelled above the motor. "I need you right NOW."

In fairness, I hadn't finished yelling before he was standing by my side.

"What should we do? What should we do?"

"Don't worry, he'll move over."

"He's not moving."

Gary watched another moment.

"Son of a ..." and he yanked the wheel ten degrees to starboard.

Our friend was indeed not moving, but playing chicken down the middle. We passed with barely two metres between us. Gary had me swing back to port so we could cross the wake head on. It was so big we buried the bow below the surface on the way back down the wave. After a couple of further sloppy waves, we came back on course. It was seven twenty-nine.

"I've just one question," said Gary.

"What's that?"

"Now can I get dressed?"

In all my panicked concentration I hadn't even noticed. He stood beside me, buck ass naked. Not even a baseball cap.

Chapter 49
Journey's End

The end of this incredible journey had been coming from the beginning but somehow I had always managed to live in the now: to breathe the air and kiss the ocean, to scent the spray and kick off my shoes, to laugh and love from the soul. I had envisioned it several times. I would step down off the sailboat, walk up the dock to the taxi waiting to take me to the airport and bid a farewell wave over my shoulder to the man standing on deck: the man, the boat, the life I had fallen in love with. But here it was – a very different goodbye. He was the one catching a flight and I was heading back to the marina.

After two days spent catching up on sleep and cleaning the boat, Gary had taken me out to lunch. We'd rolled up to a steak house where we'd split a dish of I can't remember. The food was fine, the service friendly, but the conversation overshadowed it so much, who knows what I ate.

We started talking of favourite days on the ocean, beautiful islands and funny moments. The conversation turned to Lee Stocking island where I had taken the picture of Gary doing jumping jacks in the water next to the logo of *Freed Spirit*.

"Yes," Gary said, "it was a magical day."

"That was the day things changed for me," I said.

"Changed how?"

The waitress arrived to take our order. After she left our conversation wandered down the lane of cuisine and the moment was gone.

"So," I said, "I would like to take you out to dinner before you go."

"That's kind, but not necessary."

"I know, right?" I said, in my best valley girl accent, which cracked us both up.

"If we were in Florida," I went on, "I would take you to Carrabbas, one of my favourite Italian restaurants.

"None in Brunswick," he said, consulting his phone. "The nearest one is in Jacksonville, and guess what?"

"What?"

"It's right by the airport. We could go for lunch when you drop me off?"

The thing I loved about Carrabbas was the fillet steak and Montepuciano, their house wine. I would be driving his car back to Brunswick, so a lunch gig with only water to wash it down wasn't appealing to my sense of occasion.

"I've another idea," I said. "Why don't we go there for dinner on Tuesday night, stay over in a hotel for the 'last hurrah', then drive to the airport the next day?"

Again with the waitress – this time bringing our drinks. Gary stood up to go to the restroom.

"Before you go," I said, "are you aware of my RR policy?"

"RR?"

"Restaurant/Restroom."

"Another one of your *rules*?"

"Yep, but this one has a point to it," I laughed. "The person who goes to the restroom has the prerogative to talk first when they get back."

His quizzical expression didn't bother me. I knew this was one of my finer ideas.

"You see, the person who goes to the restroom is by themselves and, therefore, has time to ponder, and think *thoughtful* thoughts, whereas, the person left at the table is distracted by the atmosphere, the waiting staff running about, snippets of other diners' conversations and whether there will be enough butter for the potatoes."

His eyebrows made that funny triangle like Fozzy Bear from the Muppets.

"OK, maybe the butter thing is just me. Anyway, when you come back you get to talk first."

"OK then," was all he said. And he was off.

Sure enough, in the time he was gone, the food arrived, the people in the next booth were talking about a dog that needed to be put down, and I'd already dropped my fork. When Gary returned, he sat down and unfolded his napkin.

"I've been thinking about what you said."

"About spending the night in Jacksonville?"

"About the day in Lee Stocking," he said, "you started to say things changed for you. What changed?"

"My feelings."

"In what way?"

"That was the day I realised I had fallen in love with you."

It was out my mouth before I could suck the words back in. He didn't speak, but put his hand on his heart and I watched his eyes soften. I wasn't expecting anything in return. He had been clear. He didn't want a relationship and this, whatever *this* was, was almost over.

"You know I'm not in a place to..."

I stuffed one of his French fries in my mouth for fear I might say something else I would regret. Don't you just love it that the interrupting waitress never shows up when you want her to, and always does when you don't?

"So," I said, "when you came back to the table and used your get-out-of-restroom-free-speech card I thought you were going to say something about Jacksonville, seeing as that was what we were talking about before you left, and all."

"Yeah, I'm up for that."

"Really?"

"Yeah, sure."

"The last 'hurrah'?"

"Yeah."

"A night in a hotel?"

"Sure."

He smiled and *All I Ask* played over and over in my head – a request to make one last night special. I smiled back. But what if Adele was right? "What if I never loved again?"

It rained the morning of our trip to Jacksonville. His car, which was supposed to have been our ride to the hotel, was stuck in the garage waiting on a part. Now what? I stood up to close the deck hatches from the inside as the first drops began to fall. Catching his plane was not an issue, I knew we could probably ask someone from the marina to give him a ride to the airport tomorrow. However, I was pleased to see Gary giving serious consideration to our options. Maybe he was just as keen on this *last hurrah* as I was.

He picked up his phone, scrolled his contacts and chose a number.

"Kris? Hi, it's Gary." Kris was the woman who had held the key to his car while we had been in the Bahamas.

"Yes, do you remember you mentioned I might be able to borrow your car? ... Uh-huh ... How would you feel if we borrowed it overnight and Niamh brought it back? ... Niamh? Oh, I thought you'd already met her ... Sure ... No, I understand ... Uh-huh ... Yeah ... no, the flight is tomorrow, but I have some stuff to take care of in Jacksonville today."

I've been called many things in my day, but never *stuff*. In fact, as you know, I have spent most of my life relinquishing *stuff*. But, hey, if it meant a long romantic night in a triple-sheeted bed, with room service and monsoon showers, then he could call me *stuff* any day of the week.

"Oh, OK. Sure ...We'll see you then. Thanks."

What was I hearing? Was the captain about to make this happen? He put the phone back in his pocket, smiled at me, and said:

"We're good."

An hour later, the delightful Kris handed us her key and waved goodbye in the rain. By the time we got out on to interstate ninety-five south, the clouds had turned black. In front of us was an articulated lorry, but within half a mile it had disappeared behind the downpour. The windscreen wipers were no match for the deluge. It had been a long time since I had been in a southern rain storm. Although we couldn't see past the end of the windscreen, it was more dangerous to try to pull off the road.

"Can you bring up the radar on the phone and let's see how long this is due to last?" Gary said.

I could see his tighter-than-normal grip of the wheel and the tension in his face.

"Well, the radar has…"

Lightning illuminated an outline of the truck ahead. A crack of thunder followed.

"Em … according to the radar we are right in the middle of…"

Another flash, another cracking rip.

"… a thunderstorm crossing the highway."

If it hadn't been so potentially dangerous we might have both laughed at the irony. Here we were, a couple of sailors who never weighed anchor unless we had thoroughly researched the tide, wind and current, awash on a Georgia Highway because we never thought to check the regular weather.

We, and the truck in front, were already down to forty miles per hour, driving with the hazard lights blinking when an SUV went screaming by. It kicked up a lashing spray, but, since our windscreen was already past the point of saturation, it didn't make a difference. I kept checking the radar on Gary's iPhone but no amount of swiping my finger would make the storm pass any faster. Twenty minutes crawled by before the wipers could keep up with the torrent of water pouring down the windshield.

"You're doing great," I said. "We're going to be fine."

As he had on our ocean passage, he drove with a steady hand and calm demeanour, but I noticed his eyes were tired.

"When we come out of this, and you get a chance, why don't you pull over and I will drive for a while?"

I was expecting a male-like stubborn response, but he gave up the wheel. Our teamwork was back in play.

"So," he said, as I drove up the ramp onto the now visible highway, "did you bring any lingerie?"

When we left the hotel the next morning, we meandered along the river towards the car. He reached for my hand, and held it in his. It was the first time he had acknowledged *us* in public. It was warm, comforting, and bittersweet – an inkling of how things could have possibly been. Instead of allowing my eyes to sting, I chose to cherish it for what it was: a reminder of final passion. I walked, living inside those moments, holding on to the now. We still had another hour.

The parking lot in Jacksonville Airport seemed rather full but we found a spot in the middle of Row G, which made both of us laugh out loud. Then it came. You know that moment when someone turns off the ignition, but does not get out of the car? He took a breath before he shifted in his seat to face me. He sighed. I held back my tears but not my love. It was free-flowing, very pure and very simple. And there was nothing I could do to stop it. He said he didn't know if he should be happy or sad for me. I asked him what made him sad.

"Well, it's not that I'm sad for you, in fact I am happy for you, even happy you did fall in love with me, but sad I cannot reciprocate in the way I feel you need. I have learned so much from you, laughed so much with you. This has been an incredible journey. I don't know what the future holds for us, but I know we will stay connected. I don't know if that will be as friends, acquaintances or lovers."

I held his hand and heard him say:

"But please know I do care for you."

My heart tumbled down a beat. The atmosphere was charged. I leaned in for the kiss, but then noticed the dashboard flashing. Could our energy do that?

"Em, Gary, do you see the flashing?"

"What?" He turned abruptly to check it out. "Oh no, you've got to be kidding me," he said, reaching around the steering wheel for the key. "This is the last thing you need today."

It didn't matter how many times Gary turned the key off and on, we were smacked down off the emotional cliff and into reality. It was time for him to check in for his flight and here was I in a borrowed car with a dead battery. Then Captain Krieger stepped up and called for roadside assistance.

He was not going to leave me stranded. The technician who came was a friendly local and within minutes the car was once again roaring with life, a life that needed tending.

"If you stop on the way back, don't turn off the engine," Gary advised.

"I won't."

Pause. Awkward pause. It was clear I couldn't leave the car and he couldn't stay. Was this it? Were these going to be the last words we exchanged – something banal from the everyday world of life on land? But then he leant up against the car and pulled me towards him.

"You said you wanted to soul gaze with me one last time – well, here we go."

Words, hand signals, touch – everything that tied us together was now no longer necessary. We stood in silence while a comet of communication arced between our eyes. Deep in his soul I saw the essence of him, the care he had for me, and a mirror of my own. We might never know the reasons we'd been brought together, but together we had come. Somewhere in that short bottomless moment we both nodded, as if we'd said:

It's time. Farewell my friend, fair winds be with you.

I took a step back and released our hold. He gathered his case, folded his sail jacket over his arm and blew me a kiss. Then he was gone.

Gone.

I collapsed into the driver's seat and finally let the sea of saltwater tears flow down my face. I turned the music to *our song* and the lyrics of John Denver's "Calypso" filled the space. I recalled all the times we had played it when we'd hoisted sails, got underway, or danced in the cockpit. Like an old friend the melody cradled my being as the sobs overtook. Yet, sitting there, in a borrowed car, in a darkly lit parking garage, miles from the turquoise waters of our love affair, I rejoiced in the truth that sailing with Captain Gary Krieger had not only opened my heart, but *Freed* my *Spirit* as well.

Chapter 50
Alone Again

Back at Brunswick Landing Marina, I began settling into life onboard without Gary. But sadness seeped in. Reminders were everywhere. Sometimes I talked to the empty seat; other times I cried. In the mornings I scrubbed bird poop from the deck and de-rusted the stainless steel. In the afternoons I wrote. I existed. Friends from Florida drove up to visit me and I was distracted for a while. But after they left a quietness descended and the sadness returned.

By the end of that first week without him I knew I had to change my thinking. I sat down and focused on the positives. I was in a wonderful marina, with hot showers, free laundry and social gatherings three times a week. There was still food in the fridge and for the next six weeks I would have a roof over my head until it was time to fly to Ireland for my family reunion. And although Gary was gone for good, living in the spaces where he had been kept me connected to his energy and to the energy of the woman I'd become. Even though another one of my romantic relationships had ended and I was single once again, for the first time in my life I didn't feel abandoned. I felt nurtured, supported, congruent. I realised the only person who could truly abandon me was the only one who'd ever done so — me. All the times I had buried my emotions, ignored my health and fitness, and criticised my failures instead of praising my achievements, I'd abandoned self-love. Now I was learning how to embrace it.

As I made those shifts in thinking, my heart began to fill with gratitude. Despite the brevity, I was grateful for the parallel journey our souls had travelled. He was right; we'd been brought together for a reason. I had become a better me.

Ten minutes after that exercise, the phone I kept for emergencies rang. The last time it had rung, it brought me the news that my mother had crossed over. What was the universe going to bring me this time? I flipped it open.

"What year did your father die?"

"Nineteen-eighty-nine, why?"

"Just wondering."

"Well, that's a funny thing to be wondering, Captain Gary," I said.

"I had a breakfast meeting with some friends from my project group this morning," he explained, "one of them is an actress and thinks she worked with your dad."

Busted. The man with an allergy to pecans and relationships had been sitting in a Los Angeles diner with alumni from his Master's degree programme in spiritual psychology, discussing *me*.

"So what else is new in your world?" I asked.

"When are you leaving for Ireland?"

"Twenty-first of July."

"I've decided to come back to Brunswick to take the boat out sooner than I'd thought."

"Oh, OK." That had always been a possibility. "Where are you off to?"

"I'm thinking of sailing up to New Jersey."

"Wow, what's in New Jersey?"

"Newark."

"Duh."

"And a cheap flight from there to Dublin."

What was he saying?

"You're..."

". . .wondering if you'd like to sail with me up the eastern seaboard of the United States."

". . .coming to Ireland?"

"Yes."

"Yes."

We both laughed.

Three weeks after that call, I drove his car back down to Jacksonville airport and stood in the arrivals hall sporting a new blouse and a silly dolphin balloon. He was last off the plane. His smile was worth the wait. We hugged, we laughed, we hugged again. But as we drew apart and he took my hand in his I saw the conflict in his eyes. Joy versus doubt, love battling fear. Those weeks in California hadn't told him he was ready to commit; just that he knew he wasn't ready to let me go. Could he be free to be himself within a relationship? Was love without borders really possible?

As for me, I knew I was no longer a woman looking for love to make me complete. In my voyage around the mind, world and heart, I had found my soul. I was whole. But what could I say to ease him on his own journey? Inspiration struck me. Instead of overwhelming him with expectations, something I might have done in previous relationships, I borrowed a phrase from Abraham Hicks.

"I like you pretty much," I said. "Let's see how this goes."

His shoulders dropped, he let out a sigh. It gave him permission to relax into the next phase of our connection.

Eight months later, on a beautiful January morning I was thrilled to be back in the blue water of the Bahamas. I was drifting a metre or so above the coral reef, enjoying the explosion of colours on a snorkel dive, when the blue fish that children like to call Dory swam right up to my face. She hung in front of my mask a moment, as if checking her reflection in the tempered glass, then darted off to the right. Perhaps she'd forgotten Nemo had been found. But I couldn't help her, I needed to come up for air. As I kicked for the surface, a shadow blocked the sun.

"Did you get the shot?" I asked when I broke through.

"Yep, wanna see?" Gary said as he handed me the camera.

"Cool."

"Race you back to the boat?"

We climbed aboard and I went to lie out on deck to dry off.

"You know what today is?" he asked when he joined me.

I knew. A woman always knows, but I was surprised he did too. But then, many things surprise me about this man.

"I've got a present for you," he said.

I sat up.

"Happy Boat-a-versary," he said as he placed a card in my hand. It had been one year since I'd first stepped on board and into his life. Since then, he'd met all my family in Ireland and I'd met all of his in the US. We'd sailed over 4,000 miles in a twelve-metre boat, up the east coast of America, right past the Statue of Liberty, all the way up to Maine and back.

I looked down at the greatest gift he could have possibly given me – our new boat card, with a picture of *Freed Spirit* under full sail on one side and a photograph of the two of us as a couple on the front – the life I had always wanted.

I looked up and saw that his eyes held no fear. The whole of me met the whole of him.

"I love you," he said.

"I love you too."

Then he grinned.

"What's so funny?"

"Just thinking. Aren't you glad you didn't let one bad night of sailing ruin a whole *month*?"

Epilogue

On 25 March 2021, as I surface from sleep, I reach for Gary as I have done every morning for the past four years. The bed doesn't roll with the swell of the sea and the Florida sun throws shadows on the ceiling ten foot above my head. Life on land. I miss the water but I close my eyes again and steer my thoughts to gratitude for our extraordinary love and the adventures we've shared.

On that first boat-a-versary, I'd sped around the anchorage passing out the new boat card. Couples who knew us recognized the significance. My sea-sisters hugged me, and their husbands slapped Gary on the back. We were loved and in love. Days were bright, full of fun, nights romantic, filled with unending conversation. When he talked about *Freed Spirit,* he no longer called her his boat but referred to her as "our home". He made space in the stateroom for my clothes, and I moved my toothbrush to the forward head. It was funny to think of it as moving in together. We'd already lived under the same deck for a year.

Now that I'd found the love I'd sought most of my life, and our relationship was official, my mind sometimes slipped out of the present and worried about the future. As Gary approached his 70th birthday in July of 2017, I fretted about how long we would have together. My dad had died at 63. The more I fixated on it, the older it made Gary feel. I had to stop that thinking. When I did, I realised the obvious. It was a blessing we hadn't met sooner because the truth was neither of us had been ready. We'd needed to undergo our own experiences, all the joys and heartaches, before we could each grow into ourselves. Once I accepted that, I relaxed about our fourteen-year age difference and rooted myself back in the present, living each day more fully, in case it might be our last together.

In December of that year, we brought the boat up the west coast of Florida for repairs and attended the St Petersburg Boat Show. I wondered how Gary would like the boating couple we'd arranged to meet for lunch. I'd never met the woman and it had been over twenty years since I'd seen the man – the boyfriend who'd brought me to America. Gone was the anguish of that break-up. Instead, it felt like catching up with an old friend, and evoked a nostalgia for Ireland. As we dined al fresco on salads, I learned that he too had been married and divorced and I was delighted he'd also been granted another chance at love. I couldn't help marvel at how we are all connected and how every person we meet may play a part in moulding who we become. I silently thanked him for the role he had played in mine and was grateful he and Gary bonded over talk of the sea rather than me. His girlfriend was delightful and the four of us got on so well they agreed to help us sail *Freed Spirit* back to the Florida Keys and even offered us a berth on the dock of their canal home. It felt both strange and wonderful to be back in Key Largo. Everything seemed just as it was when I'd left — the hotels, the supermarkets, the tourists driving rented convertibles, and my favourite restaurant was still serving my favourite dish: yellow tail snapper in a sherry sauce. When the weather offered us a window to cross the gulf stream, we waved our new old friends goodbye and headed to the Bahamas once more.

The following year we expanded our nautical horizons and plotted a course to the Caribbean. But we knew we needed help. Our friend Roland, a life-long mariner who'd solo-sailed the Atlantic, agreed to crew with us on a ten-day open ocean passage — destination Puerto Rico. We left in April. Winds were forecast Force 4 from the south, so our weather advisor suggested we sail 650 miles due east into the Atlantic until we reached longitude 65 west. Then we were to turn south on this highway in the sea, motor for two days until we picked up the trade winds from the east, which should carry us the rest of the way. What did we get? None of the above.

For the first five days, we pounded our way into the face of the wind and seas. *Freed Spirit* was heeled so far over that the deck rails were in the water. If I'd had those sailing lessons as a child, it would have felt normal, but instead it frightened me. I had to hang tight to the grab bars and swing like a monkey just to get from the stateroom to the galley. Cooking meals for the lads was akin to performing a trapeze act holding a frying pan in one hand and a spatula in the other. So many waves crashed on our bow that the hatch above our bed leaked and the salt water poured down the bulkhead, ruining all our books and soaking the mattress.

With our bed out of commission, we had to 'hot-bunk' Roland's cabin. At night, while one person stood their two-hour watch on the helm, one stretched out on the settee on the low side of the boat and the other slept in the quarter-berth. On shift change, we'd rotate. I found the quarter-berth so stuffy I set cushions on the floor in our stateroom instead, and wedged myself between the bed and the wardrobe. This kept me from rolling and worked well until we made the turn to the south. The boat now leaned over on the other side and the salt water that had been running down the bookshelf now plopped in my ear instead. The easterly trade winds that were supposed to help did not materialize and the wind blasted us from the south, right on our nose.

On day six, I was roused by a crashing sound and Roland shouting those words no sailor wants to hear: *All Hands on Deck.* The vang, designed to support the boom and mainsail, had separated from the mast and the broken end was smashing the deck as we rode each wave. Fixing it was urgent. Gary, whom I'd begged to take something earlier to help with sleep deprivation, stumbled about in a fog, throwing the settee cushions out of his way to get to the storage units underneath. He dug like a Jack Russell Terrier, duct tape, tool bags, rubber bungs flying out either side of him until he found a spare cotter pin and ring.

I raced up to the cockpit and handed Roland what looked like a large hairpin and a ring that would hold a set of keys. As nimble as you like, Roland clambered out on deck and collared the bouncing vang under his arm and somehow reattached it while waves broke on the sail above him and poured down on his head. I could almost feel the salt sting his eyes from where I stood protected at the helm. I was deeply grateful for his experience and that neither Gary nor I had to risk being out there.

On 2 May 2018, when we were two days from land, the weather forecast told us we were in a race to get to port ahead of the tropical wave bearing down on Puerto Rico. With three sails flying in Force 6 winds, we pushed the engine full throttle and gained more than half a day.

The following morning, I had only ten more minutes left on my final six a.m.-eight a.m. shift when Gary came up to relieve me. I saw his surprise when he noticed how I was braced, one foot up on the seat, the other planted on the low side.

"Look at you, 'Miss rails-in-the-water'," he'd said, pointing at the inclinometer.

"Yeah. W-h-a-t-e-v-e-r." I was past being afraid, but so ready to be done. Before we swapped places, I scanned the horizon and was delighted to utter two short words:

"*Land Ho!*"

Once we docked, I wobbled ashore, convinced one leg was longer than the other. The storm broke within the hour. It had been our longest and toughest time at sea, but we'd survived and become more confident sailors as a result.

In November, after a summer spent house- and pet-sitting our way through Europe, we were eager to set sail again and explore the Caribbean chain. We still had to head east against the trade winds, but at least the Spanish, US, and British Virgin Islands were close together. We could leave one in the morning and arrive at the next before dark. It wasn't until we reached the last anchorage in the BVIs, near Richard Branson's Necker Island, that we faced an overnight at sea. The body of water between Virgin Gorda and St Martin, known as the Anegada Passage, has tested many an experienced sailor. This time, it was just the two of us. We waited for weather and were rewarded with a glass-smooth passage and arrived just before dawn.

A short hop from St Martin's brought another full circle for me: St Barth's. What a relief it was to see Birdy back on his feet and boat. Not only had he too found a new love, he also had two more volunteers working at his home. They'd been told to prepare a wonderful meal for us, that I was volunteer royalty. Until then, I hadn't realised I was the first workawayer he had ever hosted.

We continued south, day sailing down the island chain, making new friends and visiting new countries along the way. Everywhere we went, our story touched people's hearts. Somehow, the love we shared was bigger than the sum of ourselves. We were so in sync with each other, people assumed we'd been a couple for years. Life on the ocean has a way of compressing and expanding time. We figured one year living together on a twelve-metre boat was the equivalent of seven years on land. Just like a dog. So, when they asked how long we'd been together, we'd answer them in *boat years*. By our reckoning, we were coming up on our silver anniversary.

When we reached Grenada, our intended port below the hurricane zone, we put down roots. On his 72nd birthday, Gary earned his scuba certification and we spent the summer diving the reefs and snorkeling the shallows. By this time, I was almost at my healthy goal weight, but I had reached the danger zone where people had started to compliment me. With Gary's nurture and support, instead of turning around and eating and drinking my way back to fat, I kept going on the healthy path. To celebrate my uncovered femininity, I committed to taking part in the Pretty Mas Parade held annually during Carnival. Amidst hundreds of other local and ex-pat women dressed in skimpy bikinis and leotards adorned with angel wings made of feathers, I strutted my stuff down the streets of Grenada. A proud Gary walked along the path shooting stills and video as though I was a movie star. The music coming from the float ahead of us was so loud I could feel the asphalt vibrating through my feet. It was as if the Caribbean beat was drumming three years of personal growth, emotional resolutions and dedication to health and fitness into my psyche. I felt pretty. Among all those courageous, fun-loving women, I understood that beauty is not just in the eye of the beholder, nor does it come in a one-size-fits-all, but resides in our own hearts and minds. When we accept ourselves for who we are and embrace, the twists and turns our journey takes us, we honour ourselves and share our greatest light.

On Thanksgiving 2019, we were moored at Bequia, a beautiful friendly island in St Vincent and the Grenadines. We had planned to dine ashore. Gary was off in town making a reservation for a restaurant on the water; I had champagne chilling in the fridge. When the evening sun rippled across the wavelets, we sat on deck and raised a glass, both of us spilling our lists of gratitude. When he'd finished sharing his, he held my hand and added:

"But most of all, I am grateful for you, and the joy you have brought to my life. Thank you for loving me and for your patience as I processed my feelings for you. I love you, and I love telling you how much."

I sipped on bubbles and drank his words. He reached into his pocket.

"I was going to wait until dinner," he said, "but now that I am sitting here with you on *Freed Spirit*, right where it all began, this feels right. Niamh, my love, will you marry me?"

My heart burst open.

"Yes."

The ring he placed on my finger was the epitome of us – two diamonds sparkling between a sea of sapphires. It was a moment that would live in my heart forever. I didn't know that I would have another life-changing 'moment' only three months later.

On 20 February 2020 at 5:30pm Atlantic Standard Time in Antigua, I photographed two middle-aged British men cross the finish line of The Talisker Whisky Atlantic Challenge, having rowed 3,000 nautical miles from the Canary Islands. They'd been at sea for 70 days. When they stood up in their tiny boat, lit their hand-held flares and raised them to the skies, the harbour erupted in a cacophony of horns, ships bells and whistles. I cried. This was their 'Olympic podium' moment. *Click.* As soon as my camera captured the scene, I knew I had taken *the* shot. But for what, I didn't know. Yet. After they stepped ashore and the welcome ceremony was over, Gary and I invited them to dinner on our boat for the following evening. We talked for hours. I was fascinated, not about how, but about *why* they rowed that ocean, how the challenge affected their families and how the experience changed them as human beings.

As these precious memories flood my senses this morning, I list my reasons to be grateful. It's been a year since we were moored in Antigua, watching the virus sweep across the globe, cancelling everything in its wake.

When it closed the doors on the pubs in Ireland and killed St Patrick's Day, I knew it was serious. Then came the fixation with the daily numbers. People were dying. Countries were scrambling to protect their own, some doing a better job than others.

We had been eagerly awaiting our wedding in July in Ireland. My dress hung in the quarter-berth. We debated what to do. Onboard *Freed Spirit,* we felt safe; maintaining social distance from others would be easy. But what plagued us was the unknown. How long would our supplies last and where could we re-provision when we ran out of food? Seaports were closing all around us. Bonaire, where we had planned on keeping the boat during hurricane season, was a four-day sail away with no guarantee it would still be open by the time we got there. The US State Department was urging its citizens to come home or risk remaining overseas indefinitely. On previous trips to visit Gary's family in America, I had seen how a common cold could turn to pneumonia in his lungs and dump him at death's door within twenty-four hours. If he caught Covid-19 in the islands, where ICU beds were few, it was doubtful he would receive adequate care. We felt we had no choice but to haul our home out of the water, leaving her to fend for herself against summer storms and just go. But go where? Gary's primary health insurance covered him in the USA; my ex-pat medical policy covered me everywhere *except* America. We were sure about one thing, though. No matter where we went, we would go there together. We'd heard of too many people who'd become stranded. In February, an English boating friend had flown home to the UK for a short visit and couldn't get back. This left her husband having to sail their boat across the Atlantic by himself.

The boat lift at Jolly Harbour Marina in Antigua did not stop humming. Cruisers were desperate to get their vessels strapped down on land so they could grab a seat on one of the last flights out, including our Canadian friends we'd met in Martinique. They suggested we fly with them to Toronto. If I got sick, I'd be covered. If Gary fell ill, we could drive him into the States. But by the following day, the US–Canadian border had closed. We couldn't fly to Canada, and they couldn't come to their winter home in Florida, so they offered it to us instead. With nothing but disinfectant floor wipes we'd found in the local shop, two ounces of precious hand sanitizer we'd concocted out of rubbing alcohol, aloe vera and lemon juice, and strips of tee-shirts we'd fashioned into face coverings, we boarded the plane and flew to Miami. When we eventually got to the house, we closed the door and began the fourteen-day quarantine countdown.

For every day that passed that we remained symptom free, a little more anxiety ebbed and gratitude flowed. The travel risk had been worth it; we were so glad not to have been marooned. Like much of Europe, many of the Caribbean islands had gone into lockdown. Sailors were ordered to remain on their boats offshore. In Grenada, those who violated curfew were subject to fines and/or imprisonment, the offenders allegedly being identified by police drones. We were glad we'd escaped that level of confinement, but we understood their rationale. With cases rising exponentially across the world, these islands could not afford to take chances. If the infection rate passed the tipping point, it could wipe out an entire generation within that nation.

As we settled into the expanse of our new space, we read with compassion about the hardships some families faced: having to work from home while schooling young children, paying bills having lost employment, or enduring the pain of losing a family member while not being allowed attend their funeral.

Gary and I felt so fortunate. Especially when we saw people buckle under the stress of living on top of each other. It didn't surprise us, though. On the water, we'd met several couples who'd bought a boat and sailed away into their retirement only to divorce six months later. Although they'd been "happily married" for years, they'd never realised how little time out of each day they'd actually spent in each other's company. One or both of them worked outside the home. When they came together in the evenings, they'd be busy with after dinner chores or maybe they'd watch TV till bedtime. If they fought, there was always a way out. They could jump in the car or go for a walk. But once they moved onto a boat, they were truly together for better or worse. And sometimes worse won.

Now, it was as if Covid-19 had made a houseboat out of every home and each family had to figure out how to live in close proximity.

For us, it was the opposite. Could we maintain our closeness in a 2,500-square-foot home filled with everyday luxuries we'd given up to live on a sailboat, like hot water on demand, electric power even on cloudy days, and a machine that washed our dishes? On *Freed Spirit* there is only enough room for us to sleep in a snuggle. The first morning I'd woken up here, I thought I'd lost Gary only to climb over extra pillows and a fluffy duvet and find him on the opposite side of this enormous king bed. Initially, we enjoyed the novelty of wandering from room to room looking for each other, but before long we gravitated back to our happy place, side by side. As the pandemic intensified and social distancing restrictions extended from weeks to months, we chose to appreciate and focus on the benefits land-life offered. Walking in a straight line for more than twelve metres was joyful, riding a bicycle exhilarating, and access to a range of fresh vegetables and salads, delightful. Isolating ourselves from society didn't cause a crack in our relationship as it did in many others, but rather hardened the glue that already bound us together.

That very glue alleviated my guilt for turning Gary into a writer's widower. From the moment I'd given him one of my short stories to read, he had believed in my ability, invested in my aspirations and created the space for me to write. I spent the rest of 2020 writing the story of why Paul Hopkins and Phil Pugh had rowed across an ocean. The iconic photograph I'd taken of them in Antigua would become the front cover of *Flares Up: A Story Bigger Than The Atlantic.*

Not everyone will undertake such extreme challenges like climbing Mount Everest or diving to the wreck of the Titanic, but my objective in relating their journey was to inspire all of us to achieve goals we set ourselves, push through the challenges we may face, and to live our greatest lives. After hours spent typing away each day, I would reconnect with Gary in the evenings and read passages aloud to him. It was so gratifying when a paragraph would make him laugh or cause him to shed a tear. He would listen with his heart and critique in a gentle manner. His insights were invaluable. We knew the story was important, but neither of us had any idea that three years later the book would go on to be shortlisted for The Sunday Times inaugural Vikki Orvice Award.

Compared to the grief others were suffering during the pandemic, we were blessed. The only thing it affected was our wedding plans. Lockdown forced us to cancel. Twice. Like thousands of other couples, we were disappointed, but accepted our duty to protect our friends and families by sheltering in place.

As the world paused, many of us looked inward. Threatened by disease and death, we contemplated life and our role in it. When we looked up at that blue sky, clear of auto emissions and jet contrails, we pondered our individual and collective impact. We recognised how our thoughts and actions can have a direct bearing on our neighbour, be they next door or across the planet. We asked if we were part of the problem or the solution? We couldn't be neither.

Some of our outlooks have changed.

We've focused on what is important and how we can rebalance our lives. Busyness has been replaced by stillness; we've let go of the pursuit of doing and entered the art of being. Real friends have distinguished themselves from acquaintances, and casual commitments are being re-evaluated. We are blessed to be living in this technologically advanced age where families can digitally dine with their loved ones miles away. Working from home has allowed many to leave the cities and nurture themselves in nature, others have changed professions. It's as if our global pulse has tapped back into passion, and now it's time for all of us to embrace uncertainty and cherish each moment we have. It's wretched to think it took a highly contagious respiratory disease and loss of life to show us how to breathe new enthusiasm into our existence, but here we are.

I wonder about Maureen, the diver who returned to England from Belize believing her life was pre-determined. What changes will she have made? It's my hope she's uncovered what she really wants and has found a way to create the life she desires.

Mine has been blessed and full. I've lived life as a scatterling, following sunshine. I find home wherever I lay my head. What have I learned? Every country I've visited, every career path I've followed and every relationship I've treasured has forged another spoke in the wheel of who I am. Those who wronged me taught me that forgiveness of others is a gift you give yourself. And to those I've hurt, I've sincerely apologized. Above all, I've learned that no matter our culture, creed or colour, we are intrinsically the same, each of us looking to love and be loved. When I open myself to the infinite possibilities the universe has to offer, my joy explodes.

But I am not wrapped up in a bow; I am still a work in progress. I have to remind myself to seek light when my mind goes dark. This morning, Gary's side of the bed is empty. All those times I stressed about our age difference, I could have been asking a better question: what were the benefits of him being older? It meant he was eligible to get vaccinated early and escape the virus. Today, he'll wake up in California, able to hug his kids and grandkids. It's the first time we have been apart since we'd said goodbye all those boat-years ago. But this time, when he drew me to him for the airport kiss, he said:

"This isn't Jacksonville. This time I *know* I'm coming back."

I smiled, confident in our requited love.

"And I promise you two things," he said, "*Freed Spirit* will sail again, and someday soon you'll get to wear your wedding dress and matching shoes."

THE END

Author's Note

Dear reader,

Thank you for coming on this journey with me. I hope my efforts in laying bare my story has inspired you in some small way to listen to your inner child, follow your own sunshine wherever it may lead you, and to create the life of your dreams.

If you enjoyed this memoir, you might also enjoy *Flares Up: A Story Bigger Than The Atlantic* available in paperback, eBook, and audiobook. It's a fascinating true story that reads like a novel. It still gives me goosebumps.

Meeting with book clubs is one of my favorite things to do. I offer entertaining 'behind the scenes' presentations either in person or via zoom depending on location. I love hearing from readers, and I greatly appreciate all of you who help spread the word about my books by taking the time to post an honest review on Amazon or Goodreads.

In the meantime, if you'd like to book me for an event, or attend one of my writing workshops, or just keep up with my new releases, sign up for my newsletter on:

https://www.thewriteronthewater.com

Niamh
The Writer On The Water

Acknowledgements

To Gary, every day we spend together is a gift. I treasure every moment. Thank you for believing in me, stretching me, encouraging me to lean in to my true calling as a writer. The best part of my writing day is reading sections aloud to you. You listen with your heart and critique with kindness. Our lives are forever intertwined, and I am so grateful for the work you do as my marketing manager. Together, we truly have become greater than the sum of our two parts. Thank you for the incredible joy, love, and laughter you bring to my life.

To my parents, thank you for the gift of life and for allowing me to live it on my terms, and to my siblings who have supported my journeys on land and sea as well as on the page.

To the inspiration for my wanderlust – Lambay Island off the coast of Dublin, Ireland. A private island that captivated me in my youth. I had permission to dive off its shores but never to set foot on land. I've come to believe that its inaccessibility is what sparked my curiosity to explore remote islands. To Betty Dempsey, a single woman and friend of the family, who died years ago and never knew that her solo travels to unusual places had a lasting impression on me.

My editor, Brian Langan of Storyline Editing, thank you for your perceptive feedback and for always ensuring my manuscripts are crisp and clean. Special thanks to my publisher, Black Rose Writing: Reagan Rothe, David King and the design team for the beautiful cover, and the entire crew for believing in this project. It has been an absolute joy working with you.

To Kellie Rendina and my publicist, Jane Reilly, at Smith Publicity, thank you for all your work in bringing my story out into the world.

Every writer needs a tribe, I am blessed to be the founder of an international group of nine authors. Thank you to Ben Tufnell, Billy Green, Catherine Johnstone, Conor McAnally, Emile Cassen, Lily Devalle, Nina Smith, and Sandy Foster, for your invaluable support.

Many thanks to the talented Carl Rich, and to my beta readers and fellow authors: Sinead Moriarty, Amanda Geard, Hilary Fannin, Lisa Febre, Cam Torrens, Anil Gupta, Jane Spilsbury, Rory Golden, Monika Tur, Max

McCoubrey (Maxi), Kate Durant, Paul Brady and the wonderful Domenick Allen.

I am especially grateful to the kindest, most gracious cheerleaders ever: Jeremy Irons and Liam Neeson. From the moment I first met you while I was working as the stunt assistant on the set of *The Mission*, I have followed your careers and I am honored by your support of mine.

About the Author

Niamh McAnally, known as The Writer on The Water, is an Irish-born author, former TV producer/director and scuba instructor. An avid explorer with a penchant for volunteerism, many of her stories are inspired by her world travels on land and at sea. Her bestselling book, *Flares Up: A Story Bigger Than The Atlantic*, tells the true tale of why two middle-aged men rowed a 20-foot wooden boat 3,000 nautical miles across the ocean, and how the experience affected their families and changed them as human beings.

The Ray D'Arcy radio show chose Niamh's memoir-short *Haul Out* from over 3,000 entries for a coveted spot in the anthology *A Page from My Life,* and her whimsical series *Falmouth Freddy and the Cruising Kanes* has been serialized in Caribbean Compass Magazine.

Despite the pandemic, quarantines and travel restrictions, Niamh and Gary managed to celebrate their love with three weddings: one with toes in the sand in Antigua, one in Ireland for Niamh's family, and one in America for Gary's. Blissfully happy, they are now based in Southwest Florida.

In 2020 she founded an international writer's group, with whom she meets monthly. Believing everyone has their own unique story to tell, Niamh also runs writer's workshops, both in person and online, to encourage emerging talent. To learn more visit:

www.thewriteronthewater.com

Book Club Discussion Questions

1. The memoir emphasizes the importance of living in the present moment and embracing the unknown. How does Niamh's mantra of "anything is possible" manifest in her adventures? And what is your takeaway from that? Is it something you believe too? What techniques do you use to ensure you are "living in the now"?

2. Explore the significance of volunteerism in Niamh's journey. How does her volunteer work shape her understanding of different cultures and communities? What are your views about volunteer travel? Have they changed as a result of reading this memoir?

3. Of all the projects Niamh took on, or the countries she visited, which was your favorite and why? Would you consider visiting any of these places or volunteering on similar projects? Which ones?

4. In what ways does "Following Sunshine" challenge conventional notions of success, fulfillment, and happiness?

5. Explore the significance of the ocean as a metaphor in the memoir. How does Niamh's connection to the sea mirror her internal journey?

6. Discuss the role of love and relationships in Niamh's life. How do her romantic encounters shape her understanding of herself and her purpose? If she and Gary had met years earlier, do you think they would have connected in such a profound way? Do you think your own relationship(s) would survive living in the limited space of a 40ft boat?

7. Do you think Niamh made the right decision to tell her aging mother about the molestation she experienced as a child, or should she have let it go? Discuss the difference between her mother's and Gary's reaction.

8. Discuss the theme of resilience throughout the memoir. Which characters or books do you think influenced her spiritual journey the most? How would you have approached the various challenges she faced? Would your choices differ from the ones she made?

9. Reflecting on Niamh's story, what aspects of her journey resonate with you personally, and why? Has her story inspired you to do something new or different in your own life?

10. Consider the overall impact of Niamh's storytelling style. Did you find her writing fresh and easy to read? Were there any particular passages that stood out to you? Would you recommend this book to someone? Would you read another book by this author?

Note from Niamh McAnally

Word-of-mouth is crucial for any author to succeed. If you enjoyed *Following Sunshine*, please leave a review online—anywhere you are able. Even if it's just a sentence or two. It would make all the difference and would be very much appreciated.

Thanks!
Niamh McAnally

We hope you enjoyed reading this title from:

www.blackrosewriting.com

Subscribe to our mailing list – *The Rosevine* – and receive **FREE** books, daily deals, and stay current with news about upcoming releases and our hottest authors.
Scan the QR code below to sign up.

Already a subscriber? Please accept a sincere thank you for being a fan of Black Rose Writing authors.

View other Black Rose Writing titles at
www.blackrosewriting.com/books and use promo code
PRINT to receive a **20% discount** when purchasing.